W9-ACI-833

DATE DUE

ELBERT HUBBARD

About the time he started The Roycroft Shops

Elbert Hubbard
of East Aurora

BY

FELIX SHAY

WM. H. WISE & CO.
NEW YORK
1926

FOREWORD
By Henry Ford

ELBERT HUBBARD'S writings in *The Philistine* and in the " Little Journeys," and his famous experiment in book making at East Aurora, made him one of the interesting American characters of his time. He had a rare faculty of expression and he used it to serve the cause of common sense in this country.

Elbert Hubbard demonstrated the power of an idea when conceived by an independent mind and supported by intelligent industry. His Shop became a place of pilgrimage to men and women who were interested in the handicrafts and who dreamed of a greater idealization of common life. Whether Mr. Hubbard made a permanent contribution toward that end, the event will declare, but certainly he served to keep the thought alive in his time.

I visited him at East Aurora and was a reader of the "Little Journeys" from the first. There has been so much interest in the personality and work of Elbert Hubbard that this volume descriptive of the man by one who worked with him will be eagerly sought by readers. A biography of Elbert Hubbard should find a permanent place in our libraries.

CONTENTS

BOOK I

CONTENTS

BOOK II

CARTOONS

BOOK I

CARTOONS

BOOK II

BOOK ONE
Elbert Hubbard and East Aurora

The English Who's Who for 1913 offers the following example of Elbert Hubbard's style.

HUBBARD, Elbert; editor, The Fra and Philistine Magazine; President of the Corporation known as The Roycrofters; *b.* Bloomington, Ill., U. S., 19 June 1856; father a farmer and country Doctor. *Educ.*: the University of Hard Knocks. Hon. degree of M. A. from Tufts College, and LL. D. from the Auditorium Annex, Chicago; school-teacher, printer, editor and lecturer; met William Morris in London, 1890, and went home and started the Roycroft Press at East Aurora, N. Y., on similar lines as the Kelmscott; the Roycrofters Corporation has grown out of this venture—a semi-communal institution giving work to 800 people. *Publications:* One Day; No Enemy but Himself; Little Journeys; Time and Chance; Life of John Brown; A Message to Garcia, etc., and about ten thousand magazine articles. *Recreations:* Horseback riding, swimming, rowing, and care of flowers and garden. *Address:* East Aurora, N. Y.

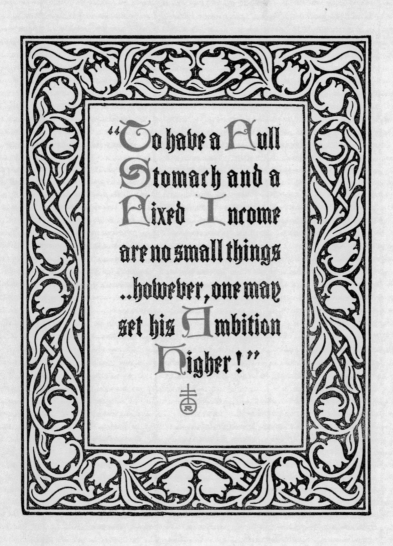

"To have a Full
Stomach and a
Fixed Income
are no small things
..however, one may
set his Ambition
Higher!"

I Discover Elbert Hubbard for Myself

THERE'S a certain period when a boy is trying to discover the man within himself, when all the world seems topsy-turvy, and the times are out of joint. Particularly is this true of the poor boy who, through force of circumstances is unable to go to college, and must matriculate in the University of Hard Knocks. When I was fifteen I ran away from school. After that, the little matter of survive or perish was strictly a personal problem. Over a period of six years (or was it six *eons!*) I passed through the Glacial Age, the Iron Age, the Stone Age, and the Stony-broke Age.

The year I was twenty-one I had succeeded in forcing and working my way into the position of " Divisional Sales Manager " for a mail order house in New York City. The position sounds more important than it was, but it paid $35 a week—and that was opulence.

That year I was supremely happy, but when I looked for a raise in pay at the end of the twelfth month, it was not forthcoming. My immediate superior, who was my friend, confided to me that the job did n't pay any more and, just between us, if I wanted to get on I would have to get out, but not to be so foolish as to throw up a good thing until I found something better.

Meanwhile, in my home-town in suburban New Jersey, a group of young men seeking for self-improvement organized

a reading circle, and round one boy's hearth-fire read aloud into the night, and looked up words, and argued "points."
❡ I am not sure all the books we read were worth while, but the arguments they provoked were distinctly worth while, and the dictionary habit which the unknown words fastened on every one of us stays with us yet.

One night, a boy who is now a successful mechanical engineer, brought along a small magazine bound in brown butcher's-paper; it was *The Philistine*.

Absurd as it may seem I can understand how Balboa felt when he stood " silent upon a peak in Darien " and looked out on the Pacific Ocean for the first time.

This was a discovery, a whole magazine of discoveries!
❡ Here was a successful business man talking a sympathetic language youth could understand, and calling it common sense—and offering Opportunity! Here were words of wisdom and helpfulness without sham or hypocrisy! Here was Inspiration!

Every page of that particular issue was read aloud, and re-read and discussed, and enthused over. His humor made him all the more attractive to us. Here was a *human* Man!

" Who is he? "
" What does he do? "
" Where does he live? "
" Will he give *me* a job? "

Then we read that *Philistine* over again!

There was an epigram on the cover: " Fences are made for those who can not fly." Only those who have lived in a community where " flying " is strictly against the rules can appreciate the stimulation in that thought to a group of young fellows who wanted to try their wings.
❡ Fly! As I walked home that night the only thought

in my mind was " How can I fly to this man Hubbard? "
❲ Next morning I wrote him my application.

I claimed for myself all the accomplishments and virtues
I could think of, and then rewrote the letter and added
a few more. I forwarded the application to East Aurora
under a special delivery stamp with another self-addressed
special delivery stamped envelope enclosed. Otherwise I
feared he might not recognize the importance and the
urgency of the communication. Nor was that such a poor
plan, because at East Aurora (I learned later) Mr. Hubbard did not receive such applications personally.
There were dozens of them daily.
But a " special " was different. The village postman knew
his book of instructions, and when a " special " read
" *Elbert Hubbard—Personal* " he delivered it to Mr. Hubbard in person, for his signature, and to no one else.
Had I not sent my letter under a special delivery stamp
I would have received the regulation, " Your letter has
been placed on file and should a vacancy occur," etc. ❧
Instead, by return mail, back came my special stamped
envelope together with a letter signed by Elbert Hubbard
himself which read: " If you are half as good as you say
you are, I think you better come at once." That was in
the morning's mail. By noon I had resigned my job, collected what was due me, and was down at the railroad
station inquiring about the first train for Buffalo.
His letter was not very explicit. It simply read, " If "
—and " come at once."
Financially, my impetuosity had somewhat disorganized
me. When I counted up I discovered that in case he said
" No," after he had seen me, I had enough to pay
railroad fare up and back, and three days there, at a
reasonably-priced hotel.

I figured I ought to be able to sell myself to him in three days, but doubt crept in, and so I rushed up town to a friend and borrowed five dollars, which in case of a prolonged discussion would enable me to stick for four days.

I boarded the noon train for Buffalo and started West. That this train arrived in Buffalo about two a. m. meant nothing to me. That a night train would have delivered me there the next morning in plenty of time, meant less than nothing. I wanted to start!

I spent the last half of the first night at the Temperance Hotel near the railroad station in Buffalo, but I was unable to sleep. I was afraid I might miss the seven-thirty a. m. train for East Aurora.

When I turned up at the Main Shop I met Bert Hubbard who suggested that I go over and register at the Inn and that his father would see me later.

The morning passed and nothing happened.

After lunch I was standing in front of the fireplace chewing my under lip, when a man in a soft flannel shirt, fly-away tie, and big soft. hat, with the gentlest eyes imaginable, came in and greeted me. He did not mention his name and I was only half convinced that he was Elbert Hubbard. I hoped he was because I was drawn to him instinctively. ⁋ He made me feel comfortable and at ease.

Now then, we 'd have that talk and get the thing settled. But No!

He was saying: " Mrs. Hubbard and I would like to have you walk down to the barn with us and see the horses."

" Of course! Certainly! Thank you! "

I understood. They wanted this conference to be strictly confidential ᔄ ᔄ

They wished to get me away from the Inn, I knew.

But on the way down he took a soft leather ball out of his pocket and invited me to play catch.

Well, *that* I could do!

Years afterwards he wrote in *The Philistine*, " I hired Felix because he was a good ball player, and had an interesting twist to his tongue."

So maybe I did have that " conference " on the way to the barn without knowing it! As was his custom, the last thing that Hubbard wanted to hear was my well-rehearsed phrases ❧ ❧

Many times after that when another such young fellow came to East Aurora to be hired (or not) he would say to me, " Take him out and have a talk with him and sound his ' A.' "

On the way to the barn he was sounding my " A," only I did n't know it.

When we reached there Hubbard saddled Garnet and Getaway with cow-puncher saddles, while I tried to help, and got lost in a tangle of straps and rigging! Had I shown that I knew which end of a horse was which, he would have invited me to ride with them.

Instead " Boots and Saddles," they waved good-bye and galloped off in a fine flurry of hoof-thrown snow.

Right then and there my optimism failed me. I figured that I came, was seen, and had not conquered. I dragged back to the Inn in a low frame of mind.

That was a Friday, and I saw Hubbard no more that day! ❡ After dinner it was snowing as it can snow only in the Great Lakes Country, while I snuggled up to the roaring hearth fire in the main hall of the Inn. Presently a group formed, bundled in reefers and scarfs and half-boots, for a walk to the Three-Mile-Camp.

One friendly lady came over to ask if I would care to go

along. I told her I was waiting to see Mr. Hubbard. " Oh, he 's busy tonight. He 'll see you tomorrow. I know you 'll enjoy the tramp to the Camp, it 's such beautiful snow."
¶ Though I had never thought on the artistic side of snow before, I was lonesome, so I went along. My derby hat, my modish suit and overcoat and thin city shoes were not meant for tramping about in a Northern snow storm. I was cold, cold.

'T was a long three miles to the camp.

I anticipated some form of entertainment, but found a bleak board shack on a wooded hillside. All that we got there was hot coffee. And a fire had to be built before we had that.

Then back ✷ ✷

I enjoyed the company, and managed to maintain my morale until almost back in the village, when the group stopped for ten minutes in a grove to admire and exclaim over the way the snow had drifted against the tree trunks. Then and there I said to myself, " This is the Nut-Family Robinson; they 're all crazy."

I was chilled through.

Next day, Saturday, nothing happened.

I did not see Hubbard at all.

Nor did I know what were the rates at the Inn. I could only guess whether or not my money was holding out!
¶ Sunday, Hubbard talked in the Chapel, and rekindled my enthusiasm for him. I thought him the most wonderful man in the world and firmly resolved that the only way he could get rid of me was to order me out of town.
¶ In the afternoon there was a cross country walk and fifty or more people went along. Hubbard insisted on loaning me a reefer, instead of my stylish coat, and a soft hat instead of my hard one. I played catch all the way with

the bunch, had the pleasure of picking a few out of the air, and enjoyed it immoderately.

That night I had my talk with Mr. and Mrs. Hubbard. They were very pleasant, and wanted to know what I could *do*. I told them at length.

After a while Hubbard said, " Very well! You come to work tomorrow morning at eight. We 'll pay you ten dollars a week."

Crash! My world came dropping round my ears!

Had n't I just told the man I had been making thirty-five dollars a week? What was the matter with him? Could n't he understand?

Then slowly I realized that he did understand, and that this was a test. So I said to him, " Will ten dollars a week pay my board and laundry here at the Inn—for four months? "

Quite unintentionally when I said " The Inn " I associated myself with the Roycroft Department Heads, because that 's where many of them lived.

The " boys " and " girls " lived at " Emerson Hall," (another Inn).

" Oh yes," he replied, " ten dollars will pay your board and laundry."

" Very good then, sir; I 'll take your offer till May First. Then I 'll tell you what I think I 'm worth, and you 'll agree, or I 'll say good-bye, and go. Is that satisfactory?"

" Yes, that 's satisfactory."

Two weeks afterwards, when he handed me my first pay envelope, he said, " You better see Mrs. Hubbard and tell her what you want; we 'll not wait till May First."

℃ That 's how I discovered Elbert Hubbard for myself.

"IS HE SINCERE?"

Drawn by W. W. DENSLOW

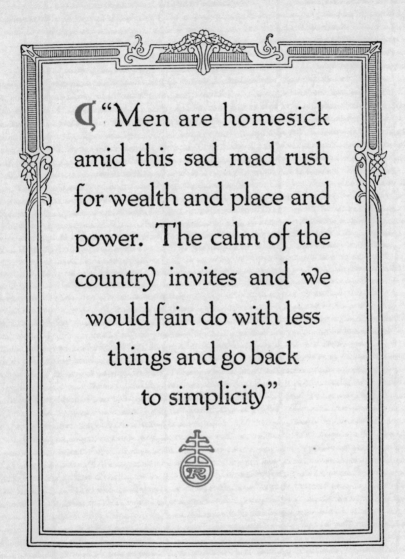

❡ "Men are homesick amid this sad mad rush for wealth and place and power. The calm of the country invites and we would fain do with less things and go back to simplicity"

Hubbard Retires from Business

EXCEPT as you read a " life " into it this is not to be a "Life" of Elbert Hubbard. Rather a setting down of my impressions of the man whom I knew at the full tide of his fame and maturity, of some of the things he told me about himself, and of many incidental things I learned through association and observation. ⁘ Hubbard was born in Bloomington, Illinois, in Eighteen Hundred Fifty-Six—the son of a country doctor who had served in the Civil War. Money was not too plentiful in his family, so he went to work on a farm when he was fifteen, to do a man's work for a boy's wages. When he asked for a raise in pay, it was refused. The boy quit, followed Greeley's advice, and went West.

That he was a cow-puncher, a lumber-jack, a printer, a school teacher, a reporter, an embryonic actor, a soap-salesman, and eventually an active partner of a nationally-known business—I know, because at various times some such incidental fact turned up in our casual conversation, or he volunteered an item of interest to illuminate a tale. ⁘ For instance, one day when we were visiting in Baltimore, I asked him if he knew the streets, the directions, in that city. He smiled a reminiscent smile and said, " Do I know the streets? * * * Why, boy, when I was a soap-merchant, I pulled every door-bell in this town! "

—and then he laughed his infectious laugh and left one to decide how much of his statement was truth.

Another time a Western business man took me into his confidence, so: " When I was a youngster—and Hubbard was little more than a boy himself—I was a member of his crew that was delivering soap in a certain city, door to door. Every morning at six a. m. sharp, Hubbard would kick his feet up toward the ceiling to get rid of the covers, and land feet foremost in the middle of the room with one bound. In the next five seconds the covers were off me! I roomed with him. I never saw such energy—and promptly at *six a. m.* every morning, too! "

But such incidents typify the youth of the typical American: a farm boy, poverty, little schooling, early to work, many and various jobs, energy, perseverance, progress, success! 'T is a familiar story!

My feeling is that Hubbard was not " born " until he was thirty-five and that he " lived " only twenty-four years.

When he was about thirty-five, he discovered that what he was doing was not what he wished to do—not entirely. Suddenly he became conscious of himself, his potentialities and possibilities.

He was a successful business man—so-called. With the years he had secured about all the money he needed, at least all he wanted. What lay ahead promised more dollars, and repetition of the same experiences. That personal development or happiness lay in that direction, he doubted. ❡ Therefore he decided on a change.

He resigned his connection in peace and amity and good will, sold out his interest for $75,000 and " retired " from business ❧ ❧

He retired to loaf and invite his soul, and incidentally to pursue the Higher Education.

He planned on going to Harvard. Below is quoted what is in many respects the most momentous letter a prosperous and " successful " man ever wrote to his mother, a letter which announces that he has torn up his " successful " life by the roots, and that he is about to transplant himself to another sphere:

My dear Mother:

Next to the selection of my parents, I have completed the most important move of my life. In fact, my death can not be a matter of as much importance—or fraught with greater moment. So, to you, above all others, I write it first—I have sloughed my commercial skin. That is to say, I have sold out my entire financial interest in the Soap Business. My last share was transferred today and the money is in the bank to my credit. Why have I gone and done this thing? Because, dear Mother, I have all the money I want and there is a better use I can make of my time.

That excellent man, S. Hubbard, M. D., and myself are probably the only men in the whole U. S. who have all the money they desire.

The next question is: What do I propose to do? I am going to Harvard College, and it is my intention to take a full four years' course. I also hope to spend a year in some university in Germany as well.

John and Frank look upon my plans as a mild form of insanity, but I am at peace with them and all the world besides. I have not paddled away from a sinking ship; the business here was never more prosperous.

I have concluded that he who would excel in the realm of thought must not tarry in the domain of dollars. Another thing, I believe that he who would live long and

well must live like a poor man, no matter what his income
is. We must be warmed and fed, of course, but we must
wait on ourselves and work with our hands a certain number
of hours each day.

Many men want to lay up enough money to give
their children a start. Money will do it all right, but it is
on the down grade. If my boys can not get along without
my financial aid, they can't with it.

I wish you and father would both write giving me
your blessing to my new arrangement.

With much love, as ever

E.H.

In this country where men pile millions on millions mean-
inglessly, for one to decide without duress " I have all the
money I want," and then to act on that decision, marks
the extraordinary man. To decide to go to Harvard at
thirty-five, for a " full four years," to start again at the
beginning, speaks of a well-rounded purpose. To abandon
a successful business career voluntarily when that success
promises millions, takes courage and vision and a certain
high seriousness.
Yet it may be that true success consists in knowing when
one has enough!
Like most self-educated men, Hubbard miscalculated and
magnified in his imagination the benefits Harvard could
bring to him. After a little while he tired of undergraduate
routine and academic formulæ.
He then decided to tramp Europe and take his learning
from original sources.
In Eighteen Hundred Ninety-two he made a pilgrimage
to the British Isles to visit the Homes of the Good Men

and Great, living and dead—and there fortune favored him. He met William Morris.

This chance meeting definitely established Hubbard's ambition, and set the pattern for his life's work.

There was much in common between Morris and Hubbard: both were writers, both were inherently artists, both were craftsmen, both leaned toward the " beautiful and good, the plain and the simple," and both were out-of-door men. ❡ When Hubbard came a-visiting, Morris was getting on toward sixty, while Hubbard was still in his middle thirties. The difference in ages made it easy for one to give and the other to take; one, in a sense, became the grateful apostle of the other. Morris tossed the torch to the hand that was ready to grasp it, and Hubbard said he " caught it! "

❡ Again in Eighteen Hundred Ninety-six Hubbard visited Morris at Kelmscott Press, Hammersmith, saw the artistic Kelmscott Edition of *Chaucer,* which took five years to plan and print, and the ultimate decision made itself ∽ Henceforth Hubbard would go and do likewise.

Years after, whenever a book auction announced a sale of the Kelmscott *Chaucer* at upwards of One Thousand Dollars a copy, Hubbard would say: " Just to think I could have brought one home wrapped in my red handkerchief for Five Pounds."

Hubbard was a rapt admirer of hand-made books, and a student of the history of books and printing, from the timeless efforts of the ancient monks in their cells, through the early Venetians, the Elzevirs, Plantin, Samuel and Thomas Roycroft, Ben Franklin, down to William Morris and his Kelmscott brethren.

His soul was in revolt against the cheap and shoddy ∽ When he saw the William Morris establishment, where they made just a few beautiful things, his business brains

clicked, and he realized that in America an institution
built along similar lines was sure to prosper. Thenceforth
his motto was to be, " Not how cheap but how good."
❧ Morris supplied the inspiration, and the Sixteenth
Century English printers, Thomas and Samuel Roycroft
supplied the name—" The Roycrofters "—which was eventually to identify Hubbard's American Craftsmen.

The word " Roycroft " means *King's Craft* or a *King's
Craftsman*. It also denotes the King's country place or
farm—so Hubbard got the pleasure of a double meaning
from his selected catch-word.

To have known him, is to know that the minute the name
was chosen, that minute he started to think of the Roycrofters as an entity. His ability to project himself into
the infinite was such that, given the proper *name*, the
Community of the Roycrofters became as real in his
mind as though it were built of granite blocks on the
eternal hills.

To him an idea was a reality—or at least once the idea
took proper form inside his head it was a very simple
matter for him to make it a reality. Soon after he returned
from his first trip abroad he printed the abbreviated
biographies, Little Journeys to the Homes of Good
Men and Great; in the Summer of Eighteen Hundred
Ninety-five he published at the local print shop in East
Aurora the first number of *The Philistine*.

Obviously " The Roycrofters " were materializing ❧ ❧

* * * * *

Hubbard lost his interest in plain everyday business in
Eighteen Hundred Ninety-two and found his life's work
in Eighteen Hundred Ninety-five in an enterprise which
permitted him to live a rounded existence and to develop
every aspect of his versatile mind and heart symmetrically.

❡ Between times, what doubts must have assailed him!
❡ What divine restlessness must have disturbed his plans!
❡ Retired, he was too energetic to rusticate, too virile
to do nothing ❧ ❧
But what to do?
Go get an education?
That's exactly what he attempted!
He went in pursuit of an education and he captured it,
but not in the place where he expected to find it hiding.
❡ Ever after he advocated the kind of education that
comes of the complete co-operation of Head, Heart and
Hand ❧ ❧
Moreover, there was something to teach as well as something
to learn. Things were not as they should be. There was room
for improvement in business and elsewhere.
Humanity needed help.
He thought his ideas were entitled to consideration.
He protested against the effects of too much centralization;
against the influence of the cities, against breeding a race
on cement side-walks. I've heard him say, " It's not so
much what a man gets in money wages, but it's what
he gets in terms of life and living that counts."
He decided that a life must mean more, or it would mean
too little; that self-expression in one's work is necessary.
Being intensely American, he believed every man entitled
to life, liberty, happiness and the opportunity to be an
Individual, instead of a *Number* on a pay-roll. Over and
above all, he believed that enough (of anything) is sufficient.
He diagnosed the national complaint as constipation, caused
by too much food, too much money, too many clothes and
chattels ❧ ❧
He wrote to his mother: " I believe that he who would
live long and well must live like a poor man." That same

sentiment turns up in his writings a hundred times in the
next twenty years.

More to the point, he did live like a poor man.

" There is no tyranny," he wrote, " like the tyranny of
useless things."

* * * * *

Pass these items in review before your mind's eye and you
will discover that the very conditions which Hubbard fore-
told and warned against thirty years ago, when he was
looked upon as a visionary and a dreamer, are our real
and pressing problems of today:

The ofttimes *excessive cost* in the selling and in the
distribution of necessities which artificially maintains
the high cost of living.

The rebellion of *machine-workers* against the forced
monotony of their daily tasks and their frantic search
for excitement, after hours, to offset the dominance
of the machine.

The penalties of centralization in concentrating uncontrolled and practically uncontrollable masses of people
in cities, living under unlivable conditions, and then
hoping against hope that they will maintain law, order
and civilization.

The *social unrest* and revolutions brought about by the
dissatisfaction of those who are compelled to live blind
lives—" The Masses "—who are paid the lowest possible
net wages, and who get little out of life but drudgery ❧

The moral and spiritual breakdown of the upper classes
who have discovered that *too much money* is just as
unsatisfying as *too little*.

No! Hubbard was not a dreamer or a theorist, but a sound
and practical thinker—and a Prophet. Moreover he had
the courage of his convictions and of his lack of them ❧

Like Lincoln he held to a thing so long as it was right, but when he concluded it was wrong, he parted with it! ❡ Ultimately, he reserved his finest contempt, his most scathing criticisms, for the man who had eyes and would not see, and ears and would not hear—and money, (which spelled Opportunity) and would not act.

" Take note," said he, " when you die all that you will take with you in your clenched hands will be the things you have given away."

Like Lincoln he held to a thing so long as it was right; but when he concluded it was wrong, he parted with it. Ultimately, he reserved his final contempt, his most scathing criticisms, for the man who had eyes and would not see—and ears and would not hear—and money (which he spelled Opportunity) and would not use.

"Take note," said he, "when you die all that you will take with you in your clenched hands will be the things you have given away."

Say!
I'm the Guy that Phils
The Philistine

With apologies to Goldberg

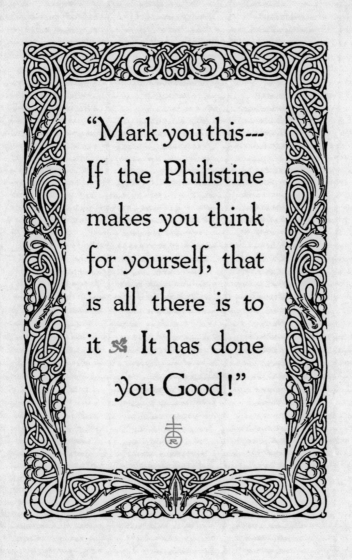

"Mark you this---
If the Philistine
makes you think
for yourself, that
is all there is to
it ❦ It has done
you Good!"

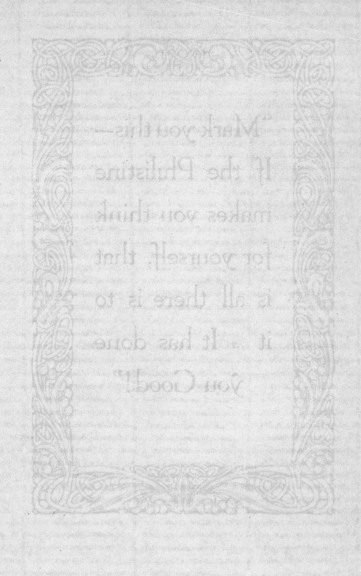

"Mark you this—
If the Philistine
makes you think
for yourself, that
is all there is to
it ... It has done
you Good."

The Philistine Presents Itself

TO appreciate *The Philistine* you must remember the age in which it was published. The first issue is dated June, Eighteen Hundred Ninety-five.

Queen Victoria did not die until Nineteen Hundred One.

In Eighteen Hundred Ninety-five Gladstone was completing his career in the English House of Commons, and the Victorian Era as we recognize it, was drawing to a close ∞

Nevertheless it still gave the tone to the whole English-speaking Civilization.

Of late there has been a tendency to glorify Victorianism from the glamorous distance of twenty-five years. But it's easier to appreciate the Victorian virtues from afar than in the near proximity.

One must have an excellent forgettery to forget or forgive the unnatural dress of both men and women, the cast-iron manners, the stilted speech, the groove thinking and the Blue Sundays. Victorian hypocrisy and surface culture were a sham, and its fetish "good form" an insult to naturalness.

¶ Then came *The Philistine,* so gay and candid and wholesome that it immediately divided sophisticated America into two distinct classes: those who " took " *The Philistine* and those who did n't know how to take it.

Across the ocean, Gladstone, in retirement at Hawarden, wrote with his own hand to Hubbard, " *The Philistine* has supplied me with several quiet smiles," which leads us to believe that perhaps Gladstone himself was a little tired of Victorianism.

Did he not address Victoria, once on a time, as though she were a " public meeting? "

Overnight *The Philistine* became a success; overnight Hubbard, the principal contributor, became known as a laugh-maker, a chuckle inspirer, a writer of sanity and sound sense, a man of Ideas!

Hubbard has testified that the original plan was to issue one copy of *The Philistine* to " say a few things and then stop." But before the ink was decently dry on that first issue there was a clamor for more, a subscription list was in the making, and *The Philistine* had become a national institution.

For years Hubbard had the urge to write, and had written, but he could find no one to publish his stuff. He told me, " I spent days cooling my heels in the outer offices of most of the famous editors of the time, just to earn myself another batch of rejection slips." One pauses to wonder what that type of editor thought of himself in after years when he realized that he or his minions had rejected this writer whose followers were to be numbered in millions so

As he wrote for *The Philistine* spontaneously and without reserve, so it was enjoyed spontaneously and without reserve. The astounding feature of his writing is that in turning back the pages one finds the same verve and vitality in Eighteen Hundred Ninety-five that there was in Nineteen Hundred Fifteen, and vice versa. Moreover there's the same quality, the same identity. Turn the unsigned pages and there is no mistaking which articles are his and which belong to others.

When the start was made in Eighteen Hundred Ninety-

five there were some half-dozen contributors to share honors
with him in the little thirty-two-page magazine. While
admitting that I am prejudiced, it's plain his " stuff "
was the attraction. Take out his articles each month, and
you have a magazine; put back his humor and his original
touch and you have *The Philistine*. As I understand it
Hubbard was the only one who ever passed a cent of money
into *The Philistine* treasury, therefore there was no necessity for the presence of the other literary contributors,
that is to say no financial necessity.

Obviously he was either a victim of good-fellowship or
excessive modesty—because on the face of it *The Philistine*
was a one-man magazine from the beginning, and there
was no mistaking who that One Man was.

But not until the forty-fifth issue did Hubbard assert himself and make the imperative decision. In the January,
Eighteen Hundred Ninety-nine *Philistine* one reads: " Beginning with the next number of this magazine I propose
to write every article and paragraph in it, including advertisements and testimonials of Roycroft books.

" If it were possible to secure any one to write so well
as myself I would not do this."

Speaking of his contributors—" All of these men I have
fed, clothed and lodged for years. To be sure, they have
slept three in a bed but I have fed them well.

" One of my legs is now so much longer than the other
that I can only walk with the aid of a crutch."

Thus and so reads his Emancipation Proclamation ✂ ✂

One searches to find and analyze the eternal charm of
The Philistine and to learn why it captured and held such
an infinite variety of minds.

Always there was the humor and the satire.

Hubbard was not only a joker par excellence and a car-

toonist with words, but he was an intelligent and pene-
trating foe to hypocrisy and pretense.

Wittily he exposed frauds and shams, and in the same breath
intimated that we are all frauds and shams, somewhat,
and called the offender " Brother."

Invariably he made a friend of the potential enemy!

Hubbard was not a killer of reputations, he was not vindictive or vicious. After he had plagued and exposed some
offender, he always found something good to say about
him. He firmly believed in that familiar doctrine " There 's
so much bad in the best of us, it hardly behooves any of
us to talk about the rest of us."

Criticism with him was a friendly, helpful, humorous
exercise ❧ ❧

While helping the world to make headway, he made men
laugh intelligently, and for that peculiar service mankind
pays the highest wage in money and in appreciation ❧
Therefore he prospered.

Most of his stuff was written with laughter wrinkles round
his eyes and his tongue in his cheek. He used ridicule as
the irresistible weapon.

One should never ask, " Is Hubbard sincere? " That 's
not the key to the man or his mood. Ask " Is he joking? "
and you 'll solve the riddle of his style. He was always
sincere, as much as was necessary, while he was writing
a thing. But when the complaints came in the next mail
which read, " I don't agree with that article," he would
answer almost seriously and say, " Come to think it over,
I don't believe that I agree with it myself."

Those who were static never knew how to take him ❧ ❧
Those who believed what they believed and nothing else,
who were their same inflexible selves yesterday, today
and tomorrow, never could understand nor appreciate a

man who refused to stay put and who believed that life is progression.

Said Hubbard: " We want honesty in literature. * * * When such small men as Samuel Pepys and J. Boswell can write immortal books the moral for the rest of us is that a little honesty is *not* a dangerous thing."

About the " respectable " publications of the day he says: " It is because we can not say what we would in the periodicals which are now issued in a dignified manner that we have made this book *The Philistine*. Philistia is a Land of Free Speech."

Ofttimes he takes a fling at his contemporaries—Mr. Bok of *The Ladies' Home Journal,* at the *Century,* at *Harper's,* at *McClure's,* at *The Forum,* at *The Arena*—friends and enemies alike.

He protests that Mr. Bok writes about " How to Carry a Cat in a Basket; " that Mr. Gilder publishes articles " beautifully printed—which nobody cares about; " that people buy the *Century* because it looks well on the library table; that Mr. Howells of *Harper's* " maunders! "

To Mark Twain he addresses himself so: " I am awfully sorry you have lost all your money. I am in the same boat, but let's not talk about it all the time."

Even though *The Philistine* was surnamed, " A Periodical of Protest," I find this kind of protest pleasant enough, and no one much the worse for it.

One has the feeling that (confidentially) these men whom he plagues may be his friends!

Quoth he, " Who are the bores? Oh, you make me weary, —the others, the others, others."

And he adds, " Subscribers to *The Philistine* not fully understanding my jokes will be supplied with laughing gas at Club Rates."

For a benediction he gives us this: " I belong to no party, to no school, to no sect. And yet I belong to each; and all belong to me, for I accept the good in all things. When anything that seems to savor of spite escapes from my ink bottle I am as innocent of vengeful intent as were the simple swaying reeds that, bending before the breezes, sighed, ' Midas, the King, has asses' ears.' Now the reeds never really voiced any such sentiment, but Midas mindful that he had asses' ears thought they did; for any man having asses' ears continually considers himself assailed."

Up to the time *The Philistine* appeared no one-man magazine in this country had ever achieved a circulation of one hundred thousand paid copies a month. Brann, with his *Iconoclast* had gained national attention—which ended in a double shooting—because Brann was a man hunter and very unconservative in his use of adjectives. He sought for trouble and he found it. Brann thought he had the sure cure for what ailed the world; Hubbard knew there was no sure cure. Brann wanted his readers to think as he thought; Hubbard simply wanted his readers to *think*.

❡ *The Philistine* captured the good will of the intelligent public with its whimsicalities, its reasonableness; the *Iconoclast* held attention for a brief hour with " sound and fury."

❡ Brann sought for enemies; Hubbard cultivated friends.

❡ Hubbard was not a professional reformer; he did not feel that he had a corner on truth. In an early issue of *The Philistine* he writes, " I think I 'll start a crusade for the reformation of reformers. I am fully persuaded that our besetting sin as a people is neither intemperance nor unchastity, but plain dishonesty. My suggestion is that for a whole year we let the heathen rest, resign all public works in the Personal Purity League, and declare a vacation in the W. C. T. U. Then each man and woman set a guard

over his own spirit and try to be greater than he who
taketh a city. In other words, practise the old plain simple
virtues of gentleness, charity and honesty—doing unto
others as we would they would do unto us. I am sure it
would be better for our nerves, and possibly just as well
for the heathen and the drunkard."

Subscriptions to *The Philistine* came in on the endless
chain principle; one person subscribed, read it and chuckled
and then subscribed for a friend. There were no high-pressure methods used to increase circulation. The list of
subscribers grew of itself. Its creator maintained that *The
Philistine* was the first magazine in the history of the
world that was self-supporting from the first issue ✒ ✒
Perhaps the secret of the popularity of the little magazine
is contained in this paragraph: " *The Philistine* seems to
stand alone in being read by people who do not necessarily
accept the editor's point of view. Its subscription list
includes names of men in every denomination, party,
profession and occupation. Philistines recognize that the
magazine which makes a person think is really doing a
greater service than is the one that does the thinking for
him."

When you understand the spirit of *The Philistine* you
understand the spirit of its author. When you understand
what this highly magnetized little side-pocket magazine
was trying to accomplish, you will realize why it succeeded.
Hubbard wanted to contribute his share to help develop
here in America a race of men and women who reason for
themselves, who come to their own conclusions and who
act on their own judgments.

To him canned thought, canned opinions, canned philosophy were anathema. What 's good enough for grand-
father is not good enough for you, not at all. You are

entitled to something at least two generations better. He
discovered that some people could be inspired to think
independently, some argued into thinking, and there were
others who had to be surprised or shocked before their
mental processes would function. He tried to serve them all.
❡ In the same issue of *The Philistine* he 'd soar into the
cerulean blue, touch the stars and then plow up the earth
with perfect equanimity—and for a purpose. Not all people
do their thinking in the sky among the angels. There are
numerous earth-bound spirits—even as you and I.
And ever and always he took as his text: " What I write,
and all that I write, is one man's opinion, worth just that
much, and nothing more."

Riding His Hobby

Riding His Hobby

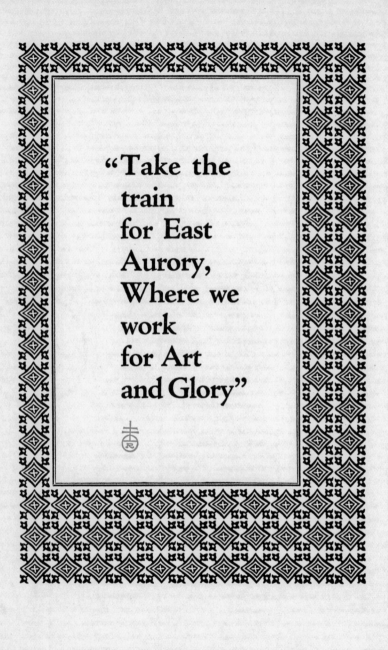

"Take the
train
for East
Aurory,
Where we
work
for Art
and Glory"

The Horsey Village of East Aurora

"EAST AURORA," said Hubbard, " is not a place; it 's a state of mind." But also it was and is a Western New York State Village, located eighteen miles from Buffalo on the Pennsylvania Railroad and a brick pike ֎ ֎

First, in the early issues of *The Philistine*, Hubbard tries to prove that East Aurora really does exist, and sometimes seriously—one is led to believe—because he takes the trouble to quote the statistical facts " Two thousand population, one bank, one newspaper, one saw mill," etc.

Then again he treats the subject humorously, and maintains that East Aurora is not on the map because it is located so many miles East of Sun-up, and states that that area has not yet been properly surveyed.

When Hubbard arrived, East Aurora was a town of farmers and retired farmers, with a sprinkling of Buffalo commuters, but more particularly of horsemen. He called it " a plain humdrum village," and " a buckwheat town " but he elected to live there because he loved horses!

When Hubbard located in East Aurora 't was but a wide spot in the road, a town of two streets, yet with the natural beauty of a New England village. The giant trees met over shady Main Street, the little white houses rested not too far back from the road and minded their own business, or not, as the case might be.

Later, when I came to know it, there were " eleven saloons
and eleven churches" and the balance of power was maintained more or less diplomatically, with fish-fries and
strawberry festivals as the counter attractions.
Originally Hubbard's business was in Buffalo, and he
journeyed to and fro each day. He describes himself as a
commuter who wore a "red vest, spring-bottom pants and
a derby hat," which description I am privileged to doubt *.*
His house was the regulation Main Street house on the
hundred foot lot.
East Aurora was headquarters for trotting horses in
Western New York and the home of the Hamlin Stock
Farms, the most famous of all the stock farms of that time.
Somewhere or other Hubbard writes, " I studied Greek
and Latin with a local clergyman and raised trotting
horses." It would seem rather difficult to associate and
synchronize those pursuits, but somehow he did it. I have
heard the Oldest Inhabitant say that in the early days
it was a familiar sight to see Hubbard, after he got home
from business, driving one trotting horse hitched to a sulky
and leading another, exercising them.
He never lost his love for horses.
The tone of Roycroft, as I first knew it, was one-third business establishment, one-third university, and one-third
horse-ranch, with just a touch of the monastic.

*   *   *   *   *

My first Spring in East Aurora (I had been there some
months) I was busy at my job one day when a messenger
came for me. Outside the main door was the Master of
Roycroft astride his stylish mare Garnet, and he was
leading a piebald broncho.
" Time you learned how to ride," he called, " Come on! "
'T was a warm sunshiny day after a thaw, and I did not

take the trouble to go back after my coat. I rode as I stood, in corduroy trousers and a soft white shirt—which is a part of the story.

" Keep behind me." That was all the advice I was given, but it was plenty. The broncho had been out at pasture, practically all winter. His coat was two inches long, he had a round hay belly and resented the rear girth of the cow-puncher saddle.

Moreover he wanted to ride abreast of Garnet.

To keep that cayuse in his place got him in a lather—and me too ✒ ✒

I crowded a whole course in horsemanship into the first hour, and I learned many a fine point and some not so fine by the simple expedient of try-it-and-find-out.

About half way along on the ride with Garnet leading by twenty yards, we crossed a lush meadow with a small stream in the middle of it. I figured the broncho would refuse the stream, so I urged him up to it, clapped both heels into his sides and over we went sailing!

But when we hit the other side, the cunning little animal landed on four stiff legs, and Hump! Hump! Hump!

Nine times he bucked! Or was it ninety?

He turned me over completely in the air, and I landed on the broad of my back—and came to my senses sitting in the middle of a pool holding the reins like an Easter Lily ✒ ✒

'T was a soft meadow.

My riding companion never so much as turned his head.

❡ That was my initiation.

After the ride a glimpse of the once-white back of my shirt where I had kissed the ground, brought forth the remark from Hubbard, " Ah! you 're one of those fellows who only ride off-and-on "—but there was a note of satisfaction in the voice because I had not asked for help, and because I had brought my horse into the barn *behind* his mare, as instructed ∾ ∾

* * * * *

East Aurora was the town of Cicero J. Hamlin, of Ed. Geers and Billy Andrews; also of the Jewett Covered Track and the S. H. Knox Stables.

'T was a horsey atmosphere, the cleanest, freest atmosphere on earth. Those who know claim that " Pa " Hamlin did more to evolve the American trotting horse than any other one man, and no one need look beyond the public prints of the last decade to learn about " Pop " Geers and " Billy " Andrews. Morning and evening, Spring and Fall, Winter and Summer, these horsemen exercised their beautiful horses hitched to spindly sulkies on their private tracks and on the high roads round about East Aurora.

Goodness me! Horses—yes!

Whenever I think of East Aurora, there comes to me subconsciously a whiff of the barn on a snowy day, that pleasant smell of feed-bins and clean straw, of warm animals, and strap-oil.

I see a half-dozen saddled horses pawing on the wooden floor, and one of the pretty girls ready to go, prancing her horse for a little preliminary excitement! Whoopee! She must have been pretty, otherwise she 'd not have dared to prance the horse!

There were always a dozen horses in the Roycroft barn and the owner of the stable was generous with his invitations to ride. When a person showed interest, the Fra showed interest in that person; he gave appreciation where appreciation was due. More! When a boy was sweet on some girl (and where are the happy, healthy boys and girls who are not sweet on each other?) Hubbard would see to it that they were both invited to ride—taking them away from their tasks to give them what he considered needed recreation—and exercise. He not only taught us to ride, but he taught us how to ride, and the philosophy of riding. After we had ridden a few miles we got off and walked awhile to " let the horse enjoy the ride, too."

If there's any pleasure more complete than a stroll down a country road in the cool of a summer afternoon, with all the world at peace—with the horse nuzzling your elbow —I can't remember what it is.

We were taught to take care of our animals on the ride, and to care for and properly protect them when we got back to the barn. Moreover, all of us, girls included, were shown by personal example how to saddle and bridle our own horses, to put our own horses away, and to be self-sufficient *◦ ◦*

* * * * *

East Aurora is a populous place in Spring and Summer and Fall, but in the old days, when the snow settled down, and the corduroy road to Buffalo was snowed in, that was the end of the visitors—except the rare ones—till the following Spring. In Winter one had to search out his own fun—and pity the person who thought that some weather was "bad" and some "good."

" All weather is good," the Fra contended, " only some is better."

I have ridden in a blizzard in East Aurora and come back in a perfect glow of health, with my hair frozen into icicles, to eat a double portion of everything for dinner. I have seen a half-dozen of the initiated rush for the barn to get out into the mad frolic of a Spring storm, thunder and lightning, wild gallops up hills with the horses jumping an extra six paces when the thunder crashed or the lightning cracked.

❡ Truth compels me to state that these escapades came to pass after we had purchased our own horses! And that E. H. was not " in the know."

Hubbard encouraged us to save and buy horses. He wished us to learn to save—and he wanted us to have the responsibility and trials and tribulations of ownership. He offered to pay me what I paid, provided at the end of ninety days I did not like the horse I had bought.

The first horse I owned was " Devil," a roan broncho, sold to me as unridable. Buck, rear, sit down, balk, bite— quite a fellow! He and I became good friends—but he never lost the habit of bucking when one mounted him on the *proper* side, which fact we never confided to the boys who thought they could ride!

The next one, I bought at the Buffalo auctions—a beautiful black. He was a runaway. I discovered that one afternoon when a farm-hand threw an armful of chains into a wagon close by. Round and round a field of live wheat we galloped, the horse in command. Every time I passed the farm-hands they rattled the chains again, and then some more speed until the acre of wheat was laid low!

Hubbard bought *this* horse from me at the price paid to maintain the peace—after he had run me one Sunday a. m. across a church lawn—and I bought my first Kentuckian ❧ ❧

Where can one find yarns so interesting as the yarns the horsemen tell? What kind of talk rivals horse talk? I 've kicked my half-frozen feet on the barn floor for an extra hour, while dinner waited, listening to my old friend, Charlie Olcott, the ex-circuit driver, tell how the little black mare came to win " by a nose," back at Erie, Pennsylvania, in Eighteen Hundred Eighty-eight!

What talk! What friendly, harmless, entertaining talk!

❡ All men claim to be able to ride a horse—some can
and some can not. I remember several. For instance,
two Philadelphia business men of prominence and position
whom we invited to go along. They were given two " dead
safe " horses who still could trot. The gentlemen were
ambitious and, as there were pretty girls in the party, they
maintained the pace.
But next day, *literally,* they were served in their rooms
with food and much free advice!
And there were others.
Again, when visitors arrived for a week-end, on a snowy,
blustery Saturday or Sunday afternoon we 'd stake them
to warm reefers and adequate boots, and then tramp up
to the S. H. Knox Stables and ramble around through
the clean warm corridors and inspect the hundred or
more finely bred animals. Then back home for a bath,
a hot dinner and a feast of reason when Hubbard presided
at the Chapel Meeting—or music on sweet zithern strings
and a flight of song in the Salon.
When only the home crowd was round about, the word
would be passed, the rendezvous appointed, and without
Hubbard's knowledge or consent the horses that belonged
to each of us would be spirited up to the Jewett Covered
Track. There protected from the storm we 'd have races
on the tanbark. Occasionally some horse would put a front
foot into a chipmunk hole and the finish would be a slide
for life ❧ ❧
This covered track was a strange anomaly; it had been
built to train horses to race on the ice in Canada in Winter,
but more particularly to " get the jump " on competition
in the Spring races.
The owners figured to train their horses *inside* all Winter
and to have them in perfect trim for a clean-up when the

outside racing season started. This covered track cost a
million or more to build—a mile enclosure. Only theory
is not practise, and "the best laid plans of mice and men
gang aft agley." The horses that were trained inside in
a dim light were afflicted with light-blindness, something
akin to blind staggers, when they were brought out to
compete. The covered track was a failure!—but when
the War came, it was wrecked for the glass it contained—
and paid back the original investment, plus.

*   *   *   *   *

Once I introduced Hubbard to a prominent national
advertiser in a Boston hotel lobby. He seemed very indifferent, distant and detached. I thought he misunderstood, so when the man moved off I said by way of protest,
"Do you know who that was? That's Mr. Blank, the
famous advertiser!"

"Do I know who that was, Felix! That son-of-a-gun sold
me the first piece of submerged real estate I ever bought,
and took the first five hundred dollars I ever earned!
Oh, yes, I know him."

Here then is the curious twist to the tale. That piece of
"submerged" real estate was located in Florida! Had
the purchaser only *held on,* as the real estate agents say
—but he did n't.

Eventually he traded (blindly) the Florida acreage for
a horse or rather a mare with a foal running by her side.
The mare's name was Sonora, a pacer with a record so.
Her colt was sired by Almont—perhaps the greatest
trotting stallion of the time. This colt became "Garnet,"
the most stylish, the most animated, and in many respects
the most knowing saddle horse in all America. Hubbard
trained Garnet himself, first to lead and later to the saddle.

She never had a harness on her back to the last day of her twenty-six years.

Shut my eyes, and I can see Hubbard coming down the road on Garnet—a string tied round his head to hold his hair in place—his reins held high in one hand—both elbows straight out away from his body to give his lungs a chance —a smile on his face—sitting his horse like a centaur, and old Garnet fancy-stepping and side-stepping and snorting, pretending to be afraid, while not afraid of a thing in this wide, round world.

East Aurora was a " horsey " Village all right!

Kid
Cupid

Champion of Champions

"Men are only
Great
as they
are Kind"

The Roycroft Idea at Work

ROUND about East Aurora is a poor farming country. More or less the land has been worked out and the small general farmers with limited holdings find themselves unable to compete against the better soil, the large landholders and the specialization of the West and the Far West. Here and there are prosperous farms, but they are conspicuous by being the exception rather than the rule. Therefore the farming community of that section is not overly prosperous.

What is true today was particularly true when Hubbard opened up in East Aurora back in Eighteen Hundred Ninety-five, because then markets were uncertain and transportation indifferent.

Though I have heard him say, "Don't feel sorry for country boys and girls, God is often on their side"— nevertheless he did feel sorry for them. There was no opportunity for the ambitious ones at home—to find opportunity they had to go to "the City."

Hubbard was a farm product himself and he loved the country. Born in what he called the "Black Mud Section" of Illinois, he grew up with the Middle West. He was proud of this heritage. He wrote of his own boyhood thus: "When I was fifteen I knew all the forest trees, all wild animals thereabout, every kind of fish, fowl, frog, or bird that swam, ran or flew. I knew every kind of grain or

vegetable and its comparative value. I knew the different
breeds of cattle, horses, sheep, or swine. I could teach wild
cows to stand while being milked, break horses to saddle or
harness; could sow, plow and reap; knew the mysteries of
apple butter, pumpkin pie, pickled beef, smoked side-meat,
and could make lye at a leach and formulate soft soap."

℃ He knew too that country boys and girls ran away from
this life, particularly in the poor farm communities to
escape the drudgery of it and that " the City " took them
in and not all returned or were heard of again. " The City "
will have much to account for on Judgment Day!

As a matter of first principles, Hubbard agreed with Herbert Spencer that before a man can be a good man he must
be a good animal—and he did not believe it possible for
a man to be a good animal " off the ground," away from
contact with Mother Earth.

So when he started the Roycroft, his primary determination
was to provide work for the farm boys and girls near by
and to make the terms and conditions of their employment
so attractive that they would want to continue it. That
he succeeded in his purpose is testified to by the fact that
many of the helpers at the Roycroft today have been
working there ten, twenty, twenty-five, and in a couple
of instances, thirty years.

It would have been easier, and undoubtedly more profitable,
for Hubbard to have started with skilled labor, found wherever it was available. He would have gotten under way
much quicker, and, in a mechanical sense, accomplished
more. But that was not his ambition.

This was what he sought to accomplish—and did: " In
one obscure country village I have had something to do
with stopping the mad desire on the part of the young
people to get out of the country and flock to the cities.

In this town and vicinity the tide has been turned from city to country. We have made one country village an attractive place for growing youth by supplying congenial employment, opportunity for education and helpful recreation, and an outlook into the world of art and beauty."

❡ His philosophy was that all boys and girls wish to make things, with their hands; that they wish to make beautiful things; that they desire to learn, get along, progress; so he supplied Opportunity for them at home. Eagerly they did the rest.

* * * * *

Hubbard was not dealing with "ideal" people, rather the average run of farmer folk. Only one who had grown up on a farm and who knew the American farmer's psychology perfectly—who knew and understood and sympathized—could have handled this peculiar and distinctive "labor problem" and accomplished what he accomplished.

❡ Mind you, these were free-born Americans right in from the hills and valleys, and not the washed-out descendants of wage-slaves.

They were a free-spoken lot, "familiar, but by no means vulgar." Many of them called the Chief Roycrofter "John" to his face—and that 's a story.

A prosperous individual drove out from Buffalo one day to see Mr. Hubbard. He wheeled up in front of the Inn, said " Whoa " to his spanking pair of bays and stopped. Raking leaves in the roadway was a person in a battered hat, a flannel shirt and corduroys. " Here, John," said the prosperous one, " hold my horses," and passed the person a quarter.

" Could you tell me," he inquired at the desk of the Inn, " where I could find Mr. Hubbard? "

" Why," said the girl looking about, " he was here just

a moment ago!" Then glancing through the open door
she said, " Oh, there he is, out there holding those horses!"
Ever after that the boys called Hubbard " John."
Fra Elbertus delighted to answer to that name!
" John " and " Zeke " and " Cy!" 'T was all right! It
really signified they considered him a Member in Good
Standing ✒ ✒
Another time, Hubbard engaged an old countrywoman,
about eighty years old, to weave rag carpets for sale at
the Shops. Or rather, he thoughtfully brought her down
from her home up-country and put her to work, because
her local market was an indifferent one and half the time
she had trouble making both ends meet. The Roycrofters
could easily sell all she made, pay her what she was
accustomed to getting, guarantee to take all she could
produce and make a profit besides. The old lady came
and brought her clay pipe to smoke while she worked ✒
Because of the fire risk and because smoking inside the
Shops was against the rules, her employer stopped one
day to reason with her. " Granny, don't you know that
smoking is bad for your health? (Puff, Puff!) You cut
years off your life. (Puff, Puff!) You set a bad example
to the boys and girls—I wish you 'd stop it!" (Puff, Puff!)
❡ Then up spoke Granny: (Puff, Puff!) " Sonny, ain't it
'bout time that you run along and found yourself some-
thin' to *do?* " And that was that!
There were no " Social distinctions " at the Roycroft.
The farm hand or teamster who would take his bath and
change into his blue serge suit was as welcome at a dance
or any other gathering as the next one, and he was considered just as good as the next one, too—if he was.
Cleanliness, conduct and intent were the only tests ✒ ✒
Most people learn quickly.

The " Guests " were invited to come in, and on the same basis ❧ ❧

Of course Hubbard was not fooled on this subject of equality. Here are his own words on the subject: " All men are created free and equal. This is absolutely true —leaving out all those who have hare-lips, strabismus, legs that are not mates, wills that do not obey, and passions not under control! "

Nevertheless, he thought that all men were entitled to an equal Opportunity and that they should be judged acceptable until they proved themselves otherwise. Rarely did the clean-limbed, clean-minded, ambitious country boy bungle his chance when it was given him.

Nor did they take advantage in business.

Largely, the place was operated on the honor system ❧

To complicate matters the Owner not only allowed two outside recesses each day, of ten-minute stretches, but it was his habit to invite the boys and girls to leave their work whenever an interesting speaker arrived, and hold a meeting in the Chapel or on the lawn.

Sometimes in Summer he 'd wave the whole crowd from their tasks and take them for a walk across fields or hail out special groups for horseback rides, or a game of " catch "—but the work always seemed to get done, probably because no one paid much attention—as a voluntary matter—to the eight-hour day. When people are interested in the task under hand, they lose track of time ❧ ❧

'T was particularly interesting to observe · what effect congenial work and friendliness had on a so-called " bad boy "—either domestic or imported. Presently he 'd forget himself and spend his energies in his work—and then the bad boy would become the good man.

Hubbard observes, " The hoodlum is very often the good boy who does not know what to do with himself or his energies." ✦ ✦

These Roycroft helpers worked in clay and designed and produced pottery, hammered copper into beautiful shapes, evolved serviceable fire-dogs and hinges, and what not, in wrought iron; modeled leather, wove rugs and baskets, set type, bound fine books, pegged together attractive pieces of furniture, designed stained-glass windows and lamps, put up preserves, made maple sugar candy, planted flowers, painted canvasses, wrote poetry, composed music —and made a profit on the investment.

'T was an extraordinary accomplishment.

To the Fra belongs the credit though he does testify: " By myself I could have done nothing. If I have succeeded, it is simply because I have had the aid and co-operation of cheerful, willing, loyal and loving helpers. No man liveth unto himself alone; our interests are all bound up together." ✦ ✦

* * * * *

Hubbard called East Aurora " The Land of Immortality." There's a passage in the Koran of the Mohammedans which describes Heaven as an orchard of choice fruits with gorgeous flowers growing in profusion there. Perhaps that is why this curious man who discovered the Land " East of Sun-up " placed his buildings in the midst of a picturesque old apple orchard and then planted round them a Magic Carpet of Flowers!

Authorities have called the Chapel at East Aurora the most perfectly proportioned building in America. It is surely pleasing to the eye. No less is the Main Shop. Both of these buildings were put together without the aid of either architects or blue-prints, by so-called "village labor!"

The "designs," worked out with the stub of a pencil, were by Jim Cadzow and the stone work by Billy Kelly, aided and assisted by the bunch. Ali Baba claims much of the credit for the finished work because he bought and selected the stones ✍ ✍

Those of you who doubt there can be such a thing as "inspired labor" should make a Little Journey to East Aurora and view these buildings.

The first Shop was a one-room affair called a " Chapel " because that word properly belongs to Printers and not to our orthodox friends at all. That original Chapel is now the Entrance Hall to the Inn.

'T was cold in the old barn where they first set up *The Philistine,* so very soon Hubbard built this little Chapel right alongside of his own house.

Hubbard writes, " I wanted it to be comfortable and pretty so we furnished our little shop cozily. The Shop was never locked and the boys and girls used to come around evenings. It was really more pleasant than at home. I brought over a shelf of books from my library. I bought the piano because the youngsters wanted to dance. The girls brought flowers and birds and the boys put up curtains at the windows. We were having a lot of fun with new subscriptions to *The Philistine* coming in almost every day, and once in a while an order for a book. * * * The boys picked up field stones and built a great splendid fireplace and chimney at one end of the Shop."

The effect of the finished fire-place was so satisfying that Ali Baba, " the man-of-all-work," was commissioned to buy all the field stones available locally at a dollar a load. These stones were the particular affliction of a York State farmer's life, and so when the announcement of Ali Baba's

74

ELBERT HUBBARD

requirements was published they thought the millennium
had arrived. They rushed into town with their loads of stones
hoping to get there before somebody discovered what Ali
Baba was doing and put him where he belonged.

Four thousand loads were purchased before the supply
inside the " dollar limit " was exhausted. Of these stones
three buildings were constructed, with walls and gate-
posts enclosing the campus.

The coloring in these field stones is rarely beautiful.

Not only did the helpers design and construct the buildings, but they felled the trees and fashioned the timbers
for the rough-hewn beams that make the interiors so
distinctive. All the way through 't was a home-made
job and a fine monument they built to themselves.

One of the criticisms aimed at Hubbard was that he paid
small wages. Fiddlestick! These poor critics mean *money*
wages, while Hubbard paid a large outlay in Happiness,
Contentment and Opportunity. One need only look at
those East Aurora buildings and learn something of their
history to understand that it was almost a religious quality,
an ecstasy, that went into the day's work!

When completed the Fra put Walt Whitman's quotation
over the door—" The Institution of the Dear Love of
Comrades." ॐ ॐ

William Marion Reedy and Fra
Elbertus Discussing Great Themes

William Marion Reedy and Fra
Elbertus Discussing Great Themes

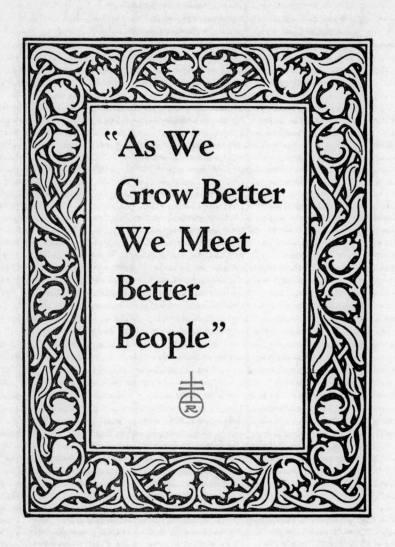

"As We Grow Better We Meet Better People"

The Inn and Its Visitors

ONE of the initiated said: "Elbert Hubbard is the only man who ever had to build an Inn to house his admirers." There was no choice. In the early days, one hears him inviting the Faithful to come and be welcome at the festive family table. He promises to find them a place to sleep too—free, gratis, without charge!

Did they come? They did.

They came by squads and phalanxes, ate of his board and filled his beds.

What to do?

The problem was somewhat complicated by the ever-increasing number of workers who had to be accommodated and cared for.

It was decided to build an Inn.

That Inn is not yet built—not completed—though it does accommodate one hundred and fifty guests. Each year something is added to it and something is taken away ❧ ❧ They called it " The Phalanstery."

Outside it is the oddest shaped building imaginable, but inside one of the most attractive.

" Twenty-five cents a meal; fifty cents for lodging "— those were the prices advertised in the early days, but not always collected.

Hubbard simply hoped to pay expenses.

As late as just before the War, the Roycroft Inn asked

but Two Dollars a day for a scrupulously clean room with three bounteous meals included. Hubbard did not like the idea of trying to make money from his " Guests;" but he did not object to letting them pay their own way. 'T was amusing, however, when some comparative stranger came along and growled because there were no bell-boys to bring him ice-water, to see the Master of the Inn engage the guest in friendly conversation and then present him with a Ten-Dollar book. The guest understood that his total bill at the Inn would be, say, Three Dollars! How, then, could the Fra afford to give him a Ten-Dollar book? He 'd go away, shaking his head over the economics of the problem—when there were no economics to it at all. It was simply a gesture by this interesting and original Innkeeper, who had his own ideas of hospitality. The impressed stranger went on his way and talked about his experiences at the Roycroft for years—and his friends came a-calling to discover whether or not he told the truth! ❡ The Inn of today is an architectural hodge-podge, but the general effect is a pleasant one. Three or four buildings are joined together and enclosed by a peristyle stretched out along a shady village street.

Inside is a symphony of polished natural woods, bright Navajo rugs and stained glass lamps and windows—like unto nothing but itself: the library, a maze of books; the dining room, a long rectangular room laid with large, round, Doctor-Johnsonesque tables that seat twelve each to encourage conversation and good-fellowship. The music room, of reflective hard wood floors and colorful murals by Alex Fournier, with modeled leather chairs and screens, is a sanctuary of art and beauty.

The trim of all the individual rooms, as well as the Roycroft-made furniture, is of matched natural woods: mahogany, cherry, ash, oak, bird's-eye maple. Cleanliness, simplicity and beauty are perfectly blended. The atmosphere is that of a cultured home—a home of wealth and refinement ๑๑ The buildings, furniture, rag rugs, stained glass, sculpture, bronze and copper ornaments, the paintings—all were made by the Roycrofters.

The individual rooms are not numbered; they are *named* —named after the famous men and women of all time— Socrates, Edison, George Eliot, Beethoven, William Morris, Susan B. Anthony.

Not only was the trim and the furniture of, say, the George Eliot room a symphony of matched woods, but there was sure to be a bit of statuary, a painting or two, and some framed excerpts from George Eliot's writings and selected volumes of the writings themselves to perpetually endow that particular room with a George Eliot atmosphere ๑๑ While on the subject of George Eliot, a village carpenter was once employed to carve the proper name on the door of that room. Late that same day—in the corner grocery —when asked what kind of work he was doing he delivered himself thus: " Just a fool job! Up at that there Inn they 're goin' plumb crazy. They 're cuttin' the NAME of the guest on the door of his room. Today I 've been cuttin' the name of a feller by the name of ' George Eliot '—and what are they goin' to do if the son-of-a-gun don't show up? "

Introductions were unknown at the Inn—and so occasionally when some visitor was a little backward in coming forward we 'd address him by the name of his room. Once so called the name was apt to stick.

" Socrates, would you care to play ' catch '? "

There 's a mining engineer, for instance—who will be known to the Roycroft forevermore as " Socrates," because that is what we called him by chance—and he liked it.

Each year thousands of visitors came to East Aurora ⁐
The names on the register at the Inn, if published, would
make a fairly complete Who's Who in America.
'T was and is a pleasant place to visit.
There "high thinking and plain living" meant something
more than a phrase.
Among the Roycrofters there was a fine flair for personal
independence. To illustrate: Once Mr. X the famous food
specialist, visited Hubbard on a Sunday.
When dinner-time came around he was placed at the
"star" table where he would meet the most representative
Roycrofters. Dard Hunter, master craftsman, (silent Dard),
chanced to be presiding at that table, serving as voluntary
host ⁐ ⁐
Mr. X said very little, and a desultory attempt at general
conversation ended in silence about the time the soup
was served.
When the roast and vegetables were placed upon the table,
country style, Dard served the guest first. When the young
lady waiting on table delivered the full plate to Mr. X
he was busy masticating a dry cracker or something
of the sort and said quite bruskly: "I'll not have that
now." The embarrassed girl returned the plate to Dard,
who flushed and then turned pale—an ominous sign ⁐
With a full sweep of his arm he placed the plate on the
window sill behind him.
After a while Mr. X said peremptorily, "Now I'll be
served." Again the full sweep of Dard's arm and the
same plate was brought back and again placed before the
guest ⁐ ⁐
"There it is!" squeaked Dard. "You'll find the food
cold and unpleasant and I'm damned well pleased!"
With that he got up and stalked out!

Another time, dear old Marilla Ricker spent a Summer with us. I believe Marilla was the first or second woman lawyer to practise before the Supreme Court of the United States of America. And back in prehistoric times she nominated herself for Governor of New Hampshire and went down and cast a vote for herself—and for that they arrested her. She was a disciple of Susan B. Anthony!—a delightful and charming old woman. She was forever plaguing her friends about their errors in English—and then correcting them. One day at dinner when Richard Le Gallienne and Katherine Yates and other distinguishables were present Marilla lapsed.

Some one asked, " Marilla, will you have some more spinach? "

Marilla replied, " Not any, thank you, I have a great plenty."

Spoke up one of the irrepressibles, right before the " company "—" I beg pardon, Marilla, but in that sentence is n't the word ' great ' superfluous? "

Marilla, caught on her own hook, while the table tittered, handed down her decision as though it were a death warrant: " Yes; I agree it is."

Nor were all the jokes played by the Roycrofters on the Guests &o &o

Sometimes the Guests took liberties with each other &o I remember once when Burr MacIntosh, the actor and Good Humored Philosopher, was vacating the William Morris room, he learned that immediately it was to be occupied by a famous and much-married millionaire &o The millionaire was coming along with another new wife, a certain Marie. So Burr sat himself down and wrote the wealthy gentleman a message in the *guest book* which belonged to the William Morris room and then propped it open on the table to be read: " Dear Bill: When you come into the quiet of this sequestered room, and at last, at last, take Marie into your arms and kiss her—I want you to kiss her again for me, and tell her, dear boy, tell her with your well known fervor, that I shall never, no, never, forget the last time *I* kissed her. Yours as ever, Burr MacIntosh."

'T was a hoax, of course, but—the millionaire and his new bride did not come down for dinner that evening!

Many, many brides and grooms stayed their honeymoons in East Aurora. 'T was an ideal place; the happy pair was neither harrassed nor annoyed with attentions. Either they could mix in, or hold hands in the library, or go tramp the hills together as they pleased. Then before the hearth fire after dinner there was Hubbard himself to present a beautiful and appropriate book to the blushing bride, autographed from " Your Uncle Fra Elbertus," and with a kindly little speech wish them happiness; while several of the sentimental ladies dabbed at their eyes with moist handkerchiefs ✍ ✍

Commercial travelers and business men of all kinds and classes—not to mention actor folk and incidental tourists —when " caught " in Buffalo over the week-end, came out and spent Saturday and Sunday in East Aurora ✍ Particularly Sunday in Summer was always a delightful day at the Inn.

East Aurora was a marvelous marriage market.

Many, many college girls came to East Aurora and took the first job that offered just to stay there. In Summer considerably more than half the helpers at the Inn were college girls.

'T was amusing to watch some young American hustler find the waitress who was serving him much to his liking

—and then wonder what he was going to do about it!
ℂ Imagine his surprise and joy an hour later to find the
same girl, in a white dimity frock, with a rose at her belt,
sitting at the Steinway in the main hall softly singing,
" Just A-wearyin' for You."

Such things are really too good to be true!

Of course the Roycroft boys were equally susceptible.
ℂ There were marriages aplenty.

Hubbard used to remark facetiously, " Put your head out
the window in East Aurora and call ' Elbert ' and fifty-
seven little boys will come running."

Somebody says that Ali Baba added, " Gee Whillikins!
That 's easy!—the Old Man gives ten dollar gold pieces
to every kid that is named after him! "

* * * * *

One could never tell who would turn up at the Inn.

" The desk " closed at ten p. m. One night I arrived shortly
after the closing hour and found a tall lean man standing
in front of the hearthfire waiting.

He inquired, " Are you Felix? "

I replied in the affirmative.

" Well, the night-watch tells me that you are a young
man of bad habits, that you come in after hours, and that
if I ask you politely you 'll give me a cigar? "

Not many of the " regulars " smoked at East Aurora,
but I did. I hurried back to my quarters and returned
with my private stock.

He invited me to join him in a goodnight smoke.

There was talk, much talk.

The late-comer was Brand Whitlock, then Mayor of Toledo,
successor to " Golden Rule " Jones.

I shall always remember one story he told me:

" Mr. Jones called me on the phone one night and asked me to go to a certain place to make a speech. I wanted to know more about the assignment, so I asked him, ' What kind of people am I to talk to? '

" He replied, ' Oh, hell, Brand—just folks.' "

Continued Mr. Whitlock: " That was a lesson to me in Democracy; since then people have been *just folks* to me."

❡ About three a. m. we retired.

Five years later when the Germans were overrunning Belgium and the German High Command had ordered the execution of Edith Cavell and that same Brand Whitlock (American wartime Minister to Belgium) was pleading for her life, I wondered whether he considered those German officers " *just folks.*"

* * * * *

Except for general supervision Fra Elbertus left the practical management of the Inn to Mrs. Hubbard and her assistants ✦ ✦

Only once I saw him take charge.

'T was a beautiful moon-light Summer night when the hours slip by unnoticed. A circle of men held forth in high good humor in one corner of the peristyle—nor noticed the flight of time—nor that it was long, long after hours.

❡ Alex Fournier had finished one story and Dicky Le Gallienne had capped it with another. The laughter was loud and prolonged, when patter-patter down the peristyle came the Fra, his trousers pulled on over his night-shirt.

❡ He was high! and going higher!

" What the blankety-blank is the matter with you fellows —don't you realize that at this time of night all honest men are in bed? "

" I 'm sorry, I 'm sorry, Elbert," wheezed Dicky. " What time *is* it? "

" It 's THREE O'CLOCK—don't you know that? "
It *was* three o'clock!
For three hours we 'd been keeping a hundred people awake
with our unseemly mirth!
" Well," said Dicky, slightly peeved, and to save his face,
" I 've seen Hubbard write a book and run a business
and give a lecture, but this is the first time I 've seen him
in the role of irate innkeeper! "

The ROYCROFTERS

ED HOWE JOINS the CLAN

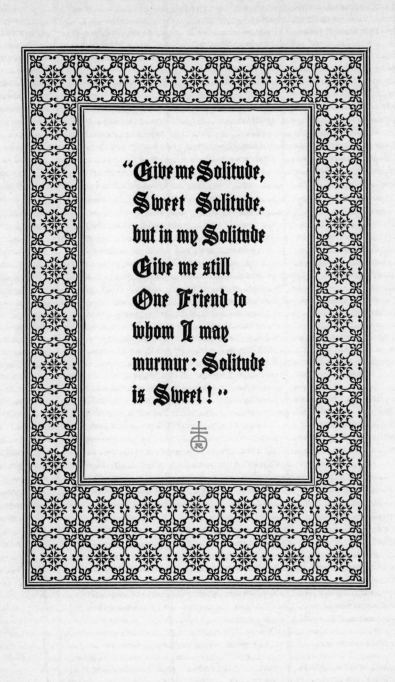

"Give me Solitude,
Sweet Solitude,
but in my Solitude
Give me still
One Friend to
whom I may
murmur: Solitude
is Sweet!"

Unconventional Conventions

UBBARD was a gregarious individual; he enjoyed the company of his kind. So, once a year there was a Convention of the Elect. Just what these annual Conventions were to decide or settle was not always clear. Rather 't was a getting together of bright minds, with results and accomplishments left to take care of themselves.

The philosophy of the occasion was that life is in the journey and not at journey's end. " We are going the same way, so let 's go hand in hand." Even so, there was a more or less serious attempt to induce mutual respect, to tolerate divergent opinions, and to harmonize conflicting personalities ๛ ๛ Every type of person imaginable was in attendance during Convention week.

One had to be tolerant or intolerant; there could be no in-between policy. A large number of those who attended were " one-idea-men."

A one-idea-man is a sincere and misguided, but usually likable citizen who is positive that single tax, or reform in the currency, or vaccination, or woman's suffrage, or Esperanto will redeem the world.

To all who would listen, he offered his cure for the ills that afflicted mankind. Of course, there was an amount of logic and specious argument on his side. To hear him the first three times was amusing, diverting, interesting, informing.

One did not agree, *in toto,* but granted the open mind, one was sure to agree in part.

At East Aurora, as elsewhere, the only way to guarantee an audience for one's self is to be an attentive member of the audience for the previous speaker.

All were given a chance to air their views.

There was an exchange, a compromise of opinions.

Anarchist and capitalist sat down together to talk it over and try to understand each other, not as members of a class, but as thinking individuals; not as orators-in-public seeking for effects and applause, but as Philosophers-in-the-Sun seeking for the Truth. When they first stood up and went at it, it was each man for himself—and the devil take all those who differed. But after a week of association, a week of fair, square discussion, there was much talk of moderation, mediation, toleration, co-operation, reciprocity.

❧ People are like that.

Wasn't it Dr. Johnson who said, "I hate that man!" His friend replied, "How can you hate him when you don't know him?"

Countered Johnson, "That's the point! If I knew him I couldn't go on hating him!"

Once a high railroad official took the trouble to cuss out the anarchists from Land's End to John O'Groat, and from Dan to Beersheba—individually and collectively—and all those connected or affiliated with them, unto the tenth generation. He wanted them all shot against the wall.

❧ "Hear! Hear!" a bystander remarked. "That listens exactly like an anarchist talking, wanting people shot against the wall! How many anarchists have you known intimately?"

"Not one—and what's more I never want to!"

"Very good, then, let's forget it and go over to the Campus and play ' catch! ' " Before they crossed the street others were invited to join in the frolic, and for half an hour there was good fun tossing the ball about in the sunshine on the green—the game punctuated with joshing, wise remarks, and other odd contributions. The railroad man and one of his playfellows became very friendly and walked back toward the Inn arm in arm.

Then I called the capitalistic friend aside and scolded him thus: " You 're a nice representative member of the monied classes, you are; an inspiring sight for your board of directors—you walking across the street with Emma Goldman's chief attorney. The man you just found so companionable is Harry Weinberger. The newspapers call him an ' anarchist! ' "

" Well," said the magnate, " I 'll be damned! "

" Console yourself," I continued, " Harry Weinberger is not really an anarchist. When a young man he decided that he would become a lawyer and espouse unpopular causes, and befriend the friendless. That policy has cost him a brilliant ' career.' He takes the cases other lawyers refuse, whatever they may be."

" That," said my monied friend generously, " is pretty fine work! "

* * * * *

Conventions ✎ Introductions are tabu ✎ Everybody knows everybody else. Good will and the laugh in which there is no bitterness prevail. Music will be a feature. There will be gentle walks afield, tramps to the Farms and the Camps, and demonstrations at the Roycroft Woodpiles. As for the Ideas—everybody is welcome to all he can bring and all he can carry away. Perhaps you had better not dress too fine—flannels, corduroys, khaki, stout shoes, and a Smile!

In the programs of the Conventions of Philistines are printed the names of Clarence Darrow, Mangasarian, Madison Peters, Alfred Henry Lewis, Robert Barr, Hall Caine, Ella Wheeler Wilcox, Bruce Calvert, Rabbi Fleischer, Winifred Sackville Stoner, Carrie Jacobs Bond, Scott Nearing, Horace Fletcher, Dr. Algernon Sidney Crapsey, and who not.

Those last two names recall an incident which emphasizes the humor, and good humor of Hubbard. One Convention period, I came back from a business trip the morning it opened up. While among the "outlanders" I had been smoking cigarets. That morning when I stepped out of the station rig I walked flush into the Fra, accompanied by the Reverend Doctor Crapsey, the famous divine, and Horace Fletcher, the world-known dietitian, and was caught with the cigaret in my hand!

Apart from all other considerations, surely this seemed a discourtesy to the Fra, who was against cigarets.

(I mean a discourtesy to flaunt one.)

Greetings over, Mr. Hubbard said, somewhat quizzically, "Felix, have you ever read my Essay called "The Cigarettist?"

"*Read* it? Hell—I wrote it!"

Dr. Crapsey and Fletcher put the laugh on Hubbard. He too laughed at my claim of authorship, and I could see I was forgiven. " Throw away that coffin-nail," he commanded, " and lend me a hand with the medicine ball." ❡ There was neither hard liquor nor a liquor-drinking crowd at East Aurora. None was for sale at the Inn, and apparently none was brought there. I never saw booze on the premises at the Roycroft. There were beer saloons downtown but they received slight patronage from the Roycrofters or their guests. The high spirits developed at these conventions did not come in bottles!

*   *   *   *   *

There was no competition in dress at East Aurora. The lady with seventeen trunks stored sixteen of them in the basement the day after she arrived and left them there till the day before she left. I remember a little actress, once on a time—whose name is known to the electric lights on Broadway—who brought along a wagon load of trunks. But we jollied her so much about her wardrobe that she turned the tables on us by spending most of her vacation in soft flannel shirts and khaki skirts! She said she welcomed the escape from the tyranny of " perpetual changes."

There was something extremely sensible about the East Aurora " uniform " of white shirt, khaki trousers and a fly-away tie, because it was particularly adapted to the environment. One can't very well kick up dust down a country road, cross lush meadows, scramble over streams on stepping stones, and climb fences in costly finery.

Such exercises were the order of the day at these Conventions! The specially advertised " Three Programs a Day " were invariably staged far afield: one morning at the farm, a mile away; that same afternoon at Pigeon

Roost in the woods, another mile and in a different direction. There was only one way to get there—walk!

Two miles before lunch and two miles before dinner, creates the perfect appetite—automatically does away with all criticism of the wholesome country fare and banishes insomnia!

One could actually *see* city folks thrive on this scattered schedule of " Walks and Talks Afield " and food and rest aplenty at the Inn.

The Pastor of his flock said, " What we seek to accomplish is a Healthy Mind in a Healthy Body, and then most of our problems will solve themselves."

The year that Major Rowan, the man who carried the *Message to Garcia,* visited East Aurora there was some talk one evening on the peristyle of the importance and dignity of proper clothes. Some one remarked, " Clothes maketh the man." Some one else said, " No." Another quoted, " Costly thy raiment as thy purse can buy." And then Edmund Burke was quoted about how a naked House of Lords creates no awe. At that moment the Master of the Inn crossed the peristyle.

Some one called to him for a decision.

Waving them aside he said, " That will be taken up in the next lesson "—and passed on into the Inn.

All the years I knew Hubbard I never saw him sit down on the Peristyle to talk or gossip.

Next day, following the talk on clothes, Hubbard induced a number of celebrities to discard their dignity and go for a swim in the creek, down at the Ol' Swimmin' Hole. They went. For a while they forgot their years and decorations and honorary degrees—and dove off the bank and splashed and floated and enjoyed themselves like small boys!

But when they came to dress, somebody had stolen their clothes—all but their shoes! These gentlemen were inclined to be a little panicky in their plight and they again discussed the all-important subject of *Clothes*—in the all-together! ❧ ❧

Just then Ali Baba drove across the nearby field in a hay-rick and Hubbard whistled for help. Mysteriously enough, Baba was able to provide a couple of dozen pairs of blue-denim overalls and as many coarse hickory shirts. And by men concealed behind bushes they were gratefully received ❧ ❧

That was the " next lesson " promised the night before ❧

When they reached the Inn amid roars of laughter, the ladies on the Peristyle were invited by the perpetrator of the joke, " come down and pick out your husbands! "

*   *   *   *   *

" We learn by doing " said the Leader of the Convention, and promptly marched the Conventioners up to the Farm and put them to work pursuing the nimble potato bug, weeding onions, or pitching hay!

Of course no one was obliged to work at all, and none to work a second longer than he or she wished to—but at least they were taken into the atmosphere of the potato patch and the hay field, mingled with the real workers, and to a certain extent these experiences changed the viewpoint of many of them.

To paraphrase the poet, it 's better to have pitched one forkful of hay than never to have pitched at all!

When they became interested in the task the Fra would say, " Keep it going till I come back "—and then disappear ❧ ❧

Eventually the Conventioners would straggle back—as, and when, they pleased.

Along with several other meanings the word " vacation "
means " the act of leaving empty or unoccupied—free
from duty—intermission of stated employment." That was
the special advantage of these East Aurora Conventions
of " Philistines and Immortals." They emptied the Elect
of preconceived notions, of hard-and-fast ideas, and put
them in a receptive mood for newer and better, for sounder
and saner ones. Besides, one can not listen to a group of
fanatics, or a galaxy of one-idea men, or an assemblage
of propagandists, without seeing a little of one's self in
each of them!

So these meetings at East Aurora helped to reform the
reformers! ❧ ❧

There were all kinds there.

A wisenheimer once inquired of Ali Baba, " Who is that
derned fool over there? "

" Which one? " asked the Baba.

Some of these visitors at Roycroft wanted to eat their
food raw, and some of them wanted to walk in the dew
in their bare feet (and did); some of them thought they
were " mystics " or " psychics," but most of them were
the men and women who are making America—a very
choice lot ❧ ❧

One can find a physical vacation wherever there is open
country or an ocean beach, but where can one find a mental
vacation and treat one's mind to a thousand ideas—new
and old? ❧ ❧

That was the need the East Aurora Conventions served,
and they 're missed, missed by a multitude of people
who found change, diversion, relaxation and inspiration
in them ❧ ❧

One paid a nominal board-bill at the Inn—that was
about the only expenditure. There was no other way to

spend money in East Aurora. High thinking and plain living and little expense!

Perhaps the newcomer did not always find what he expected—but as the Fra observed, " We go to Life, the Druggist, and we ask for what we want, and he says ' I 'm sorry, I 'm just out of that—but I have something just as good ' —and oftentimes it *is*."

This is a Remittance Man: all such
sent to East Aurora should be provided
with return tickets.

This is a Remittance Man: all such
sent to East Aurora should be provided
with return tickets.

"God will not look you over for Medals, Degrees or Diplomas, but for Scars!"

The Cognoscenti Arrive and Depart

ACROSS the country occasionally one meets the well-intentioned authority who says, " You used to be with Hubbard—well, well! I know the fellow who wrote practically everything that faker ever signed his name to."

" Is that so? "

" Oooh, yes! A remarkable chap! A genius! Told me all about how he was the *real* Elbert Hubbard. Extraordinary fellow ! ∞ Unfortunately addicted to alcohol. But drunk or sober—a gentleman. Do you remember him? "

Do I remember him?

Of course I remember him.

I remember him in sixes and dozens. Many's the time I have helped to put him or his double on the Four o'Clock Train, and drunk or sober he was not always a gentleman! When he was invited to go hence and it came to a showdown, there was usually a show-up as well.

These geniuses were the *cognoscenti,* the connoisseurs of life and living, who came in uninvited from nowhere to live the Ideal Life.

I can recite their speech of application verbatim: " I care nothing for money, I care nothing for what you choose to pay me. I wish to live the Ideal Life, and to do some worth-while work."

They cared nothing for work, either!

Some of them were "remittance-men." The Real Genius
for whom these "extraordinary fellows" posed, says,
"These men were willing to do anything—but work.
They offered to run things, to preach, to advise, to make
love to the girls. We bought them tickets to Chicago,
and without violence conducted them to the Four o'Clock
Train." ᕙ᛫ ᕙ᛫

The Master Roycrofter avowed he could get along with
blind people, deaf people, bad boys and old people, mental
defectives and jail-birds—but that the educated loafer who
smoked cigarets in bed was too much for him.

There was once a tramp-poet, self-styled, who took Hubbard's money, ate his food, consumed his substance, and
then left in high dudgeon to indite a book in which he
called his benefactor this and that. I believe Hubbard
offended him by asking him to put some of his poetry
into motion and mow the lawn!

These Four o'Clock Train boys were the knockers—and
they were also the boosters, but without knowing it. They
disparaged, but their disparagement came back to East
Aurora as profitable publicity for the enterprise they
damned. Often they turned about and referred familiarly
to "My friend, the Fra," and then tried to cash in on
that. After they had damned the man and East Aurora
to their heart's content they'd write a mournful, penitent
letter and ask for the "loan of a fiver"—and strange to
say they usually got it. It was easy for the Fra to forgive
—because he always saw the humorous side to these exchanges. Besides he believed that his life would justify
itself, and that their testimony *pro* or *con* was unimportant.
Said he, "They say what they say let them say!"

But suppose we listen to the Builder of Roycroft himself
on this subject:

" A frowsled, towsled, greasy and shiny one in a battered dinky derby and tightly buttoned Prince Albert blew into the Shop the other day and greeted me effusively. He was one of the Elect, he said, temporarily reduced and slightly disfigured by too much contact with a cold and cruel world. He glibly explained these things, although he need not, for life writes its record on the face, and the record in this case was writ large.

" Society was all wrong—the rich were getting richer, the poor, poorer—merit was never considered, all things went by favoritism—my friend longed for the Ideal Life ❧
" I started to say something but the Lubricated One shut me off with the gracious wave of the hand unmanicured ❧ ❧

" ' Oh, never mind that,' said he, ' I anticipate you—you were going to say that the Ideal Life is an iridescent dream and that all the East Aurora there is, is the East Aurora that one carries in his own breast. Truth, Truth, shining Truth, but you see I brought my East Aurora with me —my heart is right—I believe in the Brotherhood of Man! ' Where 's Ali Baba? I think I 'll have him take me over to the Phalanstery and get a bite of something before I go to work.'

" There he is," I said, " there he is out there on that wagon with the spotted pony and the load of mail bags.

" I walked to the door arm in arm with my new-found friend and as we reached the steps I pressed a big silver dollar in his palm and called, ' Oh Baba! One moment please—here 's a gentleman going to Buffalo; he wants to catch the Four o'Clock Train! '

" I now hear that the frowsy one has given a not wholly complimentary lecture on ' The Roycrofters As I Found Them.' "

These geniuses were the unhappy and the unfit. They were afflicted with ego and with eccentricities. They were the ones who wore the long hair and the sandals and struck poses in public places so that the guests might see and admire ∾ ∾

Hubbard himself wore his hair long because he was in revolt against " standardization "—but his managers and department heads were short-haired. Those who knew the Number One Men of the business organization at East Aurora will remember that while there were several very shiny pates among them, the Buster Brown hair-cut was a one man monopoly, which proves what it proves, because surely Hubbard selected his aides!

Nevertheless, whoever applied for work at East Aurora, who *would work,* was never turned away; that was the fixed rule. Therefore there was no escape for the department head from the " Ideal Lifers." No sooner did he get one rattle-brain on the train, than he got another on his pay-roll.

The rule was: " These men are entitled to an opportunity to earn their living provided they will work. Somebody must be fair to them and it might as well be us."

Ordinarily, it was no use.

Such odd ones had ability—some of them extraordinary ability. What they lacked was *consecutive* ability. After a very little while they got tired and restless—and then the Four o'Clock Train!

The experiences with the *cognoscenti* illustrate the way everything that came to East Aurora was turned into " copy." These misfits in society furnished just the right material for a series of inspirational booklets which have been used continuously in American business organizations for upwards of fifteen years: *Get Out or Get in Line,*

in which he writes the famous sentiment, " If you work
for a man, for God's sake work for him. If he pays you
your bread and butter think well of him, speak well of
him," etc. Then there was *The Cigarettist* and *Paste Board
Proclivities* and some others equally famous.

These Preachments were aimed directly at the fellow who
did n't know the rules of business or knowing them refused
to admit that they applied to him. They were to inform
the rule-breaker that the Old Man was on to him and to
serve warning.

They were written for home consumption, but like so
much that was written with only the village of East Aurora
in mind, Hubbard discovered they applied equally to the
big city. The particular problem that causes worry in one
business organization is usually a source of trouble in all
business organizations.

American business discovered these Roycroft booklets and
appropriated them. They were offered at nominal prices
in suitable quantities—and lo! they sold by the hundred
thousands, and still sell. So, out of the dead loss created
by the *cognoscenti* there was made a handsome profit ❧

Then there were the migratory meanderers. They were
a happy, friendly, irresponsible lot, who came and went.
Some of them were vags., hobos, gentlemen of brake-beams,
who dropped off in Aurora periodically while on their
perigrination ❧ ❧

Some were just plain Sunkist!

One was Bosco, an ex-actor, deaf as a post. The first time
he came along he asked for work. Not knowing him then
so well as we did later, he was given work. Highly educated,
he claimed he could " read proof." He could—but two
weeks was his utmost limit on the job. Nevertheless he
accepted his two weeks' pay with a tragic gesture signifying

it was all too little he had to give for such bounty, and
made a graceful exit—to go on a gorgeous jag in
Buffalo ᔟ ᔟ

Bosco had " played with Booth and Barrett, Barrymore
and Mansfield." 'T was a fact. One of our scouts verified
the man's history.

He was of an excellent family, and an actor of parts and
prominence, but deafness made it impossible for him to
hear his cues and had driven him from the stage. After
that his habits, plus poverty and self-neglect, had brought
him to the last level.

When he was rested and bathed and fed at Roycroft, he
was not only a charming gentleman and a delightful
conversationalist, but a kind and gentle character. Only he
was beyond redemption, frail and road-worn.

Next time he came along we offered him a ticket on
the Four o'Clock, but he waived the privilege and asked
permission to give a benefit for himself at the Skating
Rink. When the curtain rose, all the gang was present,
including sisters and cousins and aunts. It 's not often
that East Aurora reviews high tragedy—and the hand-bills
which Bosco had personally distributed from door to door
that day announced that he would present the grave scene
from Hamlet, the Ravings of John McCullough, and
Dr. Jekyll and Mr. Hyde, etc.

'T was a full house and Bosco did himself proud, only
he could not tell when the applause had stopped because
of his deafness. Once or twice he came out from behind
the curtain to take an encore which was not on the program. But that did n't matter, the applause was promptly
renewed whenever he appeared—and a grand time was
had by all!

After the performance I went behind the scenes to congratulate the performer. The touch of other days in his performance caused a down feeling in my heart.

The tragedy of such a life!

Before I came away, I slipped a five dollar bill into his hand, and to soften the blow to his dignity I said, " You must have dinner with me tomorrow."

Bosco replied he would be delighted.

I figured he would be in Buffalo on the midnight freight!

❧ The next day was Sunday. As the dinner hour drew near a Sabbath calm rested on the village—when down the street toward the Inn, stepping high, came Bosco— came to accept the dinner invitation.

Not hearing very well, he understood that the gift of the fiver was for *art's* sake, and that the dinner invitation was something separate and distinct.

I was in for it, and I knew it! Instead of going to Buffalo the night before, Bosco had collected his share at the box office and hied himself hither to the nearest hostelry— and liquored up, as the boys say. The aroma of the night before was still with him. Except for that, and a tendency to raise his voice in the quiet scenes (because of his deafness) Bosco's table manners and conduct were above reproach ❧ ❧

From that beginning, " Tragedy by Bosco " was an annual event in East Aurora. Whenever we saw the familiar little hand-bill announcing " Skating Rink Tonight " we knew that once again Bosco was in town.

*   *   *   *   *

Another familiar character at the Roycroft was Sunshine! Sunshine died this past year, and in so doing " made " the front pages of most of the metropolitan dailies. Several of them announced him as a " famous Roycrofter;" others mentioned him as " a friend of Elbert Hubbard."

I find this illuminating item concerning Sunshine in an old *Philistine*. It is a reprint of two newspaper clippings, both from upstate New York newspapers, dated a day or so apart. One states, " Mr. John R. Sunshine is in town and reports that for years now he has substituted for Elbert Hubbard, and given most of Hubbard's lectures. While the name of Hubbard was advertised it seems it was really Mr. Sunshine who gave the lectures," etc.

The other clipping dated a day or so later from a nearby city reports that " Mr. John R. Sunshine has been apprehended and returned to the Binghamton Asylum from which he had escaped."

It is on such testimony Public Opinion is sometimes based. The fact is, Sunshine was a highly educated individual— and only crazy part of the time. When he felt the " spells " coming on, he would pack up and leave for the House of Refuge where he was known and where they would care for him. He always knew in advance when to scoot for cover. Other times, he was an amusing and irresponsible rogue! I cite you an example—

Once my home in a certain city was on Sunshine's direct route North and South. Migrating North in the Spring and South in the Fall, I used to be honored by a call from him. These calls occurred with monotonous regularity. Each time there was a different tale for the inevitable " touch." The last time he called he spread his parcels all over my office, took off his overcoat, opened his undercoat, lit a cigaret, and gave evidence of settling down for a prolonged visit. I was not exactly pleased and looked it. Then Sunshine leaned across the desk and asked, " Felix, would you rather hear my story or give me a dollar to get out of town? "

" I 'd rather give the dollar."

" Sure! " he said, and with that collected his effects in a few seconds, was bundled up again, farewells said, and out the door!

*   *   *   *   *

No, the *cognoscenti* were not the tramps that hang about the water tank waiting for the next freight. They were the " intellectuals " who made up Coxey's Army and other revolutionary groups since. Between their brains and their bodies somewhere, there 's a missing link. They just seem to be disqualified for work—not all of them of course, but there were few exceptions. Yet the patient and ever kindly Fra even reclaimed some of them.

Turning the pages of a *Philistine* I find: " An artist blew in on the way to nowhere, his baggage a tomato can. He thought he would stop over for a day or two—he is with us yet and three years have gone by since he came, and now we could not do without him! "

There in East Aurora was a strange type of business man, willing to take a chance, to gamble on human nature, always hoping to win—but win or lose 't was the same. ⓠ In defense of this policy I have heard him say, " I positively refuse to discriminate between good and bad people. I will not condemn, nor for an instant imagine that it is my duty to resolve myself into a section of the Day of Judgment. I fix my thought on the good there is in every soul, and make an appeal to that."

THE SCIOLIST

BELIEVE in
Co-operation
even with people
I do not like, if it
will bring us any
nearer the Ideal"

Roycroft "Community" and the Socialists

HEN the Socialists called Elbert Hubbard " comrade " it was a case of mistaken identity. Hubbard was not at any time a Socialist, or a Communist either.

He played with words, he dabbled in ideas—but he could not change Nature. He was an American of American farmer stock and consequently an intense individualist ℘ Yet he easily laid himself open to misinterpretation talking about his " Community " and " The Institution of the Dear Love of Comrades."

Only Hubbard meant one thing and the Socialists meant something else.

The Roycrofters was an individually owned business for the first ten years of existence; the next ten, until his death, it was a family corporation. Of course a few shares of stock were held by selected people—but when they left the organization they were obligated to sell back their holdings. The stock paid no dividends—but voluntarily twelve per cent per annum was paid on all stock held by the Roycrofters —which was in reality a bonus. That income or profits were distributed share and share alike was always a myth. That Roycroft property was ever held in common by the " Communists " was always a misconception.

As in all business organizations, there was a pay-roll.

Each individual received what he received. He lived in
the village of East Aurora as a free citizen according to
his income. That was the situation at East Aurora from
the first day of the Roycrofters to the present day. All
tales to the contrary are fairy tales or lies let loose by
malignant tongues or the sorrowful hard-luck stories of
disappointed " comrades " who came visiting and were
not properly appreciated.

There was one " Boss " at East Aurora, but the fact was
rarely asserted. He was kind and generous, and when
treated half decently, forgiving.

All kinds came to the Shops. All were given work, whether
their services were needed or not. Many paid their indebted-
ness with ingratitude.

When in defiance of socialistic doctrines these " comrades "
produced only half what they consumed—refused to do
a fair day's work—and it became necessary in the course
of human events to ask them to depart, they went away
and paraded their tales and dramatized themselves at
the expense of their benefactor.

Except on very rare occasions Elbert Hubbard never
thought it necessary to defend or explain himself. " Never
explain," runs one of his famous mottoes; " your friends
don't need it and your enemies won't believe you anyway."
So the tales of the disgruntled ones went unchallenged,
unanswered—when there was an answer and a most con-
clusive one ✒ ✒

Wondrous were the stories told about East Aurora, and
some of them were perpetuated by being printed in *The
Philistine*. They excited interest, they brought visitors to
see for themselves—and besides (who cared!), they furnished amusement for every one!

So long as the critics were the irresponsibles of society,

he gave them plenty of space in the magazines. Only when hurt by the unjust criticism of some one whose opinion he valued and who should have known better, did he choose his cudgel and strike back.

Though he preferred not to defend—those who knew his ability to arrange and re-arrange adjectives in overpowering sequence did not call him defenseless.

But make no mistake—the Fra himself was in charge at East Aurora!

This was his business philosophy: " Every successful concern is the result of a one-man power. Co-operation, technically, is an irridescent dream—things co-operate because the man makes them. He cements them by his will." ∞ ∞

* * * * *

There have been many communities of socialistic or social and religious peculiarities in America—the Quakers, the Shakers, the Mennonites, the Fourierites, the Rappites, the Mormons, the Amana Colonists, the Oneida Communists, Brook Farm.

During the Nineteenth Century there were more than one hundred fifty such experiments right here in America. Most of them failed because they were unable to hold the interest of the succeeding generations, because their immediate neighbors made war on them, or because share and share alike proved an untenable and unworkable doctrine ∞ ∞

When a socialist experiment fails or when it succeeds, the same thing happens—capitalism captures it, and usually *from within*.

The history of these communities was as well known to the Founder of Roycroft as his Bible and Shakespeare. He was not to be tempted into that sort of error—yet he

believed and rightfully—that we could borrow some wholesome ideas from the old Communists, i. e.: the idea that
all work is respectable including the dirty work; the idea
that plain, clean clothes are plenty good enough for any
one; the idea that social distinctions should be tabu.

I have heard him say: " Because a man can do a clever
stunt why must he live in a big house, have servants dance
attendance on him, own ten times as many clothes as he
needs, decorate himself with diamonds, waste at every
meal enough to feed a family of six, and have obeisance
made when he appears upon the streets in an automobile? "
❡ That was The Roycrofter's true feeling about things.
But perhaps, unconsciously, *he* was just as keen for what
he wanted as the other man is for his wealth, insignia and
accoutrements, and panoply of place and power.

Hubbard wanted to be known—to stand out among distinguished men. He wanted to write for vast audiences;
to speak before the multitude; to be admired and applauded
by them; to be recognized as a power in the intellectual
sphere! That was *his* accolade.

He deprecated material possessions because they were too
easy for him to get, and too much care afterwards ✺ ✺
Each day he did a certain amount of the so-called " dirty
work "—either at the farm, in the stable, on the wood-pile,
and he held a low opinion of the man who refused to do it.
Apart from its social significance he believed that it helped
one maintain one's balance, one's sanity.

Ever and anon, he flirted with the idea of Communism,
and he liked it—so long as *he* remained in charge.

There was something essentially practical—and amusing
—in the way he sought to achieve a certain result. To pay
an itinerant printer a high wage was to invite that rap-
scallion to hold a souse-party on Saturday night after he

received his money. Then he 'd not report for work Monday
and everybody suffered.

There was a spirit of paternalism in Hubbard's method
of paying the minimum wage—and supplementing it with
gifts: perhaps a barrel of flour for the printer's family;
the winter's supply of coal; shoes and sweaters for the
Missus and the Kids; pea-jackets and heavy boots for
the worker himself—hams and turkeys for everybody ๑๐

That was all right for a certain kind of man, but the
self-sufficient, self-respecting kind resented the paternalism, and showed his attitude by shunning the gifts. This
kind of worker wanted what he was to get in his pay-
envelope, and never mind the gifts.

Some people resent being taken care of!

It brought unhappiness.

Two good-enough ideas were in conflict! They were not
workable at the same time and in the same place without
discrimination as between individuals.

When the Shops were first started and there was a happy-
go-lucky crowd accepting the bounty of the Chief of the
Roycrofters I think he was supremely happy. He gave
and they received. He played with the privileges of Communism (i. e., Paternalism) without risking its penalties.
But after a while, when the enterprise grew and the number of workers increased, and responsible positions came
into existence, another kind of man appeared who scorned
gifts ๑๐ ๑๐

Then a choice was necessary.

Either East Aurora had to be really socialistic or capitalistic ๑๐ ๑๐

There could only be one decision.

Everything was at stake.

One man had to shoulder the responsibilities and pay the

debts—therefore the profits, whatever they were, belonged to that individual.

Gradually the gift-giving prerogatives were abandoned. When there was a pay-roll for five hundred people to be met every week it was necessary to square away, drop some of the pleasant " communistic " practises and go in for modern business methods.

Then it was the Socialists shouted, " Traitor! " But they were wrong. They had fooled themselves. Essentially, Hubbard was always the same. Whatever he did or did not believe, he was sane and practical, and he knew what he knew! ◦ ◦

Hear him: " Our dear good friends, the Marxian Socialists, say that under the New Regime we will all get the same pay—eight dollars a day. (Year of Nineteen Hundred Four) * * * I know lots of men who pay seven dollars a day for *supervision*. The less supervision the more pay; the more supervision the less pay. Am I right in this? Or am I just a goldarn old jerk-water Octopus? "

There you have the essence of his social theories—supervision. He believed in the socialistic state—provided it was in charge, complete charge, of a strong man who would decide things for those unable to make their own decisions, and supervise those who needed it, and have the last word on all subjects.

He considered most people children, who needed a Little Father to tell them when to go to bed and when to get up; when to work and how much and at what! how much to spend and how much to save!

Yet he wished to share whatever good things he owned! ⁋ He said, " I would be ashamed to monopolize a beautiful thing."

He wanted paintings and tapestries, statues and fine

furniture available to all, shared and protected by all
—taken out of private collections and brought into general use for the inspiration and education of the plain
people ๑ ๑

He wanted cultural advantages—not only everyday education, but lessons in music, in painting, in the arts and
sciences—made free for all. He wanted social pretenses
and social distinctions done away with—" except the distinction of fine minds."

He wanted the dirty work of the world to be more evenly
distributed, and the easiest way to accomplish that would
be for each of us to do a little each day. He wanted to
share and share alike in Opportunity—and never mind the
money. He believed, earnestly, that when each of us took
out just enough, there would be plenty for all.

He believed that reforms should come from the top down
—and not from the bottom up. He believed that the
Capitalist should have given the Socialist about ninety-
nine per cent of what he wanted before he ever thought
to ask for it. He believed that the principal power of
money is the power of self-destruction. He believed that
everybody should have the necessities, and that necessities are all that anybody should have.

Luxuries are neither necessities nor necessary.

He not only preached this doctrine, he practised it ๑
There was neither wealth nor poverty in East Aurora,
but everybody seemed to have enough.

Of course the defect (if it *is* a defect?) of his theory is that
he always saw himself as judge, jury and chief executioner.
Under his plan there was no security of tenure for the
average individual. When he was good he was happy,
and when he was not good he was escorted out into the
cold, cold World—and that was that!

That 's the Law of Nature, too, is n't it? Likewise the principal defect of practical Socialism! What to do with the one
who won't conform destroys all brotherly love theories!

So when the Socialists called Hubbard this and that for not
living up to their ideals, and when Hubbard smeared the
socialistic leaders with ink because they dared to attack
American Business, I venture they were not so far apart
personally as they thought. Because most of these self-same
socialistic leaders are intense individualists. They were not
quarreling as men; they were quarreling as institutions.

Meanwhile Socialism remains an " iridescent dream "—and
will so remain.

Hubbard differed with and disliked the " academics "
among the socialistic leaders because he considered them
simply as trouble makers, as propagandists, as writing
men who found Socialism exciting, stimulating, and a
good attention-getter. He could n't see how they deserved
the right to represent men with calloused hands, their backs
bent with the burdens of the World.

To Eugene Debs, he gave sincere admiration, although
he said: " His success would mean his undoing. There
would be a grand scrabble among Socialists for place and
power;then there would be mob rule and Civil War.And out
of the bloody bedlam would emerge the strong and con-
scienceless man, say Alexander, Napoleon Bonaparte, or
' Fingy ' Conners, and proclaim peace with gatling guns.
The gallows tree would bear fruit, and ' Gene ' Debs would
swing and dangle between earth and sky."

Nevertheless he pays tribute by saying, " Debs is a very
superior man. He is more than an agitator, for he has a
generous, welling heart of love. Of the purity of the motives
of this man there is not the shadow of a doubt. He is ninety-
nine one-hundredths fine."

That the simplified scheme of Capitalism, and modified Socialism, and practical paternalism of East Aurora is worthy of study is attested by the fact that in thirty years there has never been any kind of labor trouble there, nor a strike!

But never officially or consciously did he take a stand with Socialists or for Socialism—not Hubbard. Once after listening to a Socialist orator I heard him say: " When fifty-one per cent of all the people want to give instead of to grab I 'll believe in Socialism."

That the simplified scheme of Capitalism, and modified Socialism, and practical personalism of East Aurora is worthy of study is attested by the fact that in thirty years there has never been any kind of labor trouble there, nor a strike.

But never officially or consciously did he take a stand with Socialists or for Socialism—not Hubbard. Once after hearing to a Socialist orator I heard him say, "When fifty per cent of all the people want to give instead of to grab I'll believe in Socialism."

ALI BABA in Original Binding.

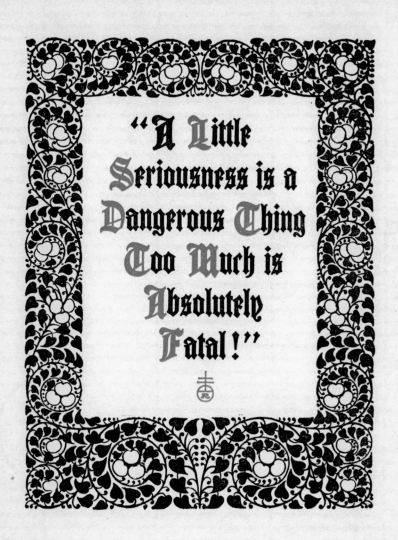

"A Little
Seriousness is a
Dangerous Thing
Too Much is
Absolutely
Fatal!"

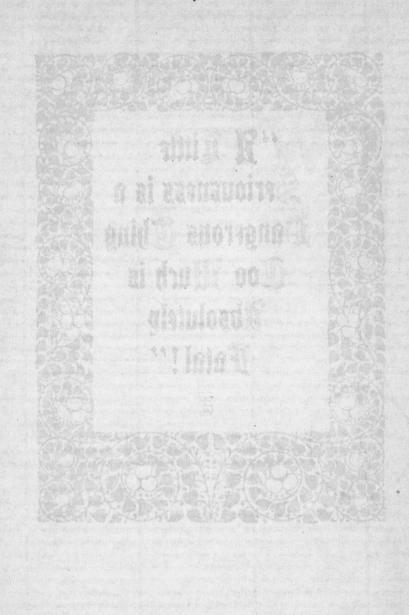

Ali Baba

RITES Hubbard: " At the Roycroft
Shop there is no more faithful helper
than Ali Baba. The Baba is grizzled
and gray, has a stubby whisker and
nice brick-dust complexion. People
who have lived in the village for
forty years tell me that Ali Baba
has not changed in appearance in
all that time, so he must be near
one hundred years old. However, he
is healthy and active; he is the first
one on hand in the morning and
the last to leave at night. He takes care of the horses,
milks the cows, carries in the big packages, and when it
rains, skirmishes around and finds umbrellas and overshoes
for all the girls. The Baba makes himself useful; but I
am sorry to say his vocabulary is not always the language
of Chesterfield."
Please note the last sentence and keep it in mind.
Another time, he is described taking his Saturday night
tub out in the orchard: six pails of cistern water properly
heated in the kitchen boiler, a gourd of soft soap, and a
gunny sack for friction. Of course, Baba timed his ablu-
tions for after dark for modesty's sake and because the
town boys were in the habit of lying under cover and
plastering him with over-ripe tomatoes. When they bombarded Baba, he was at a distinct disadvantage. Finally,
Hubbard says, he gave the Baba permission to use his
bath-room, with a lock on the door, and then all was well.

¶ Ali Baba was given his name by Denslow, the cartoonist, who accused him of stealing his tobacco—so the story goes. They set a trap for the old man, left the tobacco unprotected on Den's drawing board one night—and came back unannounced to find the Baba resting comfortably, his feet on the table, looking at the pretty pictures in the *Police Gazette.* Den is supposed to have given the Baba two kicks, properly placed on the corduroys, and admonished him thus: " Your name should be *Ali Baba or the Forty Thieves"*—and so it came to pass!

Ali Baba was Anson Blackman, a Yankee farmer, man-of-all-work!

When the three Hubbard boys were little fellows he had been their companion and protector. These kiddies called him " Ba-Ba;" that may have been the origin of the name ✀ ✀

When I knew him he was a gentle old man, with the open-eyed wonder and curious expression of a baby, a kindly character with a desire to talk—unsophisticated and friendly ✀ ✀

Early in my contacts with him, I asked Baba, " What about this stealing of Den's tobacco? "

" By cracky! " he replied heatedly, " I never used tobacco in my life. Them fellers think they 're funny! "

Then and there, I became privy to what was going on ✀ Ali Baba, as he was known to the wide world—the gentle admonisher, the censorious friend, the speaker of pertinent and pungent paragraphs—was a creation!

When they broke into print Hubbard was the Baba and the Baba was Hubbard.

In plain words the " Ali Baba " of the public prints was a hoax! ✀ ✀

For example: A summer boarder in the village is supposed

to address the Baba when he's polishing the handle of the big front door of the Chapel.

"My good man, what denomination is this church?" ▫

"Holy Smokes, Missus. This ain't no church. This place does more good than all the gol darn churches in town. This is the Roycroft Shop."

Whenever the Sage of East Aurora had the unsayable to say, whenever he wished to conceal his identity or drop his dignity entirely, that particular paragraph or story was credited to Ali Baba, and the real Baba suffered because of the improprieties, and enjoyed it because of the attention it brought him.

Baba was a good church member even though his friend described him as a "corner grocery infidel."

All the profanity was in Baba's department—Baba who never used profanity. All the bucolic humor was in Baba's department—Baba who was simple and serious-minded and who always tried to explain everything!

Hubbard got action and re-action into his own philosophy by playing with the Ali Baba idea.

Once it was announced in print that Ali Baba that season would give his famous lecture on "Art as I Know It" in a schedule of cities. Subsequently *The Philistine* gave reports of progress and quoted copiously from that lecture, which of course was never given.

Says Baba, "Build your Art horse-high, pig-tight, and bull-strong."

Again: "Art is largely a matter of hair-cut."

Denslow took his cue from this sort of stuff and worked out some very funny cartoons of the eccentric Baba, which were printed in *The Philistine:*

Baba sitting reading in a wheel-barrow of books!

Baba in the Original Binding, and Baba in Full Levant!

Baba in Work Clothes and Baba in Full Dress!

Baba on the Lecture Platform!

Baba on Function Day at the Roycroft!

Of course Roycroft had no " function days "—that was just another absurdity. There was more than a little gentle irony in the Ali Baba philosophy for the initiated.

Locally, there were some laughs in the situation too: gentlemanly visitors with high foreheads, eke women, would arrive at Roycroft, and, after a while, be sure to inquire for the Baba. The girl at the desk would direct them to the barn. Down they'd go and proceed to engage poor old helpless Baba in a theoretical, theosophical, exegetical discussion on the Bergsonian theory, on the Fifth Dimension, or the Fourth Estate, on the Nebular Hypothesis. Baba would chew straws vigorously and slap the horses —" Is zat so?—Whoa thar! Get over thar Hypatia! "

ℂ High falutin' philosophy and science was too much for him!

Once, when a group had departed, I dropped in and asked him, " Well, Bab, what do you think of 'em? "

" Think of 'em! Why, gol darn it, they're all cracked— that's what they are! "

Baba had a sincere and serious mind, humor was not in him. Always he wanted to explain, " d' ya see? "—but always those practical jokers and agile thinkers, E. H., Den, etc., were three or four moves ahead of him. The inquiring guests complicated the situation and added to his perplexities. They " wanted to know! " Never before did an ordinary man have such peculiar prominence— and problems!

* * * * *

Ali Baba was a fine hook on which to hang " copy."

Once I stood on the platform of a country railroad station

with the Editor of *The Philistine*—waiting for a train.
I chanced to see on the bulletin board a sign " Axe stolen!
Bring it back before I come and get ye! "
I beckoned to my friend.
'T was a very undiplomatic Want-ad.
The Fra reached into his pocket for one of the numberless
butts of pencils he carried and jotted down the salient
points ✿ ✿
Next month in the magazine appeared an advertisement
over the name of Ali Baba, " Somebody stole my Axe "
—and continued that he was not going to bury the hatchet
until the enemy dug up the axe! That was the sort of nonsense that made the dignitaries arch their eyebrows at
Hubbard—they could n't understand.
Another time, Ali Baba was put forward as a collector—
a collector of hats. His hobby, it seems, was hats! When
Spring came round and the millionaires of East Aurora
discarded their winter supply of hats, Ali Baba was present
to select the odd and curious styles his collection lacked ✿
" As other men collect bookplates, postage stamps, violins,
brocades, or books, so does Ali Baba collect hats. It is
his one weakness. And through his collecting is he linked
in a bond of brotherhood to all other collectors, the round
world over."
Of course this was a burlesque on the collectors of *objets
d'art*. Otherwise, there were only one or two exaggerations
in the article. Ali Baba did not collect hats, there were no
millionaires in East Aurora, and, excepting the writer of
the story himself, practically no one at Roycroft wore a
hat the year round.
Incidentally this stuff-and-nonsense somewhat explains
what Ali Baba (?) meant when he said, " Those who don't
know how to take *The Philistine* had better not." More-

over, those who did n't know that full half of *The Philistine* was ironical missed half the fun of it.

That was why the readers of *The Philistine* were called a " cult "—one had to have understanding and a sense of humor to be one with them.

When the rash of biographies started to break out in America, Hubbard sat himself down and wrote *Ali Baba, His Life*. Apparently he was going to burlesque the biographers. Then he developed another angle.

Instead he decided to write seriously the Life of an Unknown Man ❧ ❧

He reasoned, " Why is n't the Life of the Hired Man as interesting and fully as important as the Life of the Honorable Luke McLuke? "

As Hubbard wrote it—it is!

When completed, it was printed on hand-made deckle-edged paper, with specially selected type and bound in fine leather and a thousand copies of it were sold—each numbered and signed: *Ali Baba - X - His Mark*. So maybe because of this book, gruff, bluff, honest, kind old Ali Baba—who was a colorful country character and a personality in his own right—may go down to posterity.

Ali Baba (ahem!) was also an epigrammatist.

Here are samples of his quality:

" Two in a bush are the root of all evil."

" Cheap thinking and high kicking are the things that are sending this country to the demnition bow wows."

" Blessed is that man who does not belliache."

" All the belliache in the world is that which you carry with you."

" People who are old enough to know better are old enough to die."

" Do not stand under an umbrella when God rains humor! "

" As for myself, I 'd rather be a good honest wild ass of the desert with long fuzzy ears, than a poor imitation bird of paradise, stuffed by one hundred and seventeen geniuses."

" Don't be a villager—be universal no matter where you live."

" Chickens always come home to roost, which is right and natural; but when they come home to cackle and crow, that is another matter."

" Every man is a damn fool for at least five minutes every day. Wisdom consists in not exceeding the limit."

" If the Devil finds you idle he will set you to work as sure as Hell."

Ali Baba was Hubbard's dual personality, his other self *so* Anson Blackman just happened to be the happy victim. That he enjoyed being the victim there is no doubt. He knew he was famous, he knew people wanted to meet him, to talk with him, but just what he was supposed to say or do he never discovered and it sometimes caused misunderstandings and embarrassment. This Ali Baba masquerade was a curious conceit—and yet I feel quite certain that it served a useful purpose for the philosopher frequently looked on life as the hired man should have looked at it, with wonder at its absurdities and contempt for its follies *so* *so*

Once in so often, he pitchforked an epigram into place that smelled of the barn-yard, just to remind us poor creatures that we are of the earth earthy, and that the man with the hoe and the spade holds the destiny of us all in his calloused hand!

" Once," said Hubbard, " I made him the flat proposition,

thus: ' Here you, Baba, when I tell you to do things you always kick. Now, if you will cease grumbling when I order things done, I 'll give you five dollars extra each month. Is it a bargain? '

" The old man picked up a straw, chewed on it meditatively, smiled and replied, ' No, I 'm gittin' 'nough wages, I guess. You mean all right, but you give too damn many orders. Leave things to other folks a little if you can; the world will have to git along without you some day, and it might as well git used to it now as any time. Git out o' this barn now—I want to sweep up."

Art is largely a matter of hair-cut.

—*Ali Baba*

Art is largely a matter of hair-cut.

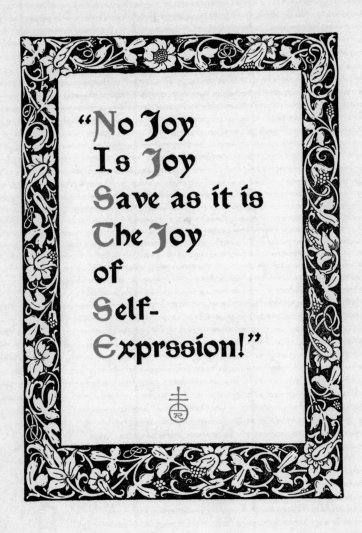

"No Joy
Is Joy
Save as it is
The Joy
of
Self-
Exprssion!"

East Aurora "Personalities"

HE Artists and Craftsmen at East Aurora were like Fuzzy Wuzzy, they did n't "give a damn." About their work—yes. About Public Opinion—well, not so much! That Hubbard was able to hold them together and synchronize and harmonize them over a period of twenty years plus, deserves honorable mention. He mixed cajolery with cussing, praise and press notices—with free tickets on the Four o'Clock, and somehow made headway. Ali Baba was not the only personality on the green!

There was the Red One, for instance, the Keeper of the Keys and of the Records, in charge of *The Philistine* subscription list and the Book of Immortals. He was also the Bursar and the Sergeant-at-Arms, who represented Law and Order. Old Red, with a golden dome like the Mosque of Omar, with his clear blue eyes and abstemious habits, who opened up in the morning and closed up at night—he was the dependable one—and is yet!

The Red was also an art critic ✍ I have heard him say to an artist with a touch of swelled head, " Huh! I could take a chew of tobacco and *spit* a better drawing than that! " ✍ ✍

Then there was Sammy the Artist, who placidly taught the young ladies to make classic initials and to illuminate them; and Von Liebich, who waved his arms and talked

excitedly and presided over music classes and evolved
sweet melodies at concerts; and husky Stacy Betzler who
" conducted the exercises " at the Woodpile!

There was St. Jerome the Sculptor, a wild Irishman with
the head of a cameo—flashing black eyes, raven hair,
chiseled jaws, a beak of a nose and the arms of a blacksmith. A huge swaggering Cossack came visiting at East
Aurora, got gay with one of the girls, and Jerome hit him
on the point of the jaw just once—and they carried gruel
to his room for a week.

Jerome's studio was the upper floor of an old barn ๛
One season he decided to make a heroic group, *The Marriage of Art and Industry*. He fashioned the heavy mass,
toiled early and late, and presently approached perfection.
For almost a year he slaved, touching here, improving
there. Friends dropped in to make suggestions. An idea
was amplified—another figure was added. The great work
for the Roycroft lawn approached completion.

One evening when a jolly group were seated on the Peristyle—a rending, tearing crash was heard. They rushed
to Jerome's studio to find it in ruins. The beams under the
second floor had given way and dropped the masterpiece to
the ground below and smashed it into a thousand pieces ๛
Years after, late one night on Broadway following a Hubbard lecture, Fra Elbertus and I bumped into Jerome all
dressed up for conquest. " Well, well, Jerome, what are
you doing? Where are you living? "

" Oh, I have this commission, and that commission and
the other commission—I 'm living in Washington, D. C."

❡ "For God's sake, Jerome, you 're becoming fashionable!
Throw away your cane, and come and have some ham
and eggs with Felix and Senator Ham. Lewis at *Childs'*
—you must not lose the common touch."

Then there was Alexis Fournier—dear old Alex—who painted the murals in the music room, painted that gorgeous historical series, " The Homes of the Barbizon Masters "— painted like an angel, and who could don paint and war-feathers himself and deliver an Invocation to the Moon in the true lingo, round a camp fire, so as to make an Apache brave shiver with professional jealousy.

There was R. D. Nott—another Red One because of his amber colored thatch—so temperamental that to call him " Red " was enough to make him sulk for a week—yet the best all around artist who ever put up at East Aurora. Pencil, pen-and-ink, crayon, water-colors, oils, they were familiar and easy mediums for the Second Red.

There was Denslow the Cartoonist, whose " What's the Use " and " Every Knock's a Boost " after twenty years are still pirated and sold by the post card emporiums: which is more than one can say of the work of most car-toonists. Den had the voice of a second mate in a storm— a fog horn voice. His sense of humor was upside-down: always grumbling about nothing, always carping, always censorious, and laughing uproariously when he secured his effects.

Fritzy Kranz the model-leather craftsman was a violent-tempered German—which did not interfere with the fact that he produced the most exquisite examples of leather craftsmanship that ever saw the light of day.

One day in a friendly game of health ball, I passed the ball to Fritzy when he was n't looking and hit him in the wrong place. Immediately, there was murder in his eye. He took after me. Either I had to meet violence with violence— or run ⚜ ⚜

To speak plain I welcomed an opportunity to cuff Fritzy a couple; he needed them. But before the bout really

warmed up, Hubbard called, " Felix—you vamoose! "—
and I vamoosed.

Kranz was always " resigning " and always asking to come
back again. He surely had the Grand Opera temperament!
Then there was Karl Kipp, Master Copper Craftsman—
quiet-mannered, easy-going, soft-spoken Karl. He worked
wonders in metal and accomplished twice as much in
volume, with half the energy that Kranz expended and
with a quarter the friction.

Kippy was a silent man!

Otto Schneider was the portraiture artist who preceded
Gaspard. I never knew Schneider, but only recently I
learned that the etchings which were priced at, say, Five
Dollars, when he was associated with Hubbard, command
One Thousand Dollars in the open market today—which
suggests that Hubbard was a good picker of men and that
the East Aurora artists were an up-and-coming lot.

Jules Maurice Gaspard was a prince of fine gentlemen ✺
There was none of the towsled or frowsy about him, and
his ethics and philosophy were as fine as he was fine ✺
Gaspard was well on in middle life when he was at East
Aurora—a man of established position, and not at all
to be numbered among the Younger Barbarians, of which
group I was a recognized member. Therefore I was the
recipient of much fatherly advice from " Gus "—much of
which I remember.

Gaspard made the portrait heads that served as frontis-
pieces for the Little Journeys. In the series to the Homes
of Great Teachers, Hubbard included Mary Baker Eddy.
Gaspard was commissioned to do the portrait of Mrs. Eddy.
'T was a work much to his liking, as he was a Christian
Scientist. He gave the best that was in him to the task
and when completed it was something superfine.

He himself was so well pleased that we all encouraged him to take it and show it to Mrs. Eddy, who was then living. She, in turn, was delighted, and made some sort of arrangement with Gaspard whereby it became the " Official Portrait." For a time, at least, it was used as the frontispiece for *Science and Health,* the Christian Scientists' hand-book.

When Gaspard returned from his successful trip to Massachusetts, he was elated and we all showered him with congratulations. But trouble followed apace.

It so happened that Gaspard had never seen the manuscript or the proofs of the Mary Baker Eddy Little Journey. After the New England trip, he took the trouble to visit the Print Shop and take an advance proof off the press. Then things began to happen.

Hubbard thought he had written a fair and unbiased biography, from the standpoint of the unprejudiced. Perhaps he had, perhaps not. Of course there were certain reservations. He not only praised, but appraised, and criticized ♨ ♨

It 's not my intention to judge the matter. I only know that Gaspard objected. He said he would not permit his portrait of Mrs. Eddy to appear in that particular Little Journey ♨ ♨

" Oh, yes, you will! " said the Author of the Little Journey. " You are under contract with me to produce these portraits. You have produced this one and it 's mine. It will be printed as scheduled."

Usually when Hubbard was stubborn he was one hundred per cent stubborn. But he slept on the subject while Gaspard did n't sleep at all, and next morning he said, " Gus, I think I have written a fair and square Little Journey about Mrs. Eddy. You think not. I know you well enough to know you are sincere in the position you take. I don't want to cross wires with your beliefs or to make you unhappy. Therefore I have concluded to surrender this portrait to you "—and he did.

Then there was Dard Hunter, the best all around Artist and Craftsman that this country ever produced—and that statement is made without apology or equivocation.

Dard had an independent income from some source or other, more than sufficient for his needs. Money meant nothing to him. He worked at East Aurora because he enjoyed it there. Years before, Hubbard had put him on the pay-roll at, say Fifty Dollars a week. Dard exasperated the Old Man by forgetting to draw this pay.

His pay envelopes would accumulate for weeks ⚹ The cashier's department would send over notes—" Come and take it away."

Hubbard would scold, " Why the blankety blank don't you collect your wages? "

" Wages! What wages? " protested Dard in his high squeaky voice as though the very thought of wages was abhorrent to him.

" Why, your money! You better hustle over and squilgee your money out of that cashier or he 'll give it to some one who is more deserving."

" Money? I don't work for money. Let him give it."

Dard was the pure Nordic—a blond Viking type of man, huge, handsome and powerful. Because he had never needed money, because he was always able to earn five times as much as he spent, he thought the race for money to be the most disgusting spectacle in the world.

Dard was no wage-slave! About ten o'clock at night he 'd pass through the Inn going from his work-shop to his room. Next morning he 'd be gone—missing.

" Where 's Dard? "

No one knew.

Finally some one would think to ask the girl at the desk!

" Did you see Dard? "

" Oh, yes, he left early this morning—here 's his address."

The forwarding address would read: " Dard Hunter, Kaiser-hof, Berlin "—or " Bristol, Vienna! "

What did it mean? It meant that the night before in an international trade paper Dard had read that some Deutsch-er had perfected a better method of staining glass, or harden-ing silver, or making paper—and Dard was en route to find out how he did it!

Six months afterward, one morning Dard would be at breakfast again—and in his work-shop half an hour later—with another trade or craft or method at his finger-tips!

❡ Sometimes he 'd be disappointed: the thing or the man would not come up to expectations; the inventor or originator would prove to be a fakir. Then we 'd ask him —try futilely to draw him out: " Well, Dard, there must have been *some* virtue to it! What *were* your criti-cisms? " ❧ ❧

With a distaste for meaningless talk, almost as much as he had for money, he 'd finally force himself to say, " Some things are so rotten you *can't* criticize them." ❧

Hunter was an architect, a designer, an artist in pen and ink, a sculptor, a potter, an iron worker, a cabinet maker, a coppersmith, a type designer and printer, an etcher, a plate maker and engraver, a paper maker and bookbinder, and an expert craftsman in the making of jewelry, lamps and lamp fixtures, stained glass windows, and many, many other things besides.

Though there were some very good workmen at Roycroft, whenever one of them was perplexed, non-plussed, stuck, it was time to send for Dard—who, without a word, would make the machine run, or the process function.

His knowledge and his touch made it right.

Finally Dard decided to do something worth while, to stop frittering. He decided to make a Book.

A Book? Yes, a Book!

Since Time began no one man had ever made a book before —not by himself alone. So he bought a place up the Hudson, an old fort, and rebuilt the old water mill for his own use. Then he wrote the book, designed and cut and set the type, designed and made the initials, and the plates, made the paper and printed it, tanned the leather for the cover, designed the cover, bound the book—and there you are! An easy enough task, when you know how, and when you have the time and inclination and money and application and the character to go on and on, for years and years ✒ Dard Hunter's Book is now in the Smithsonian Institute in Washington, D. C., carefully preserved and protected —and I learn Dard Hunter is going blind!

Well—Kismet! Kismet!

They were a peculiar lot, those East Aurora Artists— peculiar and likable.

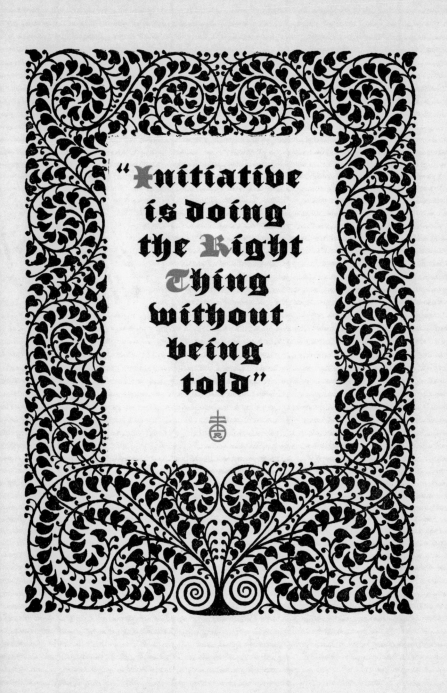

"Initiative
is doing
the Right
Thing
without
being
told"

The Message to Garcia and Its Effect

THE *Message to Garcia* has been printed and reprinted more times than any other piece of literature in the history of the world—the Bible excepted. It has been translated into some forty to fifty languages and dialects—and the end is not yet.

The presses are still grinding out the *Message*.

Hubbard described his inspiration so: " The immediate suggestion came from a little argument over the tea cups when my son Bert suggested that Rowan was the real hero of the Cuban War. Rowan had gone alone and done the thing— carried the message to Garcia!

" It came to me like a flash! Yes, the boy is right, the hero is the man who does the thing—does his work—carries the message. I got up from the table and wrote a *Message to Garcia.*

The *Message* was first printed casually in the March, Eighteen Hundred Ninety-nine *Philistine,* and run without a head, so little did Hubbard think of it. But when orders and re-orders poured in—when the entire issue of that *Philistine* was exhausted in three days—there was naturally some wonder as to what had created the interest.

" What is it that has stirred things up? " asked Hubbard of one of the boys.

" It 's that stuff about Garcia," he replied.

Then George Daniels of the New York Central Railroad asked for a price on one hundred thousand copies—rush. The Roycrofters' facilities were so limited, they estimated it would take two years to get out the order. So instead, they gave Mr. Daniels permission to reprint it in his own way ❧ ❧

The New York Central promptly issued an edition of one hundred thousand copies which were as promptly snatched up. Then four more editions were issued by them of one hundred thousand each—and then an edition of half a million. Then more and more, until everybody lost count. Millions!

For more than twenty-five years the *Message to Garcia* has been printed and distributed in millions of copies each year. The demand does not decrease. Time only mellows the tone of the tale. The lesson and the moral is still there!

*   *   *   *   *

The *Message to Garcia* officially opened the Twentieth Century: for Elbert Hubbard, for the Roycrofters, and for American Business.

Up to that time, I venture that Hubbard still thought of himself as "retired" and of the Roycrofters as an incident to his retirement. After the *Message* was blazoned on the sky Hubbard visioned his future. He decided to be the Voice of American Business.

There are thousands of American writers who can write entertainingly, interestingly, on arts and letters, but the romance of business is on their blind side. Given a business subject, they easily prove themselves writers, only writers and nothing but writers.

Their grasp of business is nil.

Yet in this country and century there is no romance that

touches the lives of so many people as does the romance of business. Here, business and the business of living are the same thing.

Hubbard had scored two distinct successes, as a business man and as a writer, so had an extraordinary advantage ✺ The average writer has no knowledge of business, no sympathy with it; often only a contempt, more or less real. The average business man once he takes his pen in hand becomes inarticulate—dumb!

So, ordinarily "business" is a badly man-handled subject.

❡ Observe this strangest of all phenomena on the American stage: the stage business man of the dramatists and the directors is a wonderful being who does not exist in fact, the scenes are strained and artificial—the "Big act" not true to life!

First, last, and all the time, Hubbard was a business man. He liked to think and speak of himself as such: — "I am a business man with a literary attachment." Freely he gave his admiration to the man who had to "look a pay-roll in the eye."

He knew the problems of business. He felt he knew the solution to some of them. Therefore, when he spoke-up he spoke authoritatively. The *Message to Garcia* was the first of a long series of essays on business problems, which, when placed in the proper hands, have helped to lighten the burden on the business man's shoulders. Inevitably, these sane, sound, practical articles attracted the attention of executives everywhere—raised the question, "Who is this man Hubbard?"—and quickly doubled the circulation of *The Philistine*.

* * * * *

Up to the time the *Message to Garcia* was printed and published and scattered broadcast, Messrs. Hirem & Firem were in charge of the business. Owners of enterprises complained that the " only way to get a job done is to do it yourself," and called their helpers an " ungrateful lot." Each Saturday night they passed out the blue envelopes to one group of inefficient helpers and each Monday morning they hired a new lot—equally inefficient.

Apart from the age old apprenticeships for the trades, business success was a matter of hit-or-miss, time and chance. No one had thought of training youth thoroughly, patiently, to insure progress. Hubbard said to Mr. Business Executive, " Yes, people are just as bad as you think they are, only more so! What are you going to do about it? " Then he wrote the First Lesson on Initiative and Thoroughness, which was the *Message*. American youth showed its liking for his matter by reading, and rereading and profiting and asking for more. Moreover they began to think on their jobs, and progress lies in that direction.

Most of the business training schools that operate on a national scale these days can trace a heritage to the *Message to Garcia*—can trace their success to the inspiration of it, whether they know it or not. The *Message* hit home and put the Boss in a receptive mood to listen to reason, and made business training possible and feasible.

Hubbard pioneered for a constructive, human-being building program! His style was so lucid, his illustrations so natural, his logic so absolute, that whoever read the *Message to Garcia,* or its companion essays, found business an absorbing subject and training a pleasant exercise— was convinced and made hungry for more of the same stuff ❧ ❧

He taught non-readers to enjoy reading.

He taught non-thinkers to think.

He easily convinced the top executives that here was one

writer who was practical—who was not an irresponsible know-nothing—and who was well worth a business man's time ✍ ✍

He put the proprietor on the defensive by proving to him in his private office that his business was not "different." For years the typical executives had flouted and defied progress by waving on high a banner which bore this strange device, "My Business Is Different."

Hubbard said, "It's a pretty phrase—but it is n't true. The ninety and nine of every hundred business problems are the same because human nature is the same."

Said he, "Think of your helpers as human beings, who are ambitious to get along, help them to do it, and you 'll all make head!"

* * * * *

Follows the *Message to Garcia,* written one night after supper in a single hour by the Sage of East Aurora:

A MESSAGE TO GARCIA

IN all this Cuban business there is one man stands out on the horizon of my memory like Mars at perihelion.

When war broke out between Spain and the United States, it was very necessary to communicate quickly with the leader of the Insurgents. Garcia was somewhere in the mountain fastnesses of Cuba—no one knew where. No mail or telegraph message could reach him. The President must secure his co-operation and quickly.

What to do!

Some one said to the President, "There is a fellow by the name of Rowan will find Garcia for you, if anybody can."

❡ Rowan was sent for and given a letter to be delivered to Garcia. How the "fellow by the name of Rowan" took the letter, sealed it up in an oilskin pouch, strapped it over his heart, in four days landed by night off the coast of Cuba from an open boat, disappeared into the jungle, and in three weeks came out on the other side of the Island, having traversed a hostile country on foot, and delivered his letter to Garcia—are things I have no special desire now to tell in detail. The point that I wish to make is this: McKinley gave Rowan a letter to be delivered to Garcia; Rowan took the letter and did not ask, " Where is he at? "

By the Eternal! there is a man whose form should be cast in deathless bronze and the statue placed in every college of the land. It is not book-learning young men need, but a stiffening of the vertebræ which will cause them to be loyal to a trust, to act promptly, concentrate their energies: do the thing—" Carry a message to Garcia."

General Garcia is dead now, but there are other Garcias. No man who has endeavored to carry out an enterprise where many hands are needed, but has been well-nigh appalled at times by the imbecility of the average man— the inability or unwillingness to concentrate on a thing and do it.

Slipshod assistance, foolish inattention, dowdy indifference, and half-hearted work seem the rule; and no man succeeds, unless by hook or crook or threat he forces or bribes other men to assist him; or mayhap, God in His goodness performs a miracle, and sends him an Angel of Light for an assistant ૭ ૭

You, reader, put this matter to a test: You are sitting now in your office—six clerks are within call. Summon any one and make this request: " Please look in the encyclopedia and make a brief memorandum for me concerning the life of Correggio."

Will the clerk quietly say, " Yes, sir," and go do the task? ⁋ On your life he will not. He will look at you out of a fishy eye and ask one or more of the following questions: Who was he?
Which encyclopedia?
Where is the encyclopedia?
Was I hired for that?
Don't you mean Bismarck?

What 's the matter with Charlie doing it?

Is he dead?

Is there any hurry?

Sha'n't I bring you the book and let you look it up for yourself?

What do you want to know for?

And I will lay you ten to one that after you have answered the questions, and explained how to find the information, and why you want it, the clerk will go off and get one of the other clerks to help him try to find Garcia—and then come back and tell you there is no such man. Of course I may lose my bet, but according to the Law of Average I will not. Now, if you are wise, you will not bother to explain to your " assistant " that Correggio is indexed under the C's, not in the K's, but you will smile very sweetly and say, " Never mind," and go look it up yourself. And this incapacity for independent action, this moral stupidity, this infirmity of the will, this unwillingness to cheerfully catch hold and lift—these are the things that put pure Socialism so far into the future. If men will not act for themselves, what will they do when the benefit of their effort is for all?

A first mate with knotted club seems necessary; and the dread of getting " the bounce " Saturday night holds many a worker to his place. Advertise for a stenographer, and nine out of ten who apply can neither spell nor punctuate —and do not think it necessary to.

Can such a one write a letter to Garcia?

" You see that bookkeeper," said the foreman to me in a large factory.

" Yes; what about him? "

" Well, he 's a fine accountant, but if I 'd send him up town on an errand, he might accomplish the errand all right, and on the other hand, might stop at four saloons on the way, and when he got to Main Street would forget what he had been sent for."

Can such a man be entrusted to carry a message to Garcia?

❧ We have recently been hearing much maudlin sympathy expressed for the " downtrodden denizens of the sweatshop"

and the " homeless wanderer searching for honest employment," and with it all often go hard words for the men in
power ❧ ❧
Nothing is said about the employer who grows old before
his time in a vain attempt to get frowsy ne'er-do-wells
to do intelligent work; and his long, patient striving after
" help " that does nothing but loaf when his back is turned.
In every store and factory there is a constant weeding-out
process going on. The employer is constantly sending away
" help " that have shown their incapacity to further the
interests of the business, and others are being taken on.
No matter how good times are, this sorting continues:
only, if times are hard and work is scarce, the sorting is
done finer—but out and forever out the incompetent and
unworthy go. It is the survival of the fittest. Self-interest
prompts every employer to keep the best—those who can
carry a message to Garcia.
I know one man of really brilliant parts who has not the
ability to manage a business of his own, and yet who is
absolutely worthless to any one else, because he carries
with him constantly the insane suspicion that his employer
is oppressing, or intending to oppress him. He can not give
orders, and he will not receive them. Should a message be
given him to take to Garcia, his answer would probably be,
" Take it yourself! "
Tonight this man walks the streets looking for work, the
wind whistling through his threadbare coat. No one who
knows him dare employ him, for he is a regular firebrand
of discontent. He is impervious to reason, and the only
thing that can impress him is the toe of a thick-soled Number Nine boot.
Of course I know that one so morally deformed is no less
to be pitied than a physical cripple; but in our pitying let
us drop a tear, too, for the men who are striving to carry
on a great enterprise, whose working hours are not limited
by the whistle, and whose hair is fast turning white through
the struggle to hold in line dowdy indifference, slipshod
imbecility, and the heartless ingratitude which, but for
their enterprise, would be both hungry and homeless ❧

Have I put the matter too strongly? Possibly I have; but when all the world has gone a-slumming I wish to speak a word of sympathy for the man who succeeds—the man who, against great odds, has directed the efforts of others, and having succeeded, finds there 's nothing in it: nothing but bare board and clothes. I have carried a dinner-pail and worked for day's wages, and I have also been an employer of labor, and I know there is something to be said on both sides. There is no excellence, per se, in poverty; rags are no recommendation; and all employers are not rapacious and high-handed, any more than all poor men are virtuous. My heart goes out to the man who does his work when the " boss " is away, as well as when he is at home. And the man who, when given a letter for Garcia, quietly takes the missive, without asking any idiotic questions, and with no lurking intention of chucking it into the nearest sewer, or of doing aught else but deliver it, never gets " laid off," nor has he to go on a strike for higher wages. Civilization is one long, anxious search for just such individuals. Anything such a man asks shall be granted. He is wanted in every city, town and village—in every office, shop, store and factory. The world cries out for such; he is needed and needed badly—the man who can " Carry a Message to Garcia."

The proper parties conferred an honorary college degree on Elbert Hubbard after the *Message to Garcia* appeared, but, as he says, "Since I did not earn the degree it really does not count."

What did count was that the *Message to Garcia* so advertised its author and East Aurora that it made possible the good work of the years that followed.

" Whatever we are, Clotilde," chided Hubbard, " we must be practical."

Is There a Personal DEVIL ?

¶ "Get your Happiness out of your Work ❧ or you'll never know what Happiness is!"

" Get your Hap-
piness out of your
Work ... or you'll
never know what
Happiness is!"

The Print Shop and Its Work

"ONCE you get the smell of printer's ink into your nose," said Hubbard, "you 'll never get it out!"

First and last he was a printer— not a mechanic (though he understood processes) but an instinctive printer ❧ ❧

When they opened up at East Aurora they worked in an old barn. Two men and a boy were employed, and Cy Rosen was the boy. Nearly thirty years after, the same Cy Rosen is Master Printer of the Roycrofters and Manager of the Printing Establishment.

Cy was and is a church member, a deacon in the church, and in addition one of the kindliest, gentlest characters that ever lived. At Roycroft he was a kind of Daniel in a Lion's Den of agnosticism. There his influence was ever a wholesome influence.

By example and precept he helped tone down the Barbarians ❧ ❧

In a pinch he 'd *pray* for our improvement.

He was the perfect type of Easy Boss who ruled by kindness and with the friendly word. Never did Cy lose control of himself or his tongue—nor of his thought. Always he was at peace with himself and the world. He got the work done by believing in his helpers and trusting them. He swore by them and not at them!

And he was a *Printer*, too!

Under Cy's guidance, The Roycrofters became the foremost
Art-Printers in America and made a reputation for themselves in European capitals as well. Roycroft books won
prizes and awards in international competitions at Paris,
Berlin, Amsterdam and Antwerp!

This fact is commentable and commendable because the
Roycroft Printers were supposedly tyros, amateurs in the
so-called art of book-printing.

Instead of following in line and doing as others were doing,
they went back to the early masters and took their inspiration direct from them. Moreover, with everything to
gain and nothing to lose, they were not afraid to break
away from precedent and defy convention and tradition.
They were called the "Mad Printers of East Aurora"
and pooh-poohed and laughed at!

Admittedly, some of their compositions were bizarre and
grotesque because they sought after effects—and learned
through experiment. But when they failed, they eliminated
and forgot about the failure; when they succeeded, they
held fast to their successes. They evolved a style.

In printing, *Roycroft Style* definitely means something,
because, while it holds the atmosphere of the old masters,
nevertheless, it does not copy them nor any one else; it
is like unto itself alone.

* * * * *

When the Roycroft Printers sought for recognition there
were precious few book-printers in America. Any number
of concerns " made " books but they made them as sau-
sages are made. They ground them out, so many at such
and such a price.

The Roycrofters supplied " The Drop of Ink that makes
the people think." They made other printers think as well.
They made them self-conscious and type conscious. By

comparison they exposed the defects of the existing work and proved in part what could be done with type, composition, color, proportion, paper, and " dress."

A new era in American printing was brought about—a renaissance. Printers everywhere began to brighten up the corner where they were. Till then job-printers were price printers—low-price printers. (Some called them blacksmith printers). Their ambition, their hope, was to produce the cheapest possible work at the lowest possible price—and they succeeded. That is to say, they succeeded in turning out a class of work that brought pleasure to no one and very little profit to the producer. The death-rate among commercial printers was devastatingly high.

The Roycrofters proved that discriminating people would buy fine books and pay a fair price for them; they proved that buyers of commercial printing (so-called) were not satisfied with what they were getting, and were glad to pay more for better work.

They pioneered in proving that an artistic book, an attractive booklet or circular that drew and held attention, was easily worth whatever it cost. For this service American printers owe the Roycrofters a debt of gratitude.

Be it said to their credit, the Roycrofters never produced a dollar's worth of printing on a price basis. The price buyers went elsewhere with their trade—and they got what they paid for, only to find that cheap and shoddy printing could no longer compete with fine printing in bidding for the prospective customer's attention.

Under pressure of the new competition, the maker of books also awoke to the fact that there were several things which he did not know about his own business. Under force of circumstances, he started in to learn his own trade again from the bottom up.

Suddenly he awoke to the fact that there was a growing
market for books " not how cheap but how good," and
he made haste to profit by a good example.

* * * * *

Good taste was shown in selecting the first books that
the Roycrofters essayed to print. Because of the monastic,
the pseudo-classical atmosphere of the place, it was right
and fitting that one of the books of the Bible should be
first, and it was, *The Song of Songs,* which is Solomon's.
Soon there followed the *Book of Job* and the *Book of
Ecclesiastes.* Before the edition of *The Song of Songs* was
well off the press it was exhausted—sold out.

Each succeeding book was equally successful.

Mail orders came in in such quantities they were kept
in common clothes hampers until it was possible to give
them attention. The printing press they used in those days
was a hand-press with a swinging pivot—an arm and an
upright and a " joint "—and the slightest haste made the
machine fall apart. Therefore, through desire and through
necessity, each book was carefully, painstakingly printed
—as carefully as the monks might have done it in days
agone ❧ ❧

To keep the balance true, another early book the Roycrofters printed was George Bernard Shaw's *On Going to
Church,* and it is to be further noted that it was an " author-
ized edition."

I seem to recall that it was Shaw who first took Hubbard
to the semi-socialistic meetings at Hammersmith and introduced him to William Morris.

Then followed Tennyson's *Maud,* Shakespeare's *Sonnets,*
Emerson's *Essay on Friendship* and later *Self-Reliance*
and *Compensation,* Coleridge's *Ancient Mariner,* Gold-
smith's *Deserted Village,* Andrew Lang's *Aucassin and*

Nicolette, The Rubaiyat of Omar Khayyam, The House of Life by Dante Gabriel Rossetti, Elizabeth Barrett's *Sonnets from the Portuguese,* Oscar Wilde's *Ballad of Reading Gaol*—and dozens of similar examples of good reading. They never produced or reproduced an unworthy or paltry work.

When they printed Ruskin's *Sesame and Lilies* the Old Gentleman himself wrote to say, " The beautiful format and attractive binding of this book goes a long way towards making amends for what other American book binders have done to my humble works."

When Hubbard—neither too knowledgeable nor considerate of copyrights—selected some odd bits of Kipling and presented them in suitable dress, somebody's " agent " threatened a lawsuit. From some incidental and half forgotten conversation, I seem to remember that Kipling himself was sympathetic even though the " agent " was obdurate. Whether facetiously or not, I remember hearing Hubbard say, " I settled with him for Sixty-eight Dollars "—and that was the end of the East Aurora attempt to dress up Kipling ✺ ✺

* * * * *

These hand-made books were rich in rubrics and hand-drawn, hand-illumined initials. They were printed on hand-made paper, when such was not nearly so ordinary as it is today, and bound substantially in boards. Next to owning such books, one gets a pleasure by proxy in reading the advertisements that Hubbard wrote about them in the first flush of his enthusiasm.

Here follows some samples of typical announcements:

The Ancient Mariner: By Samuel Taylor Coleridge. A peculiar Book made after the pattern of a Volume

devised by Horace Walpole and printed at the Strawberry Hill Press in Seventeen Hundred Sixty-one ﹏
Rubricated side-lines and initials. For this Book W. W.
Denslow has made special initials and fourteen antique
wood-cut Ornaments by way of illustration:

 900 Copies in flexible Chamois, satin lined $ 2.00
 400 Copies specially illumined 5.00
 40 Copies on Japan Vellum (ALL SOLD) 10.00

The Sonnets of Shakespeare: So far as we know this
is the only Book ever printed in America on genuine
Vellum—the material being prepared for us by the
man who supplied William Morris all the Vellum that
was used by the Kelmscott Press. This Edition was
prepared with great care and is probably the nearest
approach to a perfect Book yet produced by the Roycrofters ﹏ ﹏
On Roycroft Paper—the Initials and Ornaments made
especially for this Book—hand-illumined throughout:

 980 Copies bound plainly in boards . . . . . . $ 5.00
 12 Copies on Classic Vellum, in Full Levant
  —hand-tooled—no two alike, each (ALL
  SOLD) 100.00

The phrase " all sold " as applied to these limited editions
meant that these exceptionally fine books were purchased
before they were off the press. There was maintained at
East Aurora a list of book-lovers—people who had left a
standing order for the best the Roycrofters printed, and
whenever printed.
These book advertisements are worthy of note—worthy
of study by the psychologist, because never before nor
since have fine bindings, expensive books, been sold in

such quantities in America by mail. No natural market
for them existed, and so to discover the preferred few who
really cared, was a matter of searching and finding and
sorting. At the last 't was a gracious task.

From the certain vantage point of having been associated
with the business end of the Roycrofters I seriously doubt
that Hubbard ever made a cent—directly—on the sale of
hundred dollar books. But he made friends, and friends
are the inexhaustible assets of a business.

* * * * *

From the files I offer a half dozen letters received from
book-lovers on both sides of the Atlantic—admirers of
Roycroft books—whom I am sure you will agree are (or
were) fairly well known people:

" Her Majesty, the Queen, directs me to express to Mr.
and Mrs. Hubbard the pleasure she has had in the beautiful
copy of *Sonnets from the Portuguese*. The combination
of paper, typography, illuminations and binding is so har-
monious that the work has been given a place among the
Queen's intimate book treasures."

Helen Barstow,

Windsor Castle Librarian

" The Roycroft books are a great pleasure to me."
—Theodore Roosevelt

" It is probably true that Moses had no Christian name
but in any event the dress you have given this book is
a delight to the eye. I would be proud to have some little
thing of my own come forth from the Roycroft Shop."
—I. Zangwill

" You must send me two copies of each one of the Roycroft
books as issued, to my London address. I have just learned
where East Aurora really is and I am quite provoked to
think that I spent all last week at Buffalo and did not go
out and see how you do it."
—Ellen Terry

" I have seen some of your books, and will ask you to send me one copy each of the publications you have in stock."   Modjeska
(Countess Bozenta Chlapowski)

" The Roycroft books are a delight, and I am showing them to my friends with intent to prove that the old world moves."
—W. E. Gladstone

" Your politics seem a trifle scrambled and your theology no better, yet I have decided to chance your company for a limited time—say 99 years."
—Thomas B. Reed

Once Tom Lawson, Boston multi-millionaire, sent in an order for Hubbard's Complete Works, forty volumes, at two hundred dollars each, and while this was an unusual order and gratefully appreciated—nevertheless from the Print Shop angle the one who orderd ten dollars' worth of envelope fillers received just as good printing! Because the Roycrofters never print below their best.

* * * * *

Louis Kinder the Leipsic Bookbinder was the man largely responsible for the first fine bindings that originally came out of East Aurora. Hubbard testified he searched this country in vain to find a bookbinder. When he failed, he imported one!
Later, Herr Schwartz lent his aid and assistance.
But it is Kinder's star pupil, Charles Youngers, who carries on the tradition at Roycroft these days. They are employing the second generation now—and Charlie Youngers and his helpers are doing beautiful, creditable work.
At the Roycroft Print Shop, Cy delegates the fine composition work to Axel Sahlin, a fellow Swede. Cy saw his work in Swedish trade journals and wrote him, " Ay tank ya better come over "—and Axel came. Since his arrival

he 's won a bushel basket full of prizes for fine composition, and fine typography.

Present day printers who wish to keep abreast of the times
subscribe each year to *Sahlin's Scrap Book,* which con-
tains about the best examples of typography that adorn
and illumine this fair country of ours.

As Hubbard said, " All I can give you is Opportunity "
—but to the right man that 's enough, and plenty.

THE CONSULTATION

THE CONSULTATION

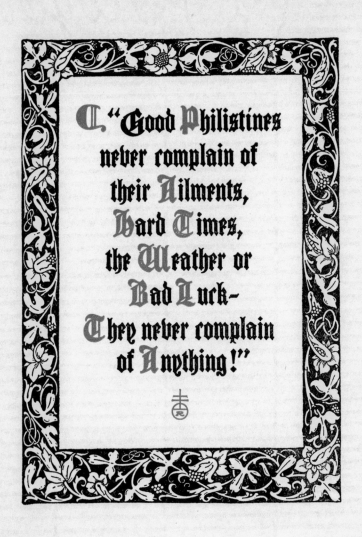

❡ "Good Philistines
never complain of
their Ailments,
Hard Times,
the Weather or
Bad Luck—
They never complain
of Anything!"

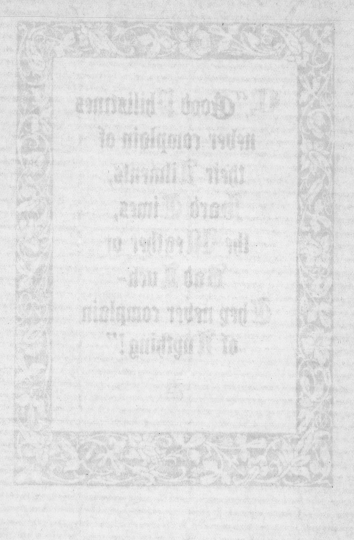

Health and Work Habits

HUBBARD was up at six each morn, and to bed at ten p. m; between times he kept busy. Though he was an easy worker, a relaxed worker, he rarely relaxed completely. For him to loaf with folded hands and do nothing was very unusual. Either he was busy, or "getting his exercise."

There was no time for sitting around.

❡ He came to the Shop before eight each morning—sometimes long before that hour. Till noon time he employed himself looking over the mail, passing from one department to another, checking up—planning, writing. Then lunch. Then perhaps, a fifteen minute nap—which he thought was a great life-giver. Then work till three or three-thirty, and then two hours of horse-back, or walking, or chopping wood or similar hard work.

After the day's exercise an hour in the office "getting out the day's mail." Then dinner and a little while for after-dinner sociability and mixing-in, talking, joking, laughing with home folks and casuals.

Then, provided there was no evening program to be supervised, back to the office to near ten o'clock—bed time ✺

His day at home was a regular one—but from September to April he was on the road on lecture trips perhaps half the time ✺ ✺

To sleep one hundred nights a year on the Pullman cars

over a period of years, to consume thousands and thousands
of miles of mileage, required a strong constitution and
perfect co-ordination of mind and body and habits ✒ ✒
Elbert Hubbard was a plain and simple liver, an abstemious
man. He practised moderation, frugality, industry, and so
kept in perfect trim. I never knew him to be ill a day.

He was neither an epicure nor a stuffer. He ate a little of
whatever was placed before him—but he never gorged!
Paunches and double chins were anathema to him; they
spelled self-destruction.

He was never a pound overweight.

He walked as straight as an Indian.

Walking and riding horse and playing " catch " and hard
rough work were his favorite forms of exercise. He was
not a player of games—though I have known him to wire
John D. Rockefeller a challenge to a game of golf. I have a
hunch, however, that this was more diplomacy than golf
—because Elbert Hubbard was not a golfer. I am not sure
that he 'd come in under one hundred fifty strokes ✒ ✒
Once I suggested to him that the main farm be converted
into a golf links to make an added attraction for the Summer
visitors. Immediately he delivered me a preachment on the
economic waste of golf courses. He 'd have none of them.
There was just as much fun on a farm, with pretense and
hokus pokus eliminated!

Though they played football, baseball, and basket ball at
East Aurora, I never knew him to attend a game. To him
life was real, life was earnest, and the goal was constructive
work, with just enough play to keep one good-humored.
But one must not make a business of play.

Card-playing and dancing seemed to him a waste of good
time that might be better employed—though finally when

dancing became a craze he countenanced it and provided for it, but not for himself.

Altogether he was a worker and an economist of time, but certainly not a sad-faced reformer. There was always time for a laugh. Those who enjoyed his kind of fun found him a delightful work fellow and play fellow, with dullness strictly tabu. He managed to make the day a happy day.

❡ Work was necessary to life; exercise was necessary to live; but play, mental play, by play, humor—that entered into every situation and toned every transaction and formed a back ground for every scene, more than made his life endurable ➤ ➤

* * * * *

Hubbard believed in exercise for health's sake and not exercise for sport's sake. He was not at all a sportsman even though he had an eye for horse flesh. Horses he admired, more than racing. Yet he really took more than an academic interest in trotters.

Incidentally, he had no scruples against " a little bet."

When the Jeffries-Johnson fight was to be staged in Nevada the subject was a very live one. Each man had an opinion, and each advance opinion was as good as the next one. Playing " catch " with him one day I aired my views, which were pro-Jeffries.

He thought the colored gentleman was going to win because he had been fighting regularly, because he was in better condition—and so on.

I differed and offered to risk the whole of one dollar on my judgment. He took me up. We shook hands solemnly.

❡ Some weeks later I had the honor of paying him the dollar I owed him—and he pocketed it!

He was an enthusiastic admirer of William Muldoon, the solid man, ex-champion wrestler of the world, who operates

a health-farm at White Plains, outside of New York City
—and his good will was heartily reciprocated. Hubbard
thought Muldoon a fine type—" a sound mind in a sound
body;" an old man with the body and enthusiasm of a
youth ✒ ✒

Muldoon's business is to take the tired business man when
he becomes too tired, and put life back in him and build
him up. While the lesson is on, Muldoon insists on substi-
tuting his will for the will of the subject.

Mr. Man must obey orders—do what he 's told to do
and no back talk! Once Hubbard visited with Muldoon
and came back with this story:

" Was it Chauncey Depew? Probably not. Well, anyway,
a famous man went to Muldoon for help! They must do
whatever Muldoon says immedjit!. He supervises the
least of their activities.

" One morning in the shower bath, Muldoon barked at
Mr. Man, ' Wash between your toes! Wash between your
toes! '

" He really wanted him to bend over.

" Said the offended one with some dignity: ' Mr. Muldoon,
I am a gentleman. I expect to be addressed as a gentleman.' ✒ ✒

" ' Gentlemen *always* wash between their toes,' sing-songed
Muldoon. ' Wash between your toes! ' "

Freddie Welsh, the then champion lightweight of the world,
was another physical culture friend who came along and
spent some months at Sun-up. Freddie, a family man, was
a student of books, an admirer of things artistic, and
altogether a fine little gentleman—not at all the type
that pugilists are supposed to be.

He was the greatest of all defensive fighters, a ring-general
and boxer supreme. He put on many exhibitions of his

skill at East Aurora. 'T was a liberal education in fisticuffs
to see him at work.

Another friend of Hubbard's was Joe Choyinski, famous
heavyweight who fought a series of highly dramatic encounters with " Gentleman Jim " Corbett, when they were
both in their prime in California. In after years Joe became
the physical director of a bon-ton club in Pittsburgh.

Jack Auer, who then operated a health emporium, exercise
and rubbing rooms, at the Biltmore in New York, was
another friend who came visiting.

I remember one enthusiast who gave The Fra a bad day
once on a time.

In a distant city Hubbard and I called on this man to
inspect his " plant." Nothing would satisfy him but that
Hubbard strip off and be passed " through the mill."

The Fra's philosophy was that he would try anything once.
So he disrobed and was outfitted with light clothing and
taken into the gym. There he was given setting-up exercises,
work with the dumb-bells and clubs, a try-out on the ap-
paratus, and then a thorough schooling in forty different
ways to throw the medicine ball. Then the electric cabinet
and the rubbing couch: the entire program.

Hubbard forgot that he was not accustomed to such violent
exercise, and not as young as he was once, and the physical
instructor neglected to use judgment.

Though in excellent physical condition, his abdominal
muscles were so sore for days thereafter that he experienced
difficulty in talking, walking, and breathing—but not so
much in talking. What he had to say about that physical
mis-director strained the language!

* * * * *

Horace Fletcher, the world famous dietitian, staged one
of his forty day fasts at East Aurora. For that period of

time he ate nothing, and drank only water. The tension affected every one, and intensely annoyed and distracted Hubbard. His doctrine was moderation: he was out of sympathy with extremes. To complicate matters there was always the off-chance the fast would prove fatal ➶ Toward the end of the self-imposed abstinence, some sort of internal decomposition set in, and actually Dr. Fletcher could be smelled almost on sight! Hubbard beseeched him to end it, and finally he did—breaking the fast with slow sips of orange juice.

To complicate a troublesome situation, in the midst of the Fletcher fast, I decided that I would try a fast to learn what it was like and to reduce my weight.

Within a year after I arrived in East Aurora my frame had filled in: I gained forty pounds, from one hundred thirty-five to one hundred seventy-five pounds: which proves what nine hours sleep, three farm-hand meals a day, proper exercise, and the regularity of that life could do for an up-and-growing youth.

Even though I was in perfect condition and could vault on a horse, I decided I wanted some pounds off.

Or was it that the fast was the thing?

At the end of eight days I had lost twenty pounds, my temper, and most of my friends. (Fasting makes one irritable, irascible, peevish!) Then The Fra issued me an ultimatum, and the fast was off!

Along about this time he wrote an article titled " Foods, Fasts and Fools," in which he says things and more things. I still cherish it—with a guilty conscience!

* * * * *

In his book *Eccentricities of Genius,* Major Pond, the impressario, says that while on the lecture tours which he managed, whenever Hubbard did not know what else to do—he took a bath.

Baths were his particular eccentricity!

He 'd stand restlessly in the lobby of a hotel for a few minutes, look at his watch and say, " Well, there 's just time for a bath! "

It makes a good story and it 's true enough, too, but I 'm just wondering, was n't the discreet Fra Elbertus seeking the seclusion of his chamber to get a little work done?

❡ His self-control and concentration were marvelous. He could work on trains, hours at a time, and turn every extra half hour in a hotel room to account.

" Work is for the worker," he said.

Surely he never slighted his work.

He admonished us, " Push your work or your work will push you "—and he promised " The reward for good work is more work! "

All of his manuscripts were written with a pencil, on canary-yellow paper. Before he turned the manuscript over to John Hoyle for editing, he scrawled in his corrections, marginal notes, strung out round and round the page!

❡ He was an emotional writer.

I have seen him at his desk laughing to himself or crying tears down his nose—completely lost in his subject.

Interrupt this, and he 'd give one a shy, self-conscious look. To cover his embarrassment he 'd say, " Let 's go and play ' bully-in-the-ring.' "

On the way out he 'd pick up a half dozen huskies, and hail over as many guests—and the game was on.

The game was played with a weighty medicine ball, the object being for the participants in the circle to keep the active one in the center from intercepting the ball as it was passed. Girls as well as men played this strenuous game. And that is one reason why the young ladies at East Aurora eliminated high heels and corsets from their scheme of things long before fashion dictated it so!

An active life makes for a natural life—and dress.

Not only was Hubbard partial to exercise and baths, but he was equally partial to sunshine and fresh air. All the rooms at the Inn were built with exposed sleeping-porches, and as much of the life as possible was lived out-of-doors. " Half our diseases are in our heads and the other half are in our houses."

Though he owned a dozen automobiles, when he wanted to go any reasonable distance, he walked. " Carry your head up, chin in, chest out, expand your lungs! Fresh air is free! " ❧ ❧

Though he owned an Inn, with a dozen farms to supply it, frequently he and Mrs. Hubbard would walk up to the one-room Bungalow and prepare their own simple meal, themselves; prepare it and serve it and enjoy it!

His health habits and his work habits were based on simple commonsense rules—except that he lived up to them!

Here's his benediction: " It's a glorious privilege to live: to feel, to know, to act, to listen, to behold, to love; to look up at the blue Summer sky; to see the sun sink slowly beyond the line of the horizon; to watch the worlds come twinkling into view—first, one by one, and then, myriads that no man can count, and lo! the universe is white with them; and you and I are here! "

When there was no other good excuse for a walk in East Aurora, at the end of the business day we'd walk out a mile to a high place to see the sunset.

Ex Libris

Ali Baba

¶ "Responsibilities
gravitate to the
Shoulders that can
carry them, and
Power flows to the
One
who Knows How!"

Hubbard The Businessman

ALWAYS Hubbard sold the Ideal—a product plus an idea, plus a word picture, plus a promise of a pleasure to come. A book was only a book until he described it, and then it was a book that you could not afford to miss. He'd suggest that what Robert Browning said to Elizabeth Barrett the night he proposed was really something extra choice—and recommend that you read the Barrett-Browning "Little Journey" to inform yourself—two dollars a copy, in Limp leather.

He'd tempt you with a part of the plot, or a sample of the text, and leave you on tip-toe, expectant, wanting more ✒ ✒

Observe how the astute book advertisers of the present day have borrowed and developed this idea of quoting a part of the plot, and have thus stimulated the book buyers' curiosity; net results have doubled.

They're all doing it—twenty years after!

The Hubbard idea was not a catch penny policy at all, but a sincere belief that the reader was entitled to know something about what he was asked to purchase—in advance. His logic was that people failed to buy voluntarily only because they didn't know; that once they saw the picture as he saw it, they quickly sent in their money. As intimated, results proved his theory correct.

He endowed each book, each product, with personality,

and it sold! The fundamental of Hubbard's sales policy
was to produce a product with "sales points," and then
to emphasize those sales points, make them so attractive
that buyers besieged the gates, and pushed their money
in under the doors! Then to ship them extra value so they 'd
come back for more!

" Give me an Idea! " invited Hubbard—and given an idea,
he quickly converted the same into sales.

His admiration went to the one who moved the goods.
Said he, " A business man is the one who *gets the business*."

❡ East Aurora would have brought up in the hands of
the sheriff in the first five years had not Hubbard had
extraordinary sales sense. One can't pay, feed, clothe, and
care for some five hundred people and their families on
ideals alone—not unless those ideals can be put up into
marketable packages and sold.

Of course there were moments of exasperation. I remember
a day when Hubbard entered the stock room and saw
there thousands and thousands of books, piles and piles
of them—enough to take one's breath away—piled from
floor to ceiling!

" Well, look at those books! look at those books! Say—
we 're not book *salesmen*, we 're book*keepers!* "

To make an artistic product was one thing—but to find
a market for this product, to educate the people to want it,
to need it, was a masterful achievement in itself, and required
a special kind of genius. Sometimes I think the last was first
in his mind, because I have heard him say, " I can find
a hundred people to make beautiful things, I can find
another hundred to record and fill the orders—but where
can I find the one who will help me to *get* the orders? "

❡ He was never ashamed of the fact that he gave a good

part of his time and attention to the problem of sales.
This practical sentiment I find in a *Philistine:*
" Am I a Business Man? If so I am glad. To refer to me
as " commercial " does not hurt my feelings. The World
of Commerce is just as honorable as the World of Art
and a trifle more necessary. Art exists on the surplus that
Business Men accumulate.
"Art, Literature and Music subsist on the sufferance, patronage and encouragement that Business Men supply."
So Hubbard was a sales maker—a business man—and
because of his abilities along these lines he " looked a
pay roll in the eye " with confidence, and the Roycrofters
prospered and pushed on!

* * * * *

Like all successful men Hubbard was a gambler in business.
Not that he played the stock market—no. But outline to
him an idea, a plan, that involved the expenditure of a
substantial sum of money, make the argument convincing,
and he 'd write his O.K. on the outlay without a murmur.
¶ I have slid off my horse on a country road to sketch
a business building plan for him in the dust—and had his
approval before I was able to climb back into the saddle:
" That looks good, go ahead and try it! "
Nor did he figure to win every time. He knew that given
a winning percentage, the law of averages would take care
of the losses.
I never heard him say, " I 'll think it over," or " I 'll sleep
on it and let you know."
'T was either " Yes " or " No," then and there.
One of his favorite mottoes read thus: " An executive is
one who makes an immediate decision and is sometimes
right! "
Given a profitable idea, he 'd put it to work, and press

forward with it until the going became difficult—until results dropped off, and then he 'd abandon it without a backward look, and get out a fresh idea! He never tried to take the very last penny out of a plan. He never sent good money after bad money, and so, while he missed some potential profits, he avoided many losses.

He was not in the squeezing business.

What he wanted was an idea—an idea—an idea! Lots of 'em! ¶ His was a mail order business, and thousands of business men bought books and things from him for the privilege of being continued on his " mail list." To receive The Roycrofters' various and sundry solicitations and communications was a business education in itself—and an education in tactics.

Because Hubbard was unafraid, because he never kowtowed to the customer or prospect, because he dared to be human, it was a real pleasure to trade with him.

There were original minds at East Aurora and Fra Elbertus made full use of them. Perhaps a single unique or unusual phrase might bring in ten thousand dollars in mail orders or apparently be responsible for the influx. Therefore he was forever on the lookout for an " attention getter."

Some of his methods were breath-taking. For instance: Hubbard never looked up credit ratings. First, because he believed the race to be honest, and second, because the average order was too small and the margin of profit too narrow to bother.

He shipped whatever was ordered " On suspicion."

Some of the *literati* did not pay up promptly. Thereafter, the first statement sent was a statement, only that and nothing more. The second carried a Yellow Slip with the word " PLEASE " in block type. The third statement was of the same violent yellow, the printed words in the

same hectic red, but—" PLEASE, DAM YOU." That
fetched them, invariably.

Some were offended and wrote in letters of protest—but
they got over it.

Besides Hubbard had a kind contempt for the sort of
people who neglect to pay small bills—who had to be
bombarded with statements till the profit on the transaction was consumed! At least if they were offended they
deserved what they got.

There 's some satisfaction in that.

Nevertheless he 'd never argue rights or wrongs. He preferred to wipe out the account and get on with the work.
" An argument makes not a right—but a riot."

So when these over due accounts would bulk large Hubbard
would write an article in *The Philistine* and say: "Don't
pay me what you owe me unless you want to. I give you
my release here and now. I 'm done with lawyers; I 'll
never sue you. But please write in and let me know your
intentions so I may clear the books."

* * * * *

He recognized that men and women were just children
grown up, and that in our hours of ease we like to shed our
responsibilities. Therefore when talking business or writing
advertising, it was with a smile on his face. He disdained
the high-pressure methods of the go-getter. He told a
" story "—a wonderful story! Of course, buy the book
was the moral of the story—but look! *With* the magazine
came a prize! (You know how us kids like prizes!) Oh, my!
❡ Nothing to do but sign your name and tuck in a dollar.
" Put the dollar bill into the envelope; we trust Uncle Sam,
and if anything happens, we 'll send you the book just the
same." ஃ ஃ

The prize was a premium. With a one dollar subscription

to *The Philistine* he gave a one dollar book; with a two dollar subscription to *The Fra,* a two dollar book. Strange but true, they were just what they were described to be, and usually Hubbard lost money on the transaction ﹏ ﹏ But he made a friend—and friends are business assets. They buy again—and again.

" Each transaction must be made as pleasant as possible, each as simple as possible. Charge even money so that bills can be put in the envelope—and be friendly."

" Trust the people and they 'll trust you, and remember it is much more important that they trust you than that you trust them! "

" Rogues are few."

" Never send a customer or a potential customer—nor anybody else—a ' dictated but not read ' letter; it may come back to you inscribed in Blue Pencil " Opened but not read." ﹏ ﹏

" Never say, ' Thanking you in advance,' because as Ali Baba warns, ' You ain't got it yet, and mebbe you ain't goin' to git it.' "

" Maybe your self-confident phrase will gum-swozzle the whole works."

" Say it and smile! "

" Give me what I want with a smile," quoth he, " and in an attractive package—and I am Yours Forever."

Just a few simple business precepts, but sane ones!

* * * * *

Inside the plant the Boss was a Humanitarian.

We worked an eight hour day with two recess periods each day. The honor system prevailed. There were really no " bosses " at all at East Aurora.

" That business is bossed best that is bossed least."

There was none of the hurry-up, hurry-up that excites

so many businesses, yet a quantity of fine work was completed. Of course some of the newcomers could not survive
the liberties permitted in the day's work: they abused these
privileges. But what more can be expected from human
nature? After a friendly talk or two, a fair warning, they
either came to themselves, or passed out.

Whenever possible there was a rotation of tasks: a printer
that imbibed too much of the indoors was put to mowing
and shaving the lawn. After the color returned to his cheeks
he returned to his trade.

Youth was in charge.

Boys and girls (literally) did the work.

All the industries were operated on the open shop principle,
and at the end of each school year dozens of apprentices
were taken in. These were fine country lads and lasses.
They were ambitious; they wanted to study and learn.
They quickly made progress. The apprentices of one year
were the artisans of the succeeding years.

This provoked the Socialistic brethren.

The New York *Call,* socialist newspaper, protested that
The Roycrofters were paid in privileges and flowers instead
of money. " Shame! " they said.

There were privileges and flowers, all right—flowers, flowers
everywhere, but there must have been money too, because
when I go back to visit East Aurora these days, I find the
boys and girls of other years driving their own cars, owning
their own homes, and sending *their* boys and girls to college.
Contentment and security was also part of the compensation ✦ ✦

The virtue of Roycroft methods was that they proved up.
❧ Hubbard said, " It 's easier to make a mechanic than
it is to make a man; I like to select my own raw material,
and I 'll abide by the results."

At East Aurora the department head, the expert, was not only an executive—he was a teacher. Instead of bossing he showed them how! Each department was a "class," and the quantity and quality of the production largely turned on the executive's ability as a leader and a teacher. ❡ Impatience and loss of temper played no part in the scheme of things. A boy or girl working at one trade might be learning another as well, after hours. Always there were volunteers to learn and volunteers to teach.

Once I developed the happy idea that I would like to learn how to make a stained glass window. I visioned Burne-Jones effects done by my hands alone. Dard Hunter offered certain evenings and rainy Sundays to the sacrifice; he, the Master, would show me how.

First, I must start on a lamp shade to learn to cut metal, to cut and match glass, and to solder corners. I took six months to make the worst lamp shade in the world, and burned all my fingers to blisters before I was forced to admit I was not cut out for a craftsman. But to the last Dard offered practical advice and suggestions to the bungler! ❡ Five o'clock ended the business day at East Aurora, but ambition recognized no such limitations. The self-help day ran on into the night. Always the Roycroft Shops were open, to render service to the boys and girls. Opportunity was not obliged to knock. It could step right in and find a welcome.

* * * * *

For the reader's edification and interest here is reprinted Elbert Hubbard's business *"Credo:"*
I believe in myself.
I believe in the goods I sell.
I believe in the firm for whom I work.
I believe in my colleagues and helpers.

I believe in American Business Methods.

I believe in producers, creators, manufacturers, distributors, and in all industrial workers of the world who have a job, and hold it down.

I believe that Truth is an asset.

I believe in good cheer and in good health, and I recognize the fact that the first requisite in success is not to achieve the dollar, but to confer a benefit, and that the reward will come automatically and usually as a matter of course ⁊⁊

I believe in sunshine, fresh air, spinach, applesauce, laughter, buttermilk, babies, bombazine and chiffon, always remembering that the greatest word in the English language is " Sufficiency."

I believe that when I make a sale I make a friend.

And I believe that when I part with a man I must do it in such a way that when he sees me again he will be glad —and so will I.

I believe in the hands that work, in the brains that think, and in the hearts that love.

Amen, and Amen.

Build your art horse-high, pig-tight and bull-strong.

ALI BABA, in his great lecture, "Art As I Have Found It."

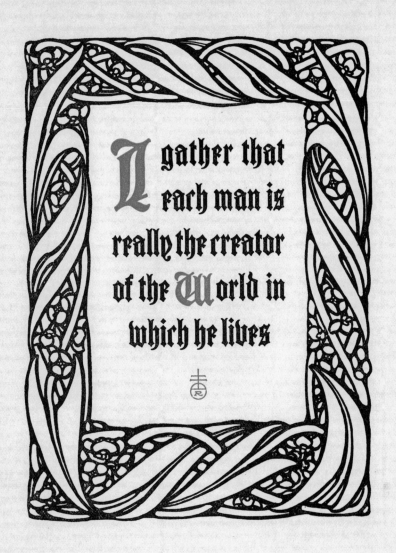

I gather that
each man is
really the creator
of the World in
which he lives

Chapel Nights

AT home and abroad Hubbard liked to think of himself in the role of pastor of his flock; particularly he liked it in East Aurora among his own people. When he was home, Sunday nights were Hubbard nights at the Chapel.

I have heard "Dicky" Le Gallienne say, " Elbert had the power to make us think, weep, applaud—and always to laugh!"

From September to April he was on the road half the time, filling lecture engagements, and meeting the men of affairs of the country.

Between dates he 'd hurry home for rest and relaxation— which really meant to catch up with his work.

But never was there a time when he was too tired or too busy to describe to us " what happened."

Perhaps he 'd played golf with John D. Rockefeller, or visited with Carnegie or talked with Charlie Schwab or Henry Ford. The first Sunday night at the chapel he 'd tell us the inside story of his adventures—and what they said—and what he said.

His descriptions made these men human and unforgettable.

❦ Or perhaps he 'd discovered a new product: a paper vest, a windbreaker, for example: He 'd bring his discovery to the chapel meeting and discourse on its merits and pass out his available supply—free, gratis, without charge—and talk himself into a fine heat of enthusiasm. This talk he 'd be sure to follow with an article on the same subject. " Thus," said he, " do we work our enthusiasm up into copy."

By convincing the home crowd he convinced himself ✺ Perhaps he had visited some shrine, some homestead, or the grave of one of the country's great dead: Lincoln, or Poe, or Lee, or Emerson, or Ingersoll. He 'd tell us what he 'd seen, what he 'd done—and then a delightful discourse on the life of the man and his accomplishments.

East Aurora was a worshipping ground for Great Names. From Moses to Ingersoll, and from Christ and Buddha to James Whitcomb Riley and Mark Twain, there was not a boy or girl, man or woman, of the Roycrofters, but who was familiar with the historic great—and some facts about their lives—what they had written, painted, said, or otherwise done ✺ ✺

Most of the *Little Journeys*—those readable, tellable, talkable biographies which he wrote—were first worked out word of mouth before the home audience ✺ And so the " narrow world " of East Aurora was peopled with an invisible host: the royal purple personages of all countries and all centuries. Hubbard introduced them, they were his friends, and they became our friends.

Fortunate is impressionable youth with such a teacher! ❡ Thinking back and listening again in memory, it seems to me that he made the personalities, the joys and sorrows, of Moses and Confucius, of Socrates and Plato, of Bruno and Martin Luther and John Knox, more knowable, more understandable than the public prints are able to make the transient personalities of the present. Those names which are limned on the tablets of eternity likewise are forever graved on the minds of those who heard the Master's chapel talks ✺ ✺

One day one of the boys " guided " a fashionable female

through the place. Enroute she remarked to him, " What do you do here in the Winter? "

" Well," answered this country boy, who was preparing for college, and earning his living, and supporting an aged mother, and playing games and frolicking besides, "Nothing much." ∾ ∾

" Are you satisfied with this narrow life? "

" Oh, yes—sometimes! "

Afterwards he remarked to Ali Baba and the bunch: " Narrow life! Huh! Jiminy Crickets! Why, when I took her into the portrait gallery, she did n't know Savonarola from Susan B. Anthony! "

* * * * *

The chapel accommodated about two hundred, and a capacity audience was the rule. Summer evenings, the lawn—as far as his voice reached—would be peopled as well. There would be a musical prelude: Jean Kerr or Rose Aaron would sing something of harmony and melody, and Bunny Hunter or Lillian Hawley would play the Steinway. Then came the Hubbard talk.

Dr. Hubbard, Elbert's father, who was a very old man, getting on towards ninety, would sit in the front row and pass audible judgment on his son's observations. They held different opinions on many, many subjects. The old gentleman was strong-minded. Whenever he was feeling good he was very contentious, and well past the point where one is open to conviction. In a lull in the talk, one could hear his thin voice saying, " I don't agree; I don't agree."

The son would look down and smile—delighted. He was glad to see the old gentleman in such a contrary mood, so normal—and go on with his talk as though there had been no interruption at all.

On this chapel platform appeared many of America's

famous men and women of the past twenty-five years:
artists, writers, painters, musicians, orators, Chautauquans,
vaudevilleians, actors, politicians, capitalists—millionaires
and radicals—Reds, Whites, Blacks, Yellows and Browns!
❡ To be permitted to attend these meetings over a period
of years offered more of a complete and comprehensive
education than it is possible to secure at any college or
university ❧ ❧
This was a free forum—this was education without restriction, with full privileges of selection and rejection.
Hubbard denied no one the right to talk, nor himself the
right to *introduce* them. I have heard him " kill them dead "
with an introduction.
To speak after a Hubbard introduction when he was opposed, was to speak in rebuttal, to participate in a debate.
❡ When his introduction was to be negative, he took the
stand that the speaker of the evening was a great and good
man, who was *mistaken*. Then he 'd anticipate, and point
out, and put his finger on the fallacies of the speaker's
utterances-to-be. Not until he 'd removed the sting from
the serpent did he turn the speaker loose to say his say.
❡ Again, when the speaker was a vain or pompous fellow
with a fine opinion of himself, Colonel Little Journeys would
give him what is known professionally as a " twenty minute
introduction." He 'd say all the fine things there were to
say about that speaker, and all the fine things there were
to say about his speech—with pertinent digressions and
discourses. He 'd make his speech for him—and please him
while doing it. But when it came the speaker's turn to
deliver his address, he generally discovered that what he
had to say was an anti-climax.
Once, however, Hubbard met his match!
A certain Spring, Stephen Marion Reynolds was invited

to East Aurora to talk on Socialism. 'T was to be a series
of talks. Reynolds was at once the ugliest and the most
distinguished man I have ever seen. The skin had been
torn and burned from his face in an explosion, and had
grown back in parchment-colored wrinkles—thousands of
them. But the eyes that looked out of this mask were the
jolliest, friendliest, most intelligent eyes imaginable ∾ ∾
His voice was so persuasive, he could have called away
the children from the Pied Piper.

Reynolds was the man who had run for Vice-President
on the socialist ticket with Debs the year of the "Red
Special!" ∾ ∾

Hubbard was no advocate of Socialism. He made that clear
in his introduction. Stephen was a good and great man,
a sympathetic and honest man—but the doctrine he advocated was *tommyrot.*

Reynolds sat there and beamed and smiled and waited
his turn ∾ ∾

Then in his soft, gentle manner, he said, "Of course the
Fra believes in Socialism!—His name '*Fra*' Elbertus,
'Brother' Elbertus, is Socialism! His institution of the
Dear Love of Comrades—that's Socialism! Every one
of his Communistic instincts is a Socialist instinct! He
does n't completely realize it—yet—but he will. All he
lacks is self-consciousness!"

He approved and praised Hubbard, and gently patronized
him as a fellow Socialist, and promised everybody the
millenium—and a division of profits!

He won the crowd, who always appreciated a masterful
performance ∾ ∾

Once or twice again they tried to put on the "Socialism"
subject. Each time "Stevie" was well able to hold his own.

❡ I was almost going to say that given an audience of non-

millionaires who would listen through to the finish, and
with Socialism as the subject, Reynolds was unbeatable.
Because, of course, he promised to those who had not
all the stuff that belongs to those who had!

Before the schedule of Socialist speeches was completed,
Hubbard cancelled the arrangement.

" This is an insidious doctrine—and a damnably false one
—and I am not going to help to propagate it, not even
passively! " ❧ ❧

So said the Roycrofter!

* * * * *

All year round the Roycrofters operated a " Lyceum "—
a home talent effort that furnished diversion and development for many. A dozen or more boys and girls who operated on that local Lyceum stage have since earned a name
for themselves, and attracted a larger audience.

Original poems, essays, stories, plays were read. Original
compositions were played; debates were conducted.

Through the Winter these amateur debates would rage
and storm until most of us became forensic sharpshooters.
Given a likely subject and a friendly audience, and we
could put on quite a show.

When Summer-time came round it delighted Hubbard to
match a hand-picked team of three of his boys against
three nationally famous personages, whenever three such
were caught in camp.

Three more equally famous ones would be selected as
judges ❧ ❧

Of course the contest was held before a home audience
and pre-prejudiced judges.

The decision always went to the home team.

I well remember one such debate on Equal Suffrage. A
United States senator, a corporation lawyer, and a million-

aire manufacturer were offered to the sacrifice. The home
team was composed of S. Jay Kaufman, who now writes
the " Round the Town " column for a New York daily,
and who was then a package of oratorical firecrackers,
the writer, and a youth who had been educated for the
ministry, (it did n't take) and who had a diaphragmatic
voice and all the airy mannerisms of a High Church bishop.
❦ The home team was given the popular side, the affirmative ๑๑ ๑๑
The judges were Marilla Ricker, Elizabeth Towne and
Toby Claude, the comedienne.
After the rocket's red glare and shells bursting in air,
the three lady judges gave proof that their sentiments
were still there or thereabouts; they decided for the affirmative ๑๑ ๑๑
Who won the decision was not important.
What was important was that from time to time the
" boys " were given a glorious opportunity to match their
minds against the ablest minds in America in free for all
debate! ๑๑ ๑๑
Beneath the fun, Fra Elbertus concealed a serious purpose.
❦ Hubbard not only enjoyed—he invited and encouraged
a good joke on himself.
Once he returned from a trip when my name was on the
list for " something original " at the Lyceum. To make
him laugh I wrote and read the foolish little poem which
follows:

What Yo'-all Gwine to Do When Yo' Die?

What yo'-all gwine to do when yo' die?
Whar yo' gwine to go when de bugle blow?
How yo' gwine to ack in de sky?
Who yo' gwine to sass ef yo're sent Below?
Say, Fra, tell me—which way yo' gwine to go when yo' die?

What yo' gwine to print on de sulphur sho'?
Whar yo' gwine to git de skins to bind yo' books?
Whar yo' gwine to hire yo' printers—fifty-two or mo'?
When all de able men are either chefs or cooks?
Say, Fra, what yo'-all gwine to work at when yo' die?

Whar yo' gwine to lecture in de Promised Land?
Who yo' gwine to hammer in dat flippant way?—
Fellers ovah yondah can't pertend to understan'
De jokes 'bout de Doctahs dat yo' always 'bliged to say—
Say, Fra, what yo'-all gwine to *disbelieve* when yo' die?

What 'll happen to yo' Tie an' big broad Hat?
When de climate calls for fig-leaves and a palm-leaf fan?
De boys wear Model Bear Skin in de Steamin' Vat—
So to keep yo' 'dentification better use de Roycroft bran'!
Say, Fra, what yo'-all gwine to look like when yo' die?

What yo' gwine to do ef dey singe yo' long brown hair?
An' 'points yo' Stoker Cap'n of de lef' han' grate?
Will yo' start a big Convention in de fire room dere
An' talk of Priests and Politics, Free Love, Bad Law—
          and Hate?
Say, Man, tell me—whar yo' gwine to finish when yo' die?

These lines were generously printed in *The Philistine,*
and it started an epidemic of similar poems on the same
subject, and in addition brought hundreds of letters from
would-be reformers who pointed to the " error of his ways "
—wanted to know in dreadful seriousness what *was* he
going to do when he died, and what was he doing " in
preparation." The Fra philosophized to me over a batch
of such letters, " Felix, you remember that Tolstoi was
ploughing in a field one day when a ministerial gentleman,
having nothing better to do, leaned on the fence and asked
him this question: ' If you knew you were to die tomorrow
what would you do today? '

" 'Today?' replied Tolstoi, 'today, I would *plough*. Giddap.' "

BOOKS TO BURN

BOOKS TO BURN

"The Great Man
is great on account
of certain Positive Qual=
ities that he possesses ❧❧
not thru the absence
of faults!"

"The Great Man
is great on account
of certain Positive Qual-
ities that he possesses
not for the absence
of Gaulier"

His Eccentricities

O NE who is ahead of his times is always considered eccentric! Hubbard wore comfortable shoes, brouges. They were "eccentric" in Eighteen Hundred Ninety-five, but everybody is wearing them in Nineteen Hundred Twenty-Six. Hubbard wore loose clothing, flannel shirts and soft hats; his early contemporaries wore tight clothing, starched bosom shirts and derbies. Please note which style prevails today.

Hubbard rebelled against the Frock Coat and the Ivory-Front. The frock coat is now relegated to the realm of the Dinosaur, and thousands of Americans have not worn a full dress suit since before the War! He affected soft, colored shirts with soft collars—and behold the *elite* are wearing soft, colored shirts and collars on the Avenue at the promenade hour! ✒ ✒

He introduced the Buster Brown hair-cut to adult America, and some ten million females (more progressive than the males) have adopted this mode; but, as Mr. Kipling says —well, you know what he says!

Here's Hubbard's explanation for his long hair: "The true driver of the quill is a virtuous person. He wears his hair long in token that he does not sleep with his head in the lap of Delilah. My advice is leave thy sconce well thatched and keep scissors at the distance of an Irish mile. Let thy shock grow like a young forest, allowing it to be tossed by the wanton Western wind, nor touched by horse clippers nor sheep shears. The Greeks were called the long-haired. Scissors were a barbarous Roman invention afterwards adopted by the Puritans. In olden times the first mark set on a slave was to shave his head, and any man who getteth even now a sentence of sixty days secures a close crop. Yea, wear thy hair long; it is a sign that thou art free! " ❧ ❧

In another *Philistine* he defends his big hat:

" The man of spirit rebels against this universal attempt of society to make all men look and act alike. The strong man knows that progress is only obtainable by the exercise of individuality. He thinks as he pleases, writes as he feels, expresses himself in his own way, and confronts ossified social smugness by letting his hair grow long when society's edict has ordered it short. Further than this he glorifies his dome of thought by covering it with a peculiar hat. To wear a hat just like everybody else, is to acknowledge outwardly that your head thinks the same thought that all other heads think! Personality first reveals itself in the hat! " ❧ ❧

He being a Westerner, his big hat was a perfectly natural head-covering, and as for his long hair I think that Ali Baba explained away that idiosyncracy when he said, " Ain't it a fact, the Old Man wears all his long hair *outside* his head? "

Once on a lecture tour the Fra left his wallet under the hotel pillow and came away without it. Not until he was aboard the train about to pay his fare did he discover his loss. ❡ Across the aisle sat a Brother Elk in a mellow mood. " Brother," inquired the Fra, " could you loan me a dollar until we reach the next station where I will meet friends? I forgot my pocket-book."

The bibulous one looked him over, up and down, and peeling a bill off his roll, replied, " Sure! here 's five—and say, if there 's any change, for Gawd's sake buy yourself a hair cut! "

* * * * *

Never was there a man who enjoyed telling a story at his own expense more than Hubbard. Some true, and some " constructive " truths.

According to him a " constructive truth " was something that should have been said but that was not said.

Here 's a fair sample:

The Superintendent of a New York insane asylum invited him to address the inmates: " Never did I have a more attentive audience. Of course some of them laughed in the wrong place—but that always happens. Halfway through the talk I was going strong, when a gaunt old woman stood up, flapped her arms and shrieked in a high falsetto, ' My gracious! I can't stand this damned foolishness any longer ! ' —and stalked out! Afterwards the Superintendent told me that was the first sign of returning sanity."

Only a sane man can laugh at himself.

Hubbard greatly enjoyed to tell and listen to stories— the humorous more than the yellow edged variety.

Probably because he seemed unable to master the dialect, his favorites were " coon " stories. A harmless, high falutin' " coon " story was a delight to his soul. He 'd laugh till the tears ran down his cheeks.

Also, he appreciated the absurd type of story, and he 'd remember one and identify the man who told it to him by a particular story.

Once I told him a story about a sweet girl graduate who was taken to Washington to be presented to President Roosevelt. When the sponsor spoke the words of introduction, the sweet young thing gushed, " Oh, Mr. Roosevelt, I 've often heard my father speak of you! "

That tickled him—" I 've heard my father speak of you " —and he 'd quote that phrase at odd and inappropriate times ✎ ✎

The stories he told best, the ones he liked to tell, were of the bucolic variety—he could make the most of the farmhand joke. Barnyard humor he called it—and most of his good ones were told at the expense of poor old Ali Baba ✎ Hubbard was of the earth earthy—a farmer. That 's the key to his character. Unlike the popular conception of a " genius," he was neither ascetic, neurotic, nor a sensualist. His hands were scarred, his nails were broken with hard work of his own choosing.

The only time I ever knew him to take to his bed, incapacitated, was when he cut down a tree, which fell in the wrong direction and partially crushed his foot.

His most outstanding characteristic was his love for children. They came to him naturally. They accepted him without fear or hesitation. Whenever a small child was " lost " in East Aurora it was common practice to look for the kiddie in Hubbard's office first. Either he picked them up and carried them along with him, or they came visiting of their own free will.

All year round people sent him presents, souvenirs, samples: goodies, fruit, candy, a clutter of marvelous things. These gifts, irrespective of value, he gave away to the kiddies ✎ One day I met a six-year-old going down Main Street with an electric lantern—value about Fifty Dollars. I knew where it came from and so I spoke about it.

Said the Pastor of his flock, " That will only belong to the little fellow till his father sees it; you wait, we 'll hear from the father pretty soon."

Sure enough, within half an hour the father dropped in.
He wanted to know, etc. ⁋ " It 's all right, Bill. I sent that
to you so you would n't fall over your feet going out to
bed down the horses at night! "
He loved horses, but I never saw him with a dog.
Much of the play was out of doors in East Aurora, and
some of it was rough. He participated in that, too, and could
laugh when the joke was on himself.
Once cutting wood with the bunch on the Woodpile, to
start a little excitement, the father surreptitiously threw
chips at his son, Sanford. " Sandy " was huge, strong and
powerful, and his father was very proud of him. When
Sandy caught him in the act, he said, " John, you hit
me with another chip, and I 'll come over and stand you
on your head." John tempted fate. He threw another chip
and then ran for it, but Sandy, fleeter of foot, quickly
caught up with him, and much to the amusement of all
observers, stood his father on his head!

* * * * *

The Fra came nearer to being a free man than anybody
in our time because he had the courage to live his own life.
Said he, " What others think of me concerns me little;
what I think of myself concerns me much."
" To thine own self be true " was his private and personal
doctrine—and it 's not always easy to be true to one's self
when pressure is being put on from the outside, and mis-
representations are being made, and lies are being told ✸
The gossips had it that Hubbard smoked. He never did.
He tolerated the cigar- and- pipe smoker, but of the cigaret
fiend he said:
" I say, do not promote the cigaret-smoker, for the time
will surely come and shortly when you will rue the
hour when you ever placed him in a position where he

can plague you by not doing those things he should
have done! "

The gossips had it that he drank hard liquor. Twice
in a period of ten years I saw him touch it.

Once at a Waldorf-Astoria banquet, I saw him lift his
champagne to his lips and take a sip of it, apparently out
of curiosity ❧ All that was left in the glass remained un-
touched through the dinner.

Once I attended a private dinner given by John Merriam,
the cigar manufacturer, in Chicago. I remember that it
was a very small party and that Dick Outcault, the creator
of Buster Brown, was present.

The dinner extended itself and distended us, from about
seven p. m. to about ten p. m., when we were due to take
a train West. The conversation was intimate, friendly,
personal. Our host jollied his distinguished guest and joked
him, and finally prevailed upon him to take a cock-tail.
When the champagne came, he insisted: " Have just one! "
which Hubbard did.

I shall always remember that night.

The dinner was held in a " loop " hotel in Chicago, and
the train left the station on the far side of the river.
When it came time to leave, farewells were said and we
checked out. But no taxi!

" What we need, my boy, is a walk! "

It 's a long walk from the " loop " to that station across
the river—and the wind blows cold in Chicago in January.
We stepped it with two heavy suit cases per each.

Upon arrival, red with cold, he put his burden down, rubbed
his ears and said, " Well, that feels better "—and never
another word again on the subject—and never again did
I see him experiment with intoxicants.

The mention of taxis recalls that Hubbard never rode

when it was possible to walk. Head up, chin in, chest out,
off he'd go briskly toward his destination. I remember
a day in New York: we had an appointment with George
Batten, the advertising agent, at eleven a. m. Going South
on Fifth Avenue, it was apparent we were going to be late.
I insisted that we hail a taxi; my friend was equally determined not to.

Before a taxi came along he settled the argument by taking
off his hat and starting down the Avenue at a running walk,
a double quick. There was nothing to do but follow after
—but being young, I nearly died of embarrassment. It
looked like a chase, and I got the full benefit of the inquiring
stares! ∞ ∞

We arrived on time!

Which illustrates another trait of Hubbard's: when he got
all set, he could be very, very stubborn—immovable ∞
Certain bluffers, blackmailers and rascals who tried to get
easy money out of him learned this to their sorrow. They
got the excitement, but not the money.

* * * * *

Ofttimes when he wrote a joke or a funny story he'd "try
it" on me.

"Well, what do you think of it?"

Perhaps I would say, "I don't think much of it." Immediately he'd tear it up and throw it in the basket.

"You see, Felix, you represent the Common People. If
you don't like it, they won't like it—so I'll destroy it ∞
Come on out and play 'catch.'"

In writing, his habit was to describe a prosperous American
millionaire as a "barefoot boy who used to warm his feet
where the cows lay down." Whenever a prosperous man
had been farm bred, he was supposed to have kicked up

the cows on frosty mornings, and then laid down on the
spot to warm his bare feet and to steal an extra nap!

And I 'm bound to say he used it more than once! 'T was
a typical Hubbard word picture.

One month in the *Fra* magazine he used this expression
to describe one man, and Mrs. Hubbard used it to describe
another, in the same issue. I marked the two places, and
took the magazine into the office where Elbert and Alice
shared the same desk. Hubbard read, and for a brief second
was inclined to become provoked. Then he passed it across
the desk, and after Mrs. Hubbard had turned the pages
the absurdity of it struck him. He said, " Well, Alice,
where do you plan to warm your feet *next* month? "

The Fra was no sit-down conversationalist. To talk over
a subject with him it was necessary to walk, to ride, to
play ball with him. His mind was most active when his
body was active.

I remember a walk with him one afternoon, up through
the farm and back. On the way we passed a palatial pile
of a house being built by the Knox family, the five-and-
ten-cent-store millionaires. Hubbard stopped to admire it:
" Just look at that, Felix! I would have enjoyed building
that house—and when finished, to go away and leave it.
The *fun* would be in building it—not in living in it."

Sometimes when Fra Elbertus returned from a long lecture
trip—say to California—before he reached East Aurora
he 'd take the trouble to convert his cash into five dollar
gold pieces. When he reached the Shop he 'd go about
shaking hands and passing out the gold pieces—" See what
they grow in California! "—the while a smile adorned his
face, his luminous brown eyes alight.

He was always glad to get home and the home folks were
always delighted to have him back, because it was a happier

day when he was there. " Blessed is that man who has found his work " applied particularly to himself. His was happy work and working with him was happy work.

After his death, Bert Hubbard very thoughtfully gave a preferred few the privilege of taking a keepsake from among his father's personal effects. I took his old everyday slouch hat, pinned up on one side with a gold pin, engraved with the words, " Man Can Achieve What Man Can Conceive." ❡ I thought it the most expressive memento of this odd and lovable man—the old broad-brimmed hat—and conceiving—and achieving!

Function Day at the Roycroft:

Ali Baba in Full Levant

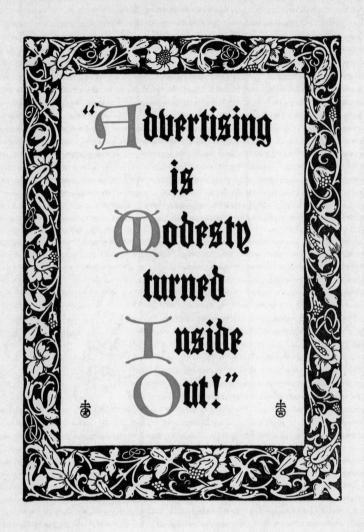

"Advertising is Modesty turned Inside Out!"

Putting East Aurora on the Map

RA ELBERTUS was an advertiser —a first-class advertiser! He iterated and reiterated, " The man who is afraid of advertising is either a nincompoop, or has something to hide."

Know the Truth and the Truth will *not* set you free—not unless the judge and the jury and public opinion know it too!

Whatever was, was advertising under his touch.

He never let an opportunity pass to bring East Aurora, the Roycrofters, or himself, before his public.

Some of his advertising squibs and quirks were amusing to the *nth* degree. Some of his advertising quibbles were real humor.

His full name was Elbert G. Hubbard, and Judge Gary's name was Elbert H. Gary. They both were born in Illinois so Hubbard always facetiously referred to himself as Elbert *Gary* Hubbard and to Gary as Elbert *Hubbard* Gary ✒ He insisted they were named after each other. This of course provoked a smile in the proper quarters.

Judge Gary was just another important citizen who admired the East Aurora genius, read his stuff, and attended his lectures ✒ ✒

There was no dissembling here, no currying favor. On Hubbard's shield was engraved the slogan " I am for Big Business and more of it! " There was no secret about it;

he advertised the fact! He *was* for Big Business and Big Business Men—openly—avowedly!

His personal advertising policy read like this: " I do not apologize for being alive."

He set the style for his friend, Henry Ford, by reprinting all that people said about him: good, bad, and worse. He even originated stories on himself to set the tongues wagging. " They say—Let them say what they say "—

He stated: " The only prophet without honor or mazuma is the one who does not know how to advertise."

Ever and anon he discusses his text pages in the advertising pages—and for a fair exchange he talked about the advertisement in the text. Thus does he get a double-barrelled cross-fire effect—and this explains why *The Philistine* was really read from cover to cover. They were afraid they 'd miss some choice bit tucked away in a corner.

His annual subscribers to *The Philistine* (one dollar each) were Members of the Society of the Philistines. His life subscribers (ten dollars each) were Members of the American Academy of Immortals, with their names down in the Book in red ink, so specified!

And there were a few hundred subscribers at one hundred dollars each—called Thirty-third Degree Members.

That this sort of hokus-pokus pleased people is attested by the fact that twenty-five thousand became Life Members and some hundred thousand subscribed to *The Philistine* in face of the fact that his critics called the little butcher-paper magazine a " house organ."

His " amusing rot," as he labeled it, lifted life out of the humdrum and drear, and gave zest to it.

When he advertised the Inn he never failed to mention, " Special attention to guests without baggage." Whether Ali Baba would show them to the Four o'Clock Train

without delay, or what the "special attention" might
prove to be, was not specified—but the phrase provoked
a friendly smile, and such spells good advertising ✒ ✒
He advertised free use of the Woodpile as one of the attractions for his guests!

He advertised the neighboring city of Buffalo by saying,
"The very best thing in Buffalo is the train for East Aurora," and that the town itself was called Buffalo because
it was almost extinct.

It is hard to believe that certain of the serious-minded
citizens of that fair city took umbrage at this caricature
of fact—and never quite forgave him.

He advertised to send packages of books "On suspicion"
to unknown people, whose names were not in Dun's or
Bradstreet's, and he made money so doing.

He told and printed stories that glorified himself. He published similar ones that disparaged or made fun of him ✒
The Atlanta *Constitution* wrote: "He looks like a member
of the Georgia Legislature togged out to attend a funeral,"
and Hubbard reprinted the compliment.

He believed in the Rooseveltian policy, i. e.: Make the
people talk, give them something to talk about, keep three
or four paragraphs ahead of them, and—never explain ✒
For years the title of his lecture was "East Aurora Folks,"
and wise and sensible people paid money at the door to
hear him talk about his own business and his own people.
Primarily that was because he stood for something. They
recognized that life is co-operation and that without their
help the Good Work could not go on.

If they did not recognize it—he told them.

He christened himself Fra Elbertus—Brother of the World
—but that did not prevent him from publishing the fact
that a Denver editor referred to him as Fra-Hell-Burnt-Us,

called himself the Sage of East Aurora, and proved his
wisdom by getting results and turning in a profit.

East Aurora was not endowed, and to be self-supporting
in a competitive age it had to advertise.

He advertised to give a one dollar Premium with a dollar
Magazine. He made the premium distinctive by offering
it " free, gratis, without charge."

He always referred to East Aurora as Sun-up and the
Land of Immortality, and so created an aura—and the
aura enveloped the Land.

Hubbard dared to take the customer into his confidence.
He dared to risk giving offense to the ultimate consumer.
He treated them as human beings and fellow sinners—
no more and no less. They liked it. He maintained that
there was so much bad in the best of us and so much good
in the worst of us, that there could be no embarrassment
in speaking frankly on the subject.

He defends his policy so: " The grown man who leaves
the room because some one says ' Pooh ' is probably in
debt to his grocer, and is a grouch who is attended by a
thousand glooms."

Consequently he was free, unfettered, outspoken.

Turn the pages of the average periodical of the last twenty-
five years, scan the scandal sheets, and you will find the
ninety and nine afraid of ideas. These were his competitors,
and he joked them, jollied them, made fun of them, scored
on them ❧ ❧

He had no fear of them either—and it was good advertising
for *The Philistine* to tell the truth about them. Some of
his most consistent subscribers were the men he so humorously damned up hill and down, and then patted on the
back. Customers or competitors, neither were sacred to
him. He said (and advertised), " All articles in this maga-

zine are written for the benefit of the man who writes them "
—and he added, " Write as you feel, and your work will
be appreciated by all who feel as you do. Be natural and
proper, but not too proper! "

He was kin to all kinds of men, but no class achieved protection from his pen. His attacks on the doctors, the lawyers and the preachers were relished most by the progres-
sives in those three professions.

Most publications fear to have an opinion or at least to
print one; they 're afraid Old Subscriber will cancel. To
the contrary any month *The Philistine* did not draw some
hundreds of cancellations it was recognized as a poor issue.
New subscribers always doubled cancellations and most of
the " cancels " missed the Hot Stuff; and after a while
like Oliver Twist came back for more.

Each of us deserves to be criticized, either as individuals
or as a class. When we think of ourselves as sacrosanct and
above criticism—when we resent it—then we 're becoming
smug ᎧᎧ ᎧᎧ

Ironically he advertised: " East Aurora has in it three
men who have attained perfection. It may be well for me
to shut off the scoffers by explaining that I am not one of
them. They are Uncle Billy Bushnell, Kerosene Jones,
and Old Cy Gifford, (three corner grocery celebrities).
None of these men read *The Philistine*. From this on let
East Aurora receive the respect that is due."

Hubbard had no nostrum to sell—no panacea—except the
Ideal. When advertising for Members of the Society of
Philistines he made it clear that the " duties of each member
consist in living up to his highest ideal, as nearly as possible,
and in attending the annual dinner if convenient."

Free thinking and self-determination!

" But why did he do and say such extraordinary things? "
ask the carping critics.

" Why, don't you see, he was not ordinary, and so it was
impossible for him to be ordinary!

" Besides he did not wish to be ordinary! "

Hubbard wrote the quotation which he mischievously
credited to Emerson, (so proved by the *Literary Digest* investigation), and which first saw the light of day in a
Hubbard publication: " If a man can write a better book,
preach a better sermon or make a better mouse-trap than
his neighbor, though he build his house in the woods, the
world will make a beaten path to his door."

Afterwards he wisely repudiated the sentiment.

If *he* had lived in a forest and built mouse-traps *he* would
have carved out leafy lanes through it, and put artistic
benches in shady nooks, and named the benches and the
lanes and the forest, and named the mouse-trap, and advertised that name on billboards, in street cars, newspapers and
magazines—and thrown a scare into the entire mouse family.

* * * * *

A part of the success in advertising the Roycrofters may be
attributed to the fact that the man who wrote the copy
was interested in everything—sincerely interested.

His was the hungry mind.

Whenever Hubbard had an unusual experience—when he
picked up a human-interest story he quickly passed it along
to his readers. Therefore the contents of *The Philistine*
covered the map and all human activities.

He appealed to many groups.

He spoke the " language " of many kinds of people. They
understood him. He abhorred the specialist, whom he
thought afflicted with an ingrowing ego. Always he practised what he preached, lived what he taught. That gave

life and vitality and understanding to his " copy." Before
he wrote, he knew! He never strove for effects; his effects
came naturally.

Said he, " Make the thing *live* and it will appeal to people."
❡ The side-show barker's cry, " It 's *alive!* " is still the
most potent attention-getter ever devised—and the fundamental of all good advertising.

Unto this day the attraction of *The Philistine* is that " It 's
alive! " ❧ ❧

The joy of his publication is that it was not edited, not
spoiled by the caution of the counting room. Before
any one had time to be careful it was printed and off the
press ❧ ❧

Letters come in from formalists asking what Philistines
are supposed to believe. Answers Hubbard, " You are not
supposed to believe at all. You are supposed to think and
decide! " ❧ ❧

All of us like to be thought of as self-sufficient individuals—
and to accomplish that " editorial policy " was good advertising ❧ ❧

The Editor of *The Philistine* made it his business to know
everybody worth while.

They found him interesting and talked about him, and
word of mouth advertising is the very best kind. He interested himself in everybody and everything and talked and
wrote about them and it, and made friends.

Friends are the best advertising media.

" To have friends, be one."

He circulated, moved about, established new contracts,
located untapped reservoirs. He named one of his lectures
" Untapped Reservoirs."

Whether he was at home or on the road he was so natural
he seemed artificial. Therefore he presented a problem—

and puzzles are always good advertising. He was unusual in a world that was trying with might and main to become standardized.

Years ago when he took the " gang " into Buffalo to see the Pan-American Exposition, he outfitted them with checked shirts, farmer straw hats, red suspenders and red bandannas. When they arrived everybody knew that East Aurora was present and accounted for. The only question to be decided was whether Mahomet had come to the Mountain or the Mountain had come to Mahomet. At least 't was the Roycrofters that got the press notices and had the fun, and diverted a portion of the crowd and the gate receipts to East Aurora.

* * * * *

The Shops employed approximately five hundred people, and each was a personality. He saw to that. The traits, the eccentricities of each were emphasized by a nick name— and when the visitors came along, looking for the strange or bizarre, the odd and curious ones were there to greet and entertain them—and that was good advertising ❧ ❧ Ali Baba did not have the front porch to himself, not at all ❧ ❧

But the Fra gave the Bab very little competition in gabby-jacking the visitors. One thing he had no time for, and that was strutting, or showing off.

Hubbard knew the market value of a scarce commodity ❧ Once I saw a letter signed with his name which read something like this: " I will yet be famous as Carlyle—if I can keep from mixing too much with the crowd! "

Every Knock is a Boost

Every Knock is a Boost.

I AM NOT IN THE BUSINESS *of* DEFAMING AMERICA *nor* USING AS A DOORMAT THE THINGS THAT ARE BUILDING IT UP: I BELIEVE IN BIG BUSINESS *and* MORE *of* IT!"

Knocks and Boosts

AN acid-tongued critic once decided Elbert Hubbard's writings appealed only to " chambermaids and chauffeurs." ✺ ✺
The easiest way to establish fact is to take a peek into his personal letter files and find out who were his friends and admirers. One finds letters from Theodore Roosevelt, William H. Taft, Woodrow Wilson, William G. McAdoo, Elihu Root, Booker T. Washington, Richard Mansfield, Arthur Brisbane, Edward Everett Hale, Tom L. Johnson, Charlotte Perkins Gilman, James Whitcomb Riley, Dr. Charles H. Parkhurst, John H. Patterson, Ogden Armour, Elbert H. Gary—in brief, from all of Who 's Who in America! There are epistles from pugilists, bank presidents, cabinet officers, literary lights, United States senators, railroad presidents, business men, educators and actors ✺ ✺

He knew them all and they all knew him.

There existed a fine fraternity between Fra Elbertus of East Aurora and the men who are making America ✺ ✺
Here are offered excerpts from a few such letters:

Princeton, N. J., May 29, 1908.
It would give me a real pleasure to be a guest at the Roycrofters' Inn and in some way show my genuine interest in what the Roycrofters have undertaken and succeeded in doing. It just so happens that my life is caught in a

great drift of things, important and unimportant, and that I am hardly my own master. * * * the coming Summer I am planning a bicycle trip in Scotland and England.
—Woodrow Wilson

There are other letters from Mr. Wilson, one as late as January Fifth, Nineteen Hundred Fifteen—just four months before Elbert Hubbard went down on the *Lusitania*

You say some mighty good things in a mighty good way.
—Theodore N. Vail

Your golf game was good, but I shall hope to get even with you the next time we play.
—John D. Rockefeller

I have not seen or heard from you for a long time, but reading your wonderful article in today's *New York American* has given me so much pleasure that I want to congratulate you.
—Nathan Straus

In your issue of *The Fra* for October I notice you have a picture of Eugene Grubb at the Roycroft School, and I have wondered if you could without too much inconvenience send me a copy of the original. * * * Mr. Grubb is a very warm friend of mine. The picture will be valued all the more because you and your good wife are in the group.
—W. C. Brown, President,
New York Central Railroad

When we succeed, as I hope we shall, in electing Governor Wilson President of the United States, I hope that the necessary reform of which you speak so effectively will be brought about.
—Wm. G. McAdoo

I congratulate you on the quality of this issue of the magazine.
F. A. Vanderlip

I was very glad for having the opportunity of meeting you, and I now know why *The Philistine* and your *Little Journeys* are so interesting.

—J. Ogden Armour

May God continue to give more power to your elbow.

—Frederick D. Underwood, President,
Erie Railroad

Your photo is framed and has the place of honor in my Hall of Fame.   —Joe Choyinski

You are as remarkable in your business ways as in your writings.   —(Sir) Herbert B. Tree

I constantly wonder how you are able to keep up the record.   —Booker T. Washington

Salt Lake City, Utah
Such generous sentiments as you express towards a maligned, misunderstood and much-wronged people makes one proud * * *   —Joseph F. Smith

We have to keep in touch in order to steady one another through this journey of life. I feel so grateful for being allowed to live in this beautiful age, in this beautiful world.

—Wm. Muldoon

Are you here? It seems a kind of magic: Perhaps you will call at the theater—or will you come some morning?

—Ellen Terry

My publishers have forwarded to you at my request one of my new books. * * * Really, my dear Mr. Roycroft, we have excelled you.

—Ella Wheeler Wilcox

I should like very much some day to go and look at the things you are doing. But I am a mechanic with a seven-day job.   —A. Brisbane

How I prize your work—hand-made and heart-made. What a difference between that kind of work and manu-

facture! Yet the word means the same as hand-made:
it is the accent only that is changed. After all, accent is
the spirit of life. You have it.

—Henry Van Dyke

Where smooth the Roycroft presses grind,
Their virgin hand-wrought reams of snow
To russet chamois, silken lined,
Unrivalled volumes—marked as low
As Two Dollars per copy—No
Pelf-hanking parsimony yet
May hold the ducats I let go
For Aucassin and Nicolette.

James Whitcomb Riley

One could go on and on and print hundreds and hundreds
of these letters because the recipient was a voluminous
correspondent and his friendships were infinite.

Quoth he: " No man in America has so many friends as
I have. Never a mail arrives that does not bring me love
letters from men and women, old and young, rich and poor,
high or low—they are my own. They tell me of a sympathy
that does not fail and of a hope that does not falter: they
tell of faith and trust."

He had a rare gift for friend making.

The typical Hubbard letter contained not more than one
hundred words—but always a happy, personal phrase,
and always a subject, an idea. One who fell under the spell
of this magic letter-writer was often his avowed enemy,
his rampageous critic.

The fellow who wrote in and called the Fra this and that,
and accused him of the seven capital sins—who lost his
temper and acted disgracefully—was labeled simply " a
friend in the making." Likely enough the Fra sent him
" The Essay on Silence "—with Love and Blessings.

Hubbard recognized a mood—and that moods pass ✥ ✥

" I don't agree with such and such an article," wrote the
self-appointed censor, and added much free-for-all advice
for emphasis.

When the answer was dictated it was to say, " Come to
think it over I don't entirely agree with it myself. Not
everything I write yesterday appeals to me today. I am
glad to learn what you think on the subject. The next time
you are in the neighborhood you must visit us and we 'll
get this subject threshed out for all time. So here is a hand-
clasp over the miles, and I am Your Sincere "—

Of course the critic being the right sort at heart was brave
enough to write again, and say " forgive me;" and soon
he came a-visiting.

* * * * *

'T is strange, but a letter of admiration and friendship,
when printed publicly in a magazine, defeats its own purpose. Most intelligent people look on them with something
akin to suspicion. The " testimonial " in the hands of the
sophisticated is a doubtful form of advertising—except
when it is put forward to repel an attack.

Or, in plain words, when one prints a " boost " he must
also print a " knock." One counteracts the other, and
much mirth and good feeling results. Therefore Hubbard
printed both, indiscriminately. He was not at all fearful
of his reputation.

In fact I have seen him searching for " knocks " to print
when there were plenty of available " boosts " under his
hand ❧ ❧

To maintain the proper perspective on one's self, he believed
both sides must be heard. Of course his calumniators were
chance-impressionists. They did not know him. What they
repeated was hearsay, or an attempt to be humorous ❧
Instead of resenting, he encouraged them.

I believe he held the theory that the more vindictive our enemies, the more steadfast become our true friends ❧ ❧
" My enemies," he said, " are my friends who don't know me." ❧ ❧
Moreover there was a humorous side: the man could not resist a bright and clever remark—even when it was said at his own expense.
It is a trick to turn a frown into a smile!
Here, then, are fair samples of the " knocks " as he published them himself, in opposition to the " boosts."

Boston *Good Cheer:* " The most saintly and the most devilish man I ever saw."

Indianapolis *News:* " The idol of silly sentimental women."

New York *Nation:* " He says he 's not a college graduate, a fact that need not have been stated."

The Straight Edge: " We called at the Shop and found him lallygagging with two female visitors. He had no time for us. We consider him a fraud."

Albany *Argus:* " A freakish combination of impudence and art." ❧ ❧

New Orleans *Picayune:* " In his youth they thought he might be a great man—alas! "

Kansas City *Journal:* " Supremely selfish."

Buffalo *Times:* " An enemy of religion and good order."

Cincinnati *Examiner:* " Ungrammatical and untaught." ❧

Hartford *Courant:* " The P. T. Barnum of art."

New York *Sun:* " Eminently crude and outrageously vulgar." ❧ ❧

Boston *Transcript:* " Disgustingly frank."

Buffalo *Express:* " Bizarre and barren. Why not bind in tin and copper-rivet the cover! "

Des Moines *Leader:* " It is said that he drinks."

Chicago *Journal:* " His egotism is insufferable."

Chicago *Tribune:* " His motto is Love One Another and Knock."

Toronto *Globe:* " The whole scheme seems to be founded on hypnotizing talented men and women into the belief that they are having a good time."

Kansas City *Independent:* " We are glad to know that our prophesies concerning this all-around rogue are being fulfilled."

Louisville *Courier-Journal:* " The admittance was one dollar, the lecture two hours long, and the subject himself."

Peoria *Star:* " The chief aim in his life seems to be to deprive the local barber of all joy in his work."

Syracuse *Standard:* " The only man we know who has the supreme crust to charge a dollar for hearing him advertise his own goods."

Jackson (Mich.) *Patriot:* " The Roycroft vogue happily has now come to an end." (1912)

Hornellsville *Times:* " His success is owing to the fact that : there are many suckers born ' Every Little While.' "

Washington *Star:* " So far Elbert Hubbard has not been indicted for producing sickly, silly, and stupid stuff."

Worcester *Spy:* " Elbert Hubbard has been defending the multi millionaire and now he has succeeded in putting himself in their class."

Milwaukee *Sentinel:* " Fra Elbertus states that morality is merely a matter of geography. Then he should lose no time in consulting an atlas to find out where he belongs."

St. Paul *Dispatch:* " Those Philistines in East Aurora have gotten up a Bible of their own—the other one forbidding several things that the Philistines do."

Of course these bright boys, the newspaper paragraphers, did not mean all they said. They simply desired to appear smart before the home folks. Their good-natured victim did not mind so long as they observed the rules of their partly-civilized warfare.

But when they carried over into the " rough "—when they lost their sense of fair play, then he struck back, and inasmuch as there was no editorial policy to restrain him, and he was a master of epithet, he usually gave a little better than he received.

His tremendous advantage in such encounters was that he took the trouble to know what he was talking about before he opened up. And when he had finished, the offending smart aleck was no longer a pretty sight for the neighbors to look upon.

Offhand I can think of less than a half dozen such exchanges in the twenty-year life of *The Philistine*, because its editor was slow to anger, and quick to forgive, with the insight to recognize all extenuating circumstances. Even so, certain unprincipled loud-speakers still carry their scars.

Then there was the " gentle josh " type of press notice or letter, usually written by a friend with a desire to be funny. Such were supposed to make two smiles grow where only one grouch grew before:

Quincy (Illinois) *Herald:* " Anything you read in the newspapers about Elbert Hubbard positively is. He says so himself." ๑๑ ๑๑

New York *Sun:* " Elbert Hubbard has written a book on Henry Hudson in which there is a deal about Hubbard and precious little about Hudson. Hubbard has the rare faculty of making everybody look small in comparison."

Boston *Herald:* " All these are dead: Bill Nye, Mark Twain, Iconoclast Brann, Bill Barlow; but Fra Elbertus still employs two magazines. Let 's see, what was it P. T. Barnum said? " ❧ ❧

Buffalo *News:* " An unknown man well dressed and seemingly intelligent was picked up by the police at the Union station yesterday. He said he was on his way to East Aurora to buy the Roycroft Shop. He is in the observation ward of a local institution."

Oil City *Derrick:* " *The Philistine* has been printed for sixteen years. Its editor says that during this time there has never been a day when he has not been able to sit up and take nourishment. This is a great tribute to the patience of the American people."

Butte *Miner:* " He has an insignificant stage presence, and no rule of oratory or rhetoric can account for the mephitic spell he throws over his audience."

Chicago *Tribune:* " From announcements in the daily papers we are led to believe that Fra Elbertus is in town and is about to take up a collection."

Indianapolis *News:* " We consider him by right of fitness, the true successor of the late lamented Baron Munchausen."

Boston *Commercial Bulletin:* " Elbert Hubbard is fully convinced that the world is growing better. Elbert is a shrinking timid creature, but we can guess to what extent he holds himself responsible for this marked improvement."

Chicago *Tribune:* " If Fra Elbertus had a crop of hair similar to that which graces the head of John D. Rockefeller the Roycroft Shop would only be a hole in the ground."

The real joke was, my friends and fellow countrymen, that there are about twenty-five thousand publications in America of all varieties. If the editors and sub-editors and paragraphers felt it their duty to keep tabs on Elbert Hubbard—well, it cost them about four dollars a year *each,* at regular subscription rates for the Roycrofters' publications.

Rather a sizeable subscription list of and by themselves, these editorial gentlemen—and in dollars and cents an important annual contribution to the Roycrofters' prosperity ๑ ๑

One thing sure, they were not on the free list!

The Fra De Luxe

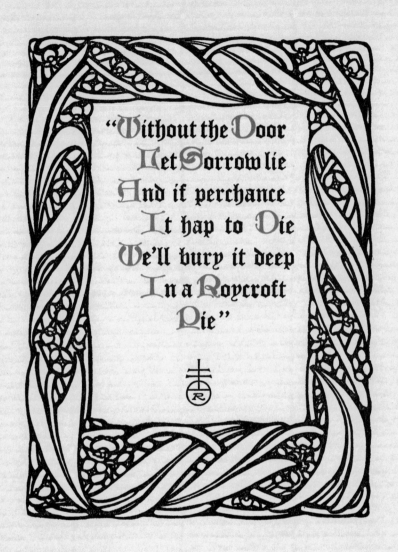

"Without the Door
Let Sorrow lie
And if perchance
It hap to Die
We'll bury it deep
In a Roycroft
Pie"

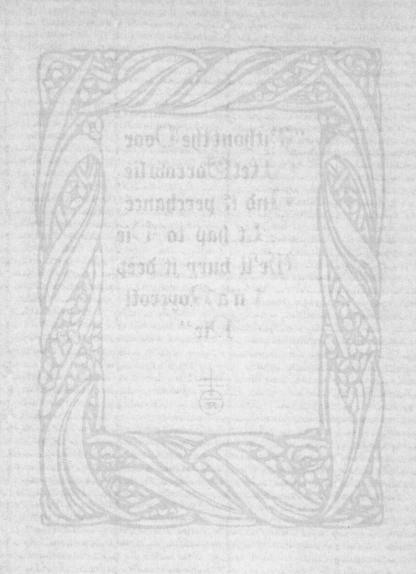

Jokes and Hoaxes

HEN Hubbard was billed to speak in St. Louis a crowded house greeted him. He stepped out upon the stage, bowed to the applause, and seemed about to begin, when a large rotund figure rose up in the right hand stage box, lifted his hand like a traffic cop, and said "Stop!" Then up onto the stage climbed William Marion Reedy, editor of the St. Louis *Mirror*. With some heat the editor addressed the audience: "Ladies and Gentlemen: This man is not Elbert Hubbard! The Sage of East Aurora is my personal friend—and this fellow is an impostor, a pretender, a fraud. I take this opportunity to denounce him, and defy him to proceed."

¶ Reedy climbed back into his box amid thunderous silence! Everybody had recognized him, everybody had accepted his indignant protest as genuine. The audience waited breathlessly.

The figure on the stage stepped forward, slightly abashed, and with an apologetic quaver in his voice, announced: "What the gentleman says is true, I am an impostor, I am a fake, I am a fraud. I am not the Sage of East Aurora at all! My name—my name is William Marion Reedy!" This confession brought down the House.

Reedy and Hubbard were play boys—they played into each other's hands and enjoyed themselves almightily in so doing ❧ ❧

Once Reedy insisted that Hubbard get his hair cut. He urged it for the public good. He insinuated that once his locks were shorn, Samson-like he 'd lose his power. He dared him!

The Fra accepted the challenge—a date was set—an imaginary wager was made; from time to time bulletins were issued ✍ ✍

The newspapers fell into the trap, and across the country the item of interest appeared: " Elbert Hubbard is to have his hair cut! "

When the day of reckoning arrived, Hubbard defaulted. ❡ " Public clamor has induced me to change my mind. Thousands and thousands of the fairest in the land have written me to say they will shun my lectures should I sever my artistic locks. It must be apparent that one can not disrupt a career just to humor a monastic Milesian who lives in St. Louis."

Probably the best known of Hubbard's hoaxes was the *Essay on Silence*—a little book which ran through fifty editions and is still being issued. From everywhere fellow jokers who knew how to catch the ball wrote in, " Unquestionably this is your masterpiece, the best thing you have ever written—wholly unobjectionable—a gift that any husband can give to any wife, or any lover to any sweetheart! "

❡ Of course these kind words were published in *The Philistine* or *The Fra*. The *Essay on Silence* was a book of plain white pages with nary a word written on them at all.

❡ In *The Philistine*, at home, on the lecture platform, Hubbard enjoyed a joke.

In a certain city, the Men's Club billed him for an address. On the night appointed he stepped out upon the stage to find the auditorium crowded, except for the first three rows ✍ ✍

His subject was " The March of the Centuries," but as he started to speak the door opened and down the aisle marched an absolute replica—a duplicate—of himself ◄► Long hair, Byronic tie, flannel shirt, everything was exactly as it should be. Hubbard was nonplussed!

Again he opened his mouth to begin, when in through the door hurried two more figures dressed the same as the first one—except that one wore a fly-away tie of a robin's-egg blue, and the other of red.

Then the Honorable Exhibits began to arrive by twos and threes—scurrying like the white rabbit in Alice in Wonderland—until the first three rows were completely filled with grinning caricatures of the speaker of the evening!

" Before we go on with the lecture," announced the much-imitated one, " now that the inmates have arrived—will the sergeant-at-arms please see that the keepers are all in their proper places! "

After that, when in friendly localities, Hubbard carried a foot-note to his announcements: " So as not to offer unfair competition to the star of the evening, gentlemen with artistic hair effects will please take seats well back! "

* * * * *

Alexis Fournier, the painter, was a Frenchman born in Minneapolis, who spent much of his youth in the great woods. His was a slight handsome figure, with a spot of a goatee and Frenchy moustache, rather dapper. When he arrived in East Aurora the center of activity was at the Ten Mile Camp where the huskies were cutting down trees for rafters and beams. Alex was invited to get into the game—and he accepted, while the wise ones smiled and promised themselves a treat.

On Alex' first day at the camp Hubbard selected a nice full-weight axe, and pointing out an ironwood tree, invited

him: " Take off your kid gloves and let 's see you knock
it over." *s&* *s&*

The gang looked on from under cover, because it is an
established fact that it takes three strong men a week
(more or less) to knock over an ironwood.

Alex removed his kid gloves and his pearl-gray fedora,
his swagger overcoat (which he folded) his collar and scarf
and scarf pin, his coat, fancy vest and outer shirt—while
Ali Baba and the bunch nearly chortled themselves pink
in anticipation of what was going to happen to the " dude."

℄ " That tree you have selec', she is so beautiful, I prefer
to destroy one not so arteestic! "

Before they could head him off he selected for himself a
soft straight chestnut, and with the practised, sure swift
strokes of the professional woodsman dropped the trunk
in the grove in just five minutes by the watch!

Some one paid for the apple cider all around—but it was
not Alex *s&* *s&*

My first year in East Aurora, the Head Roycrofter gave
me a birthday celebration up at the main farm—out in
the open, round a huge camp fire. Any excuse was a good
excuse for a potato-roast, or a camp fire with stories *s&* *s&*

Fournier delivered his Indian Oration to the Great Spirit
and various and sundry performed their stunts. Then there
was a birthday cake to be cut and distributed.

Under Brother Hubbard's supervision, dear old Mother
Grant, the culinary expert at the Inn, had made a cake
two feet across and iced it to perfection. The cake was
exhibited on top of a soap box, on a gorgeously beautiful
silver salver.

It was up to me to make the birthday speech and divide
the confection.

The first time I pressed the knife into the cake I struck

something solid. Again I pressed and again I came against
an unyielding substance. I tried it the third time—and
then suddenly it dawned on me that the " cake " was a
block of wood cut to pattern and iced!

So lifting the knife overhead I struck a pose and said,
" And so death to all traitors! " and plunged the knife
into the cake.

Only this time the blade struck *cake,* nothing but cake—
and passed through the cake, and through the silver tray!

❡ Among his hoaxes some that deserve honorable mention
were the folderol advertisements he printed in *The
Philistine,* samples of which are appended:

To All Guardians, etc., Greetings:
On no account are you to consign Remittance Men to the
Roycroft Shop unless you make an arrangement before-
hand for a Native to listen to the sad stories of their lives.
Remittance Men who are graduates of Trinity College,
Dublin; Oxford and Cambridge Men, and Alumni of
Yale and Harvard should also be provided with Setters
in double shifts, who will consider their schemes for the
Betterment of Society, and see that they do not interfere
with persons who desire to work.

Good obese listeners can be had in the Village for Three
Dollars a week and tobacco.

FOR SALE—Sandpaper for Poets
Testimonial—Since using your Number 6 on my epigrams
they are luminous; before they were voluminous.
                                        —Edgar Saltus

East Aurora Summer School of Literature:
The Season opens July First and will last for two months.
The idea being to prepare beginners that they may score
a success in the Fall publishing season.

Note: I am in receipt of a letter from a gentleman in Cuya-
hoga Falls, Ohio, who says he hesitates about sending his
dollar for Membership in the Society of the Philistines

because he is slightly bow-legged, and not looking well in a dress suit could not attend the Annual Dinner. His case will be considered by the School of Philosophy at its next session *so so*

To Herbert S.: Thanks for your well-meant letter. But the Roycroft holds no copyright on the Song of Solomon and can not therefore " stop that man Mosher from pirating the stuff! " as you suggest. None of Solomon's stuff is covered by copyright.

Prof. Scipio Smith of East Aurora begs to announce that his Barber Shop will continue open as usual on Wednesday and Saturday afternoons. Cadaver and urgency cases will be accommodated at all times by applying at Membrino King's Box Stall, Village Farm. Artistic Hair Cuts a Specialty *so so*

Don't Worry Syndicate: Noting the fact that a great many people spend much time in Worry we have opened a Clearing Office where our various trained assistants will worry for you while you wait. Ladies who nag are earnestly requested to call. There is no use wearing yourself out in worry and nagging when at a trifling expense you can get the work done. We only employ expert Naggers. Send two-cent stamp for samples and testimonials.
—Rev. Loco, President and Head Neurotic

Reward—$500-Prize
I will pay Five Hundred Dollars to the person who will send me within six weeks a better Essay than I myself can write. A further prize of Five Hundred Dollars for a better Sketch than I have written or can write. All articles submitted will be judged by me—after a precedent established by those who offer prizes for similar work.
—Address Editor, *The Philistine*

That is a most slanderous remark I find in a recent issue of the New York *Tribune:* " In Summer most of the citizens of East Aurora drink buttermilk to excess, and in Winter nothing much is done but playing checkers and cracking hickory nuts."

Right here it may not be amiss to say that Pierp and Jondee did come to East Aurora together, with a bedtick full of yellow-back notes aggregating twenty-nine million dollars and begged to buy *The Fra*. Mr. Hubbard refused to see them and then Ali Baba cornered the Pair and put them on the Four o'Clock. We aim to please—Both Phones ✆

Perhaps the funniest hoax of all was the serious-minded review which the Editor of *The Philistine* published about and concerning a dramatic book with a sex appeal, supposedly written by a Chicago packer who had gone in for literature. 'T was the story of a musical comedy troupe, the chorus of which was composed of young widows each with a secret sorrow—or was it sweet young things who were " pure " and pure of heart? Well, no matter—

Came a day when the show was stranded!

Things happened, that 's all! * * * * *

The review introduced and exposed salacious interludes of the plot—and suggested hidden beauties that for lack of space the Editor was unable to betray! * * * *

What happened then?

What happened was that the Chicago gentleman received about seven thousand mail orders saying " Please ship book to address supplied "—and there was no such book!

❧ The pseudo-literary gazabo was a good sport who decided he liked his humor inverted, so he simply hired another secretary to answer the mail and return money-orders, and wrote Hubbard a letter of thanks and appreciation—mentioning that the very last edition of the " book " was exhausted.

Another time Hubbard and a fellow conspirator decided to take Marshall P. Wilder, the little hunchback comedian, to New York on a half-fare ticket.

Marsh was a man of middle age.

When the conductor asked, " How old is he," they replied,
" Oh, he 's *eight* all right! "

They even took little Marsh into the dining car, tucked
a napkin under his chin and made him eat his dinner with
a spoon ✺ ✺

Next morning, when they were getting off the train, the
conductor, who was a Brother Elk, came along and passed
Marsh a quarter and said, " For heaven's sake, get yourself
a shave before you ride on my train again! "

I guess it was true, what Harry Lauder said about Hubbard: " Fra Elbertus is the only man in the profession who
wears his make-up on the street."

It was also true that he wore his humor next his heart:
because no one was ever harmed or made unhappy by a
Hubbard joke.

BOOK TWO

Elbert Hubbard and The World

THE SEA

The sea knows all things, for at night when the winds are asleep the stars confide to him their secrets. In his breast are stored away all the elements that go to make up the round world. Beneath his depths lie buried the sunken kingdoms of fable and legend, whose monarchs have long been lost in oblivion. He appropriates and makes his own all that is—dissolving the rocks that seek to stop his passage—forming, transforming, rearranging, never ceasing, tireless. Tireless ever, for he gets his rest in motion. With acute ear he listens along every coast and lies in wait for the spirit of the offshore wind. All rivers run to meet him, carrying tidings from afar, and ever the phosphorescent dust from other spheres glimmers on his surface. It is not to be wondered that men have worshiped the ocean, for in his depths they have seen mirrored the image of Eternity—of Infinity. Here they have seen the symbol of God's great plan of oneness with His creatures, for the sea is the union of all infinite particlse, and it takes the whole to make the one. Men have fallen on their faces to worship the sea. Women have thrown him their children to appease his wrath. Savagely yet tenderly has he received the priceless treasure and hidden it away where none could recall. He has heard the dying groans of untold thousands, and drowned their cries for help with his own ceaseless roar; but still his ear has not failed to catch the whisperings of confession that have come from souls about to appear before their Maker. And yet how beautiful and kind is he in his apparent relentless cruelty, for he keeps only the transient part, and gently separates the immortal and wafts the spirit back to God who gave it. And what does the sea do with all these secrets, mysteries and treasures? Go shrive thyself, and with soul all in tune to the harmonies of the Universe listen to the waves and they shall tell thee the secrets of life.

—Elbert Hubbard.

Gaspard's Conception of Rameses II.

Gaspard's Conception of Rameses II.

ELBERT HUBBARD
From one of his last photographs. By Strauss, St. Louis.

BLESSED
is that man
who has found
his Work"

Hubbard The Homo

IS no easy task to try to step back three paces, the better to see Hubbard as a stranger would see him —to attempt to answer without too much prejudice the quetion, *What kind of a MAN was he!*

First, he was a farmer. No honors or glory can wipe out that impression. He was a farmer—a *Yankee* farmer ☙ He valued every cent of every dollar for what it would do, for the good it could be made to accomplish. He was thrifty, and that he had once endured poverty his abstemious habits clearly betrayed.

He wasted nothing, and wanted nothing wasted.

Understand he was thrifty, but not selfishly thrifty, not grasping. Money was not miser's gold to him—something to be hoarded. It was the stuff with which to buy land and equipment, build buildings, create Opportunity. Always he was buying more farms, more land; like many a farmer he was usually land poor!

But occasionally, it seems to me, in his practise of thrift, he was penny wise and pound foolish. While going in for de Luxe editions at the Shop, he bought herds of nondescript cattle, bargains in odd sizes of horses not suitable for his work, and pigs that could not have recognized their own grandfathers.

Perhaps he thought they needed encouragement too!

It may be he got satisfaction in trying to improve the breed—but it lost him money.

In business he experimented in humans after the same fashion. Once I went to him and told him that a certain young department head was perpetuating a series of expensive errors through ignorance and inability and that he was costing the firm a substantial amount of money. I wanted him replaced.

He did not thank me; he cussed me out from Dan to Beersheba: " That boy is a good boy—instead of reporting him, why don't you teach him? Why don't you show him how? " ꙮ ꙮ

Improving the breed again!

Or was it patience?

Catch him before his mind was made up and he was easy to influence, particularly if he was not pressed. Because his was a quick mind and he was naturally enthusiastic. But approach him after he had thought out the subject and then attempt to sway him and he was obdurate— stubborn. Right or wrong, once he convinced himself he carried through to the bitter end. And he never apologized although perhaps he might atone.

After he 'd reviewed the matter and decided it, one could boil him in oil and he 'd not change his conclusions—provided they were important.

There was bone and substance to this man!

Once he opened his eyes real wide and started to stare straight ahead into space, that was the Danger Signal— lay off! ꙮ ꙮ

One day I heard him urging to have his own way with Mrs. Hubbard. He wanted to do something about a business deal—to cut a price on a lot of expensive books to *move* them—and her economical sense said " No."

He argued, and she held firm; she would not be convinced.
⁋ " Shucks, Alice! " he said, exasperated, " Anybody can
be a *brake*—but it takes a man to be an *engineer*."

And he moved the books at his price! And lost money!
First, he was a farmer and a worker; and then he was a
business man. After that, a writer, an orator, an artist,
a genius ∾ ∾

He says of himself: " I am a business man with a literary
attachment."

That was true.

Before he started anything he figured the possibility of
a profit, and his instincts were unerring. Not all of his
profits were *direct* profits. That 's how he confused the
Wise Ones. Oftentimes he made two plays with no profit,
to make a larger profit on the third play.

Nevertheless his business brains were always in good order
and clicking. There 's nothing unmoral nor immoral in such
a procedure—because in a competitive age there must be
a profit or there 's a failure. And at the last what does it
benefit a man to gain a whole world of Fame or Renown
and then land in the bankruptcy court?

No! Hubbard was right. It was the thrifty farmer, the
hard worker, the shrewd business man that made the
genius possible and enlarged the field of his influence ∾

*   *   *   *   *

Three weeks before Elbert Hubbard went down with the
Lusitania I chanced to be a-calling with him in New York
City. We dropped in to see Jac Auer, physical instructor
at the Hotel Biltmore. Jac insisted on giving Hubbard
his periodic going over, and found him in excellent condition for a man of fifty-nine.

I remember Jac's one recommendation: " With a little

systematic, well-planned exercise your chest and shoulders
could be built up considerably."

Twenty-five years of writing—bending over a desk—showed
in his chest proportions. That in face of the fact that when
he walked he carried himself straight as an arrow and
balanced with the ease and grace of an American Indian.
⁋ Follows Hubbard's measurements taken on that date.
I insert them because they give a detailed idea of the
physical man; they furnish a basis for comparison, and
satisfy a natural curiosity:

Neck	14½ inches	Forearm	10¼ inches
Shoulders	43 "	Waist	34½ "
Chest, normal	35½ "	Thigh	20½ "
Chest, expanded	38¼ "	Calf	13¾ "
Upper arm	12⅜ "	Weight	162 lbs.
Height	5 feet 9½ inches		

There's a normal man, finely drawn, with no surplus weight,
with a waist line smaller than his chest line, in condition
to do a day's work, mental or physical.

Never did he miss his " daily dozen," only they were not
calisthenics. His exercise was hard physical work—pitching
hay, plowing a furrow, shoveling snow, cutting wood so
Thus he exercised and helped to do the work of the world
as well. "The more we stick to simple foods and work with
our hands, cleave to the great out of doors and the sunshine—the better for us."

His doctrine was *Health, Wealth, and Happiness* and he
scored *Health* first. Summer or Winter whoever came along
to East Aurora was introduced without delay to the health
ball and the soft base ball.

One-O'-Cat we used to play, and it was pitiable to see a
highly successful business man who, perhaps, had been
a famous college athlete in his youth, struggle with jumpy

nerves and juggling hands to catch a soft ball when it was tossed to him.

To see that spectacle was to be convinced that Nature takes a toll for neglect of one's body and that the Law of Compensation works day and night.

I have seen a look of fright and self-pity come into the eyes of an ex-great when he tried to play an easy game of " catch " only to discover that his mind and body had ceased to be partners and refused to synchronize.

Hubbard said, " Nature intended that each animal should live to an age approximately five times the number of years it takes to reach its bodily maturity. Man reaches his height and maximum strength at twenty, and should therefore live to be one hundred."

Taking into consideration the way in which he divided his periods of mental work, rest and play, I earnestly believe he would have achieved the century mark. His father, old Dr. Hubbard, lived to be ninety-six, and his mother ninety-five. * * * But the *Lusitania* sailed away, and never returned.

* * * * *

Hubbard has said and written: " I am no ten-thousand-dollar beauty and do scant justice to a double-breasted Prince Albert."

Of course no man is a beauty—but Hubbard had a fine head—finely , sculptured with a clean cut profile and a noble brow, and the most expressive, winning eyes imaginable. After one full look into his face an intelligent person was never quite sure whether he wore his unconventional corduroys and flannel shirt or whether he wore the Roman purple ❧ ❧

Over all he had charm of manner.

To meet Hubbard and not to like him was impossible—

and if you think this statement strained or artificial then you never met him, that's all.

I remember once, at Cambridge Springs Hotel, a health resort, I introduced the Fra to a tired business man in bad condition. His nerves were all outside his clothes, and to say the least he was not an agreeable companion. At the time I found myself interested in his ward—and I wished to create a diversion so *we* could escape unnoticed.

" Mr. Hubbard, this is Mr. Smith "—

" Oh, yes! Mr. Smith," said Hubbard, " I know you." Replied the Old Boy himself, garrulously: " How can you know me when I never met you before in all my life? "

❧ " I know your work!" said the Fra, and smiled beautifully, and His Nibs was much pleased and warmed up immediately. They were engaged in the friendliest conversation when *we* turned the corner of the porch and lost the perspective.

Putting aside his abilities for the moment, I believe half of Hubbard's accomplishments were made possible because people *liked* him. Certainly his magnetic, sympathetic personality was the cement that held the East Aurora group together in the early days, and the later days too. I remember once following him out through the deserted Shop after quitting time, just before dinner, and coming on the scrub woman leaning against the door jam crying as though her heart would break.

I stopped to ask, " What's the matter—what can I do? "

❧ " Nothin' now," she told me as she brushed her tears away with the back of her wrist. " He did it. He's got my boy Bill out of trouble again, and he's going to give him a job: put him to work to help me."

And once more she burst out crying.

I thought I was close to E. H., but here he was quietly

helping to get Bill out of trouble "again," and I knew
nothing about Bill's predicament.

Though Hubbard was a play-boy and something of a show-
off when he was in high good humor and feeling extra good,
when it came down to human realities he was a modest,
kindly, unselfish man.

* * * * *

There was no intolerance in the man, no hatred of anything. He was essentially pro the people, and pro human
effort. He recognized us as a lot of poor devils trying to
get along, and was sympathetic.

He understood and cheered us on. That we were unworthy,
ungrateful—well, that was to be expected, too. Nevertheless
when things went from bad to worse he'd perk up and
call, "Are we down-hearted? *No-o-o!*"

I never knew him down-hearted or discouraged for more
than a minute. He took what Life offered and found it good!
He loved Life.

And what a capacity he had for forgiving his enemies!
When they pestered him too much he'd swat them with
the blunt end of his vocabulary—but he had no time for
getting even, for vengeance. Always he was more than
willing to meet them more than half-way and to make up.
❡ His was a friendly disposition.

Yet he had the courage to live his own life, to stand for
what he stood for, to speak up and to speak out—ofttimes
the courage of his lack of convictions. He was not ashamed
to say, "I don't know."

False pride was not in him. A dozen times I have seen him
trot down the street to meet an incoming guest—man or
woman—to greet them and to help them carry their bags.
They were as embarrassed by this unusual service as he
was at home rendering it.

When he was not at his regular table in the dining room it was almost a sure guess that he was downstairs in the Help's dining room eating with the " servants "—of which we had not one in the employ of the place.

" *If you would have a friend, be one.*"

Instead of preaching his " principles " he set the example, supplied the inspiration. When giving orders to underlings he never commanded, he suggested, and invited suggestions, and encouraged them to think and speak for themselves. Nor did he expect a perfect performance. There was a lot of give and take to his philosophy.

So everybody co-operated—except Ali Baba, who was an anarch ﾟ﹀ ﾟ﹀

" What part do you do in making books? " a farmer quizzed Ali Baba.

" Holy smokes, man! Don't say a word. Besides being mascot, I answer all of the damn fool questions asked by farmers." ﾟ﹀ ﾟ﹀

Hubbard was never harsh with his employees. When it came to a place where he was compelled to discharge one for cause, and there was no chance for redemption, he usually waited till he was leaving on a trip and then wrote a note of dismissal—gave his reasons and suggested that the man get the money due him and go.

Usually the culprit was packed up and gone long before Hubbard himself returned.

Thus were " scenes " avoided and unkind truths made unnecessary ﾟ﹀ ﾟ﹀

Finally he was a man of high courage—beyond despair. His were words of gratitude, of hope and good cheer ﾟ﹀

" Yes, faith, you are right," said he. " When one reaches the so-called jumping-off place, he discovers that by God's gracious goodness the World is round! "

The Roycroft School of Life

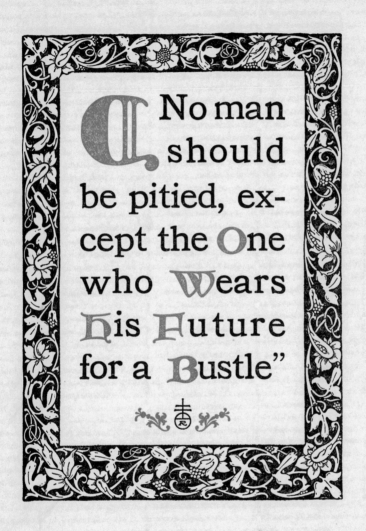

"No man should be pitied, except the One who Wears His Future for a Bustle"

No man
should
be pitied, ex-
cept the One
who wears
his Future
for a Bustle."

All in the Day's Work

I N going over my papers I find hundreds of notes and letters from Elbert Hubbard including the first one he wrote to me, and the last written the day before he sailed on the *Lusitania*. * * * * I find another written just a while before he went away wherein he states, "You know me a little better than any other living man." ❦ ❦

True, I knew him well enough to have a deep and abiding affection for him; I knew him well enough to fight for him—and to fight with him!

When I first joined his forces I was a high-spirited barbarian, just a little more than twenty; when I became General Manager of the Roycrofters, I was still high-spirited, not nearly so much a barbarian, and something less than thirty. Between times I had come under his civilizing influence ❦ A glance through the old correspondence proves he "handled" me with patience and impatience as merited and deserved—cuffed and encouraged me. Often, after the manner of thoughtless youth, I was ungracious and ungrateful and kicked up many an unnecessary rumpus: and it was imperative for him to tone me down in no uncertain terms, which he did, thank Heaven!

When I first reported there I was given an open assignment to make myself useful. With forethought and purpose, and without particular permission, I placed a desk for myself in the private office of the Chief Roycrofter, as near to the Throne as possible, and went to work.

He was always on the side of individual initiative so he said nothing and waited to see!

Defensively I testify that I really did want to *work*—and to work for Elbert Hubbard. The purity of my purpose was unquestioned; that apparently was excuse enough ✒

I got busy and raised quite a lot of dust, and tried to "reform" everything, and thereby (through the law of averages) managed to turn up an idea or two that appealed to him ✒ ✒

Some of my ultra activities pleased and amused him. For instance, I went to the librarian and insisted on taking to my room *all* the books and pamphlets Elbert Hubbard had up to that date written. 'T was a large order. Even so, my first year there I succeeded in reading his "complete works," including all available *Little Journeys*.

Not only did this assiduous reading give me a basic education and a practical equipment, for which I am eternally grateful, but it made me a work-a-day authority on his subject—and gave Mr. Hubbard much satisfaction as well ✒ ✒

Because I was absolutely "on my own," with an undivided interest, and with more than enough hero-worship in my cosmos, I tried to emulate him, to live the life he lived, to work the hours he worked, to stick as close to him as possible, to be his right hand.

How enthusiastically he encouraged and stimulated my efforts! ✒ ✒

I was there less than a year when he presented me with a beautiful gold watch—a Howard watch—inscribed " To Felix in appreciation of Good Work Well Done, May, 1908 —Elbert Hubbard."

Of course, this tells only one side of the story ❧ One Christmas season the annual Roycroft book catalog was delayed past the danger line ❧ Something beyond my ken was the cause. It was not especially my work (though my activities were neither prescribed nor proscribed) but because I was interested in sales volume I made it my work ❧ ❧

I wanted to know why the delay and warned and warned again that unless they made haste they would not get it out in time for the Christmas business.

On investigation, I discovered that several of Mrs. Hubbard's bright young ladies were playing around with it, and through not knowing how, they were getting nowhere, while maintaining a great dignity.

To pass the buck they called a " conference."

There were bookbinders, artists, coppersmiths, furniture makers, designers, printers, steamfitters and plumbers present—a sure way to never get anywhere—and Christmas due in just a few weeks.

The dear girls explained their theories, and the craftsmen present, nothing loath, explained theirs. They theorized and suggested and moved and rejected till it came time for the meeting to adjourn. I said nothing, but I was disgusted—and perhaps I showed it.

Always I have believed that the way to get a job done is to start at once with the fewest possible people and *do* it ❧ ❧

With time slipping by, another " conference " was called for another evening—and I took my horse and went for a ride ❧ ❧

I did not attend.

The next morning I received this letter from Mr. Hubbard: (Of course some one had told him half a tale—and when

he asked me *not* to defend myself I suspected he suspected
something of the sort himself.)

> Dear Felix: In reference to paying a salary to a man
> for doing a thing and then giving the work to others:
> I understand that you were offered the work but that
> you said it could not be done by Christmas Time—
> that it should have been begun earlier, etc. That is,
> instead of cheerful co-operation you began to criticize,
> forgetting that the past is dead. Usually you try to
> meet a request, but occasionally instead of getting busy
> you give 57 reasons why it can't be done, and enter into
> an argument. If you would cultivate the co-operative
> attitude instead of the censorious one, it would be
> easier for you—and others.
> If you start an argument and a lengthy explanation
> on this, I 'll know I have written in vain.
> In all good-will ever
>
> > > Elbert Hubbard.

I buttoned up and said nothing, as instructed.
Some one else produced the catalog.
It came out late.
The firm lost Christmas trade.
I did the next Roycroft catalog without assistance.

*　*　*　*　*

Always he was writing me short notes—checking, suggest-
ing, advising, stimulating. I find one that reads: " Get
your Ozone—and say, you must ride horseback with us
too." His theory was that the structure of accomplishment
was built on good health.
Another time he writes: " I am glad to see you cut out
the tobacco. At the best it does no one any good—and at

the worst it fastens on him a habit that is costly to both walletoski and health. We want power—fresh air and exercise, and a good woman (say like————) will help you get it. The world has an overplus of dubs and muts but the men of power are few. I have great hopes for you. You have the requisites—God has been good to you—it now lies with yourself. It really looks as if you might break into Class A."

Of course this was sweet music to the ear of a boy who was trying to do things—but while he was generous with his praise he never spared the rod.

One day he said to me, " Certain of the boys are patronizing the saloons—I have proof. They are coming in late and climbing up the front porch to reach their rooms. I think it would be a good thing to vote this town dry— what do you think? "

" I think so too—I agree."

" Very well, then, just before election we 'll have a parade with banners, make it an issue, interest everybody, and vote for prohibition. I 'd like to have you lead that parade on your broncho. Will you do it? "

" Hot stuff! Sure! "

That was when prohibition was the national issue—and local option optional.

Preliminary plans were made, and all went well till the day before the parade day when Hubbard himself tacked a notice on the bulletin board to the effect " Everybody on the Roycroft pay-roll will walk in the dry parade tomorrow."

That started something!

To volunteer to walk was the privilege of a free-born citizen; to be commanded to walk was something different. There was grumbling and more grumbling.

To my mind it was poor psychology. Hubbard was very busy with his preparations, excited, happy, and undoubtedly there was little forethought behind the offensive notice. He just happened to word it as he did: " Every one on the Roycroft pay-roll will walk!" I should have gone to him and suggested—instead I sulked.

The night before, both of us chanced to work till about ten p. m., and quit at the same time to walk across to the Inn together. Half way across, in the very middle of the street, he broke the silence to ask: " Well, how do you think the parade will go off tomorrow? "

" I think it will go off fine—if you 're not arrested! "

He stopped dead.

My tone was offensive.

" Arrested—what for? "

" Arrested for intimidating voters! " and I threw down the challenge. " I don't know whether I will be on the Roycroft pay-roll at three p. m. tomorrow—but if I am I won't be in that parade! That notice you put on the board is something to be proud of—nix! "

Right there in the middle of the street he took time to tell me what he thought of me. Some one has said he knew more words than Shakespeare, and I am inclined to agree! ✣ ✣

But he did not discharge me, as I certainly expected. ❡ Next day he saw to it personally that every man and woman, every boy and girl, walked. He stopped every piece of machinery, he closed up the Inn except for the desk girl, so there would be no absentees! He called out both the Roycroft band and the Roycroft fire company and uniformed them. The parade was a stupendous success!

Meanwhile I sat at my desk in solitary splendor, alone with my thoughts.

That night he left to lecture in Cincinnati without a word to me—though I was expecting the storm to break. Next day I received this letter:

> My dear Felix: I suppose you are aware that I am not wholly pleased with you. And I have been wondering if Felix is wholly pleased with himself. Felix has health, energy, youth, and usually enthusiasm. Also he has intelligence that should evolve rather than decrease. These are his limitations:
>
> 1. The handing out of off-hand advice to folks who have a carefully considered plan.
> 2. A jerky, sudden, abrupt manner when approached on a Business Matter.
> 3. A habit of (at times) knocking.
> 4. Indisposition at times to co-operate, holding out and hugging a sore toe.
> 5. Criticizing others who go ahead and do things, which he had failed or neglected to do.
>
> All these things put Felix in Class C when he should and might be in Class A.
>
> Class C gets its salary. That is well. It earns it. But commissions are for Class A.
>
> I owe commissions to Felix on October and November business. The check will be handed him on my return. This commission proposition was a voluntary one on my part and I now withdraw it.
>
> If in the future Felix shows a desire to subdue himself and devote himself I may reconsider the matter of commissions.
>
> With love and blessings
> Elbert Hubbard

When he returned in the middle of November he ignored

me. I was not invited to walk or ride or play " catch " in business hours—so I worked. I dug into my job and said nothing ✒ ✒

But when the commission due date came round again, I presented him a statement as though nothing had happened. It was his practise to pay these commissions to me personally and they amounted to much more than my salary. In turn he ignored the statement.

December Twentieth chanced to be the *next* commission date and I sent him the *accumulated* statements.

The day before Christmas he placed on my desk a promissory note which read: " I, Elbert Hubbard, promise to pay Felix Shay all accumulated commissions provided he is still with the Roycrofters on June First of next year."
❡ He thought I was getting ready to leave.

When I read the " note " I folded it and went over to him and poked it into his upper vest pocket and said, " That 's a certificate of good behavior, and I don't need it. If you don't owe me these commissions you don't owe them at all. If you do owe them—they are *overdue!* " and walked out of his office.

Later the same afternoon he passed me his personal check for all commissions due to date, with this note:

" Dear Felix: Here it is. I don't care a damn so long as you keep a civil tongue in your Irish head. * * * Come in, I have a present for you.

Love and blessings

Elbert Hubbard."

And thus ended the only passing-serious quarrel I ever had with my friend the Fra.

¶ What some men think will happen when women get the Right of Suffrage

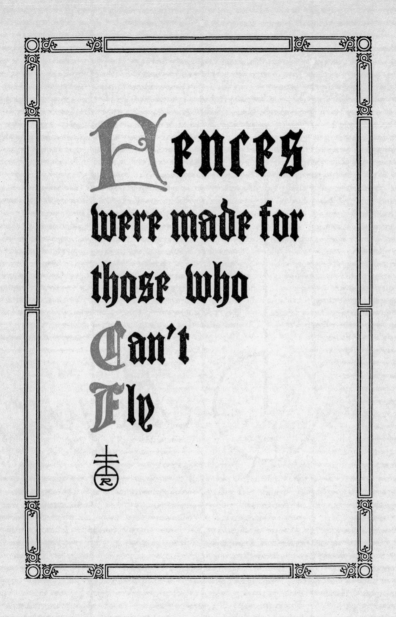

Fences
were made for
those who
Can't
Fly

The Gospel According to Fra Elbertus

A NY man who criticizes the existing order is criticized in turn.

They call him a destructive force.

They say " He knocks down without building up."

They say " He takes away without giving anything in return."

" He destroys existing beliefs while not supplying others."

They said those things, and more about Hubbard.

From time to time he took the trouble to put into print the things he believed, the things he advocated. He made them plain for all to see.

Hubbard's Philosophy was one of Affirmation.

Moreover he believed in practise more than precept ✒ ✒

His complaint was that we talked one way and lived another ✒ ✒

In the matter of Christianity, he said, " I am for it— and I only hope that some day we 'll give it a trial."

As for a future life, he was not nearly so much concerned with the next life as he was with this one.

" One Life at a time " was his doctrine.

And as for his belief in " God " I have heard him say, " Surely the Power that protects us Here will not desert us There."

Even so, his " religion " dealt almost exclusively with the Present ✒ ✒

Be it said to his credit, he *lived* what he *believed*, and if

this life is but a " preparation " there was no need for
him to fear about any life to come.

* * * * *

Hubbard was a Prophet—an apostle of the Here and Now
and the " laws " he laid down were for this world alone.
Those that follow will serve for analysis:

1. *" I believe in Fresh Air, Sleep of nights, and the moral
effect of old-fashioned Work with one's Hands."*
He believed that to have a sound mind in a sound body
one must give systematic attention to the conditioning
of that body. He believed that spiritual well-being only
came to pass when there was a harmony, a unity of Head,
Heart and Hand—the word " Heart," of course meaning
the *Spirit*. He believed in a philosophy of simplicity, of
Naturalness, of Realities—and that no man should consider
himself above manual labor, nor lose his touch with common
things, nor people. White-collared jobs were all right—
but not when they were flaunted in the face of the hand-
laborer to make him restless, dissatisfied and unhappy ❧

2. *" I believe in equal Opportunity."*
He knew very well that men were not created equal—
but he wished that the trap door of Opportunity should
be always open so that the exceptional man might climb
up through. He knew that in the course of human events
the Great Genius was more likely to be born in a hovel
than in a castle: because God made so many of the common
people they have the other kind outnumbered. He knew
that men were never so miserable as when they were made
to feel themselves to be members of an Inferior Class ❧
Therefore he advocated that the strong should hold themselves responsible for the weak, to the end that the " pursuit

of happiness " might be something more than a race that goes to the swift, and only to them.

3. " *I believe in the Equality of the Sexes and in the Good that comes in a generous comradeship between men and women in their work, mental occupations, and recreations.*" He knew his history well enough to know that among savages and the lesser tribes the women do all the hard laborious work, and that in such high civilizations as that of China the women carry the " hod " all day through— carry a load of bricks up a ladder on one shoulder with a baby slung across their back for good measure. He recognized that woman is man's physical as well as mental equal —in a certain sense—and he wanted artificial restrictions taken off. He knew that the " protected " woman who was used as a clothes-horse and jeweler's show-case by the man of her family was a cheated woman who was held in bondage and bribed with doo-dads and denied participation in the game of life. He wanted women set free and permitted to develop their powers and abilities. He wanted " equality " to mean considerably more than the right to vote. He wished it to mean the right to live.

4. " *I believe in Frankness of Speech.*" He felt that there was altogether too many tabu subjects and that no subject should be denied to intelligent adults; that when the " mystery " was taken away, salaciousness went with it; that it was the clean-minded man who dared to speak his thoughts openly, frankly.

5. " *I believe in charitable Good Nature towards those who differ from one's opinions.*" He never expected that different types of men should think alike. He anticipated no unanimity of opinion. The intellectual life was a matter of give and take. A world full of

" yes-men " would be a tragic place. He was willing that each man should think his own thoughts, come to his own conclusions, have his own beliefs, suffer his own disappointments—provided he approached his brothers in a spirit of tolerance and comradeship.

6. " *I believe in Cheerfulness of Disposition.*"
He had little respect for the tyrant or the superman, that boresome individual who believes himself self-appointed by the Deity to lord over and wreck and ruin the lives of others. He believed that life should be made a happy place, and that one smile was worth a dozen frowns. I have heard him say that temper and anger and abuse were despicable things when practised on inferiors. When a man was able to conquer himself and make himself pleasing to others, then and then only was he master of his environment ᴓ ᴓ

7. " *I believe in Big Business.*"
Human endeavor should not be restricted or held back. He believed that all things came to him who waited and labored while he waited; that none of us could foresee the future, nor foretell the benefits of human enterprise ᴓ Progress and salvation lay in going on—and on—and on.

8. " *I believe in a sufficient change in occupation to give Buoyancy, Zest and Pleasure to every task.*"
He said that no man can find happiness in feeding things into a machine all day long. He felt that the forced monotony of the standardized task is a tragedy of our Industrial Age. Under no circumstances should we forget to remember to *live*—and to let others live. He believed that Everyman had the inherent right to express himself in his work—and that a money profit was not nearly so desirable as the growth and development of the individual.

9. " *I believe in Culture and Refinement and Mental Reach.*"

To his mind unselfishness was the higher culture, and that it expressed itself through a desire to serve, and to share without duress. A man was a gentleman when he was gentle, and in no other way could he achieve that end. He preached that what we clutched for eluded us and that what we gave away came back to us ten fold.

10. " *The true Philistine does not claim to be any better, worse, or wiser than others.*"

The pride that stinketh was an abomination to his nostrils. The man who held himself superior was a ridiculous figure in his eyes. He believed that there is so much good in the worst of us, and so much bad in the best of us, that no man was permitted the privilege of setting himself on a pedestal. Actually he estimated the proud man to be an ignorant man, one not versed in the human verities. He calculated the misuse of power to be one of the capital sins.

11. " *I believe in the paradox of Success through Failure.*"

He expressed the belief that a man did not know the true sweetness of life until he had tasted the dregs of defeat and failure. At the last, there is very little difference between Success and Failure except as thinking makes it so, and that no man is a failure who has a friend.

12. " *I believe in Freedom, and to that end consider this country needs less Law, not more.*"

By twenty-five years he anticipated the present Lawless Era, due not so much to criminal intent, but to contempt for contemptuous laws. He believed that the individual was governed best who was governed least. He believed in the Honor System. He expected the best of men, not the worst. He depended on them, trusted them, had confidence

in them to do what was right. He believed that the spirit
of rebellion always rose up to counteract the spirit of intolerance. That one was no worse than the other—and that
probably one was necessary to the other to hold it in check.
He had a contempt for Busybodies and professional Reformers ᔧ ᔧ

13. *" I believe in Temperance, Moderation."*
The pendulum of life must not swing too far in one direction; that Sin lay in excess. That there can be an excess
of Good as well as an excess of Bad, because none of us
can be too sure that what we call **GOOD** is good, and
that what we call **BAD** is bad. He expounded that *Enough*
was plenty, and that when we had *Too Much* we became
swollen and bloated and unpleasant to see.

14. *" The true Philistine does not believe in political,
religious, or domestic BOSSISM."*
He was all for the Rights of Man and for the Rights of
Women, too—and Children—the Rights of the Individual.
To him unfairness and injustice and tyranny—particularly
tyranny—were unworthy things ᔧ He granted no man
the license to govern another man or woman without that
one's full and free consent.

15. *" I believe that all men and women should take an
interest in politics."*
He believed that a responsible government *of the people
and for the people* could only be brought about by full
participation *by the people:* that it was each man's duty
to accept the full responsibilities of citizenship as well as
the privileges; and that he should not only vote each
election day but that he should seriously interest himself
in government so that the representative and legislative
bodies of this country would be truly representative ᔧ

16. *" The true Philistine does not believe that Luxuries are a Recommendation, that Poverty is neither a curse or a Blessing, nor that Rich Men are ' bad ' any more than Poor Men are ' virtuous.' "*

Primarily, he believed that poverty was poverty of the mind, and that riches were a richness of the spirit; that no man was poor who held on to his self-respect, who was willing to work; and that no man was rich who had a cent which did not honorably belong to him. He believed that there were things above money, place and power. He believed that a man could risk riches and risk poverty, but that he could never risk degradation of the soul.

17. *" I believe I have no enemies that I recognize as such."*

"Enemies are only friends who misunderstand us." He never sought for revenge; he never held hatred; he never hesitated to forgive. When he criticized a man he first attempted to set down all there was good to say about that man before he marshaled his arguments against him or his act. When he completed his indictment, he always left the door open for a reformation, and parted with a kindly word.

18. *" I believe in a humanity towards all dumb animals and in a gentle and kindly treatment of children: for the Strong can always afford to be generous."*

He believed that the Weak had the right to look to the Strong for protection and help, and that in this Little Journey through life, from the Here to the There, we were all partners; that a helping hand and kindly word was worth a thousand sneers or ten thousand alibis. I have heard him say, " When we die, the only things that we will take with us in our clenched hands will be the things we have given away."

19. "*I believe that a return to simpler Times, simpler lives, simpler Recreations, is necessary to insure vigorous Health and reasonable content—a peace with God and Man.*"

Long years before, he anticipated and warned against this age of complex, high-pressure living, when the struggle for existence becomes so intense that life itself seems not worth while. He advocated that those who *had* make a definite fight to get along with *less*, so that those who *had not* might have *more* of the desirable things of life. He put the emphasis on Contentment and Happiness— and he reminded us that we passed this way but once ๑

20. "*I believe that the Universe was planned for Good.*" His was a philosophy of Optimism and Good Cheer. He said by living one day at a time, giving our best to the work in hand, keeping ourselves in a receptive mood, all good things would come to us.

21. "*The Philistine is aware that to very many this life seems one long struggle for right adjustment: but still, even though existence be sure Death at the falling of the curtain in the fifth act, Life is yet full of joyous moments and there's many a rift in the clouds. To feel, to think, to live, to know, aye, to suffer, are not small things—I'm glad I'm here.*"

His was a philosophy of Hope, and Faith, and Charity ๑

* * * * *

"Ah," but you say, "this is nothing new; I have heard it before!" ๑ ๑

The question and the answer is not, "What have ye heard?" but, "What have ye done?"

Unless we *do something* about this eternal Problem of Life and Living, how will we feel when we reach the End

of Things and the Beginning of Things? The test is not,
" Can we recognize Truth? "—the test is, " Once we have
searched for and found The Truth, will we accept it, will
we permit it to affect and modify and improve our lives
and the lives of those who are in duty compelled to associate with us! "

Remember 't is written that all things shall pass away
but words—words of truth and light!

of things and the Beginning of Things? The test is not "Can we recognize Truth?"—who can?—but the test is, "Once we have searched for and found The Truth, will we accept it, will we permit it to affect and modify and improve our lives and the lives of those who are in duty compelled to associate with us?

Remember it is written "that all things shall pass away, but words—words of truth and light."

The Tax Payers' Burden

The Tax Payers Burden.

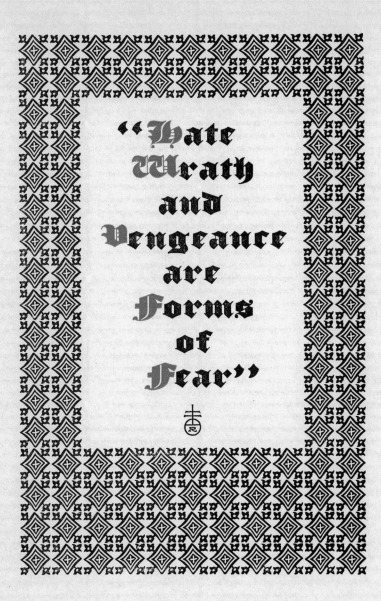

"Hate
Wrath
and
Vengeance
are
Forms
of
Fear"

What Hubbard Fought Against

THIS chapter might be written in a single sentence: " He opposed nothing." ໒໐ ໒໐

He proposed, endorsed, believed in, stood for, advocated.

But when one attempts to find evidence of negation, there is very little ໒໐ ໒໐

As an index to his character that in itself is sufficient.

Turn the pages of his Complete Works and you will find articles approving eugenics, good roads, child welfare, prison reform, thrift, higher pay for school teachers, Health, Wealth and Happiness, disarmament, world peace, protection of minorities—but where shall we look for data on damning man's mistakes? ໒໐ ໒໐

Perpetually he used the word *do* instead of the word *don't*.

❡ I remember a simple little story he used to tell to point this moral:

" Once I met a little boy and asked him, ' Sonny, what 's your name? ' ' My name,' he answered, ' is Jimmy Don't.' "

❡ Of course he " razzed " the three learned professions—the doctors, lawyers and preachers—but he had only the kindliest feeling for the individual members of these professions. His own father was a general practitioner and for years had lived the life of a country doctor so the son well knew the self-sacrifice that profession entailed.

More than once he had accompanied his father on a " call "

in the middle of a cold Winter's night out into the country ten miles to visit the sick.

No! The doctors themselves were his friends. It was their medicine, the drugs they administered (some of them) that called forth his condemnation.

He wanted the medical doctors to become *health* doctors. He wanted them on the side of the prevention of disease —and please note that in these enlightened days that 's exactly where one finds the intelligent members of the profession aligned!

Of the ministers of the Gospel he called every man friend who preached brotherly love—and who did not preach *fear. Hell* and *damnation* were hellish and damnable doctrines to him, and *fear* itself was poison to mankind. I feel sure that oftentimes he overstated his attitude toward the D. D.'s just to prove to the more timorous of his magazine readers that he himself had no fear of them. He helped to ridicule the Devil to death. But of those gentle, kindly, spiritual leaders who preached a religion of *love* and helpfulness, he had only respect and a kindly, friendly word ✒ ✒

So long as an ordinary every-day man lived up to an ideal he cared not what church he attended or to what particular sect he gave his loyalty.

He abhorred buncombe and pretense, and the holier-than-thou attitude invited his mirth and his scorn.

Said he, " *Be,* don't merely *seem.*"

Be real, be earnest, be genuine.

Better to be a real renegade than a bogus Christian.

Of the " reformer," particularly the professional reformer, he was suspicious. He was equally suspicious of instantaneous reformations. He believed that a man's life represented the total of his acts, nothing more or less, and that " reformation " was not by a proclamation but by a change of policy. He believed that the Week-day as well as Sunday should be kept Holy.

Of the lawyers he said, " Well, let us agree that only *half* of them are rogues." Nevertheless I could start with Elbert H. Gary and end with Clarence Darrow and name a full thousand lawyers of whom he held a high opinion. Therefore he must have had in mind only the *rogue* fifty per cent when he was criticizing the " lawyers."

Of the things he opposed, these are fair samples:

Society and Social Stratas. Because the race can not learn, nor progress unless the worst are brought in direct contact with the best, and so taught by example; because the spirit of mortal has no right to be proud; and because pride and exclusiveness goeth before a fall!

Dignitarians. Because dignity is ofttimes a cloak for ignorance ❧ ❧

Gossip. Because it is the lowest form of human activity ❧

Agitators. Because education, not agitation, is the solution to most of our pet problems, and because " stirring up " the people helps not at all.

Destructionists. Because any DF can tear down, but it takes patience and skill to build, to improve.

Vaccination. Because it is an unproven fetish and a dangerous one, being practised on helpless children: a cure-all that occasionally inflicts a worse disease than the one it is supposed to prevent.

Vivisection. Because to mutilate dogs and monkeys and guinea pigs, to cause poor dumb brutes to suffer intensely, while attempting through them to anticipate the subsequent physical reactions on a *man*, seemed to him to be beside the fact, futile, unnecessary and brutal.

" Vivisection," said he, " is blood lust screened behind the sacred name of Science."

Organized Religious Dogma. Because it no longer serves the needs of mankind; because we need the *spirit* of religion more than the forms; and the truth of religion more than the superstitions.

Art for Art's Sake. Because Art should be for Humanity's sake.

Poverty. Because the only poverty was poverty of the mind and that should not be glorified or held up for praise ๛

Lily-white Hands. Because no man should be above honest physical work, and ought to take pride in setting a good example to his lesser brethren.

Capital Punishment. Because crime is not an individual proposition but a group proposition; that usually the criminal is the one sinned against by the group; because we manufacture our own criminals deliberately and then punish them for being such; because a policy of an eye for an eye and a tooth for a tooth never decreased crime.

Blue Sundays. Because God is everywhere, not only in churches; because to search for and to find happiness in joyous pursuits is the true spirit of religion; because a game of base ball played out in God's sunshine is just as much an act of worship as praying indoors.

Flunkyism. Because man was born to be free and courageous.

Idle Rich. Because they are poor ignorant people who have missed the purpose of life: " Give us this day our daily Work." ๛ ๛

Static Learning. Because the discovery of Tomorrow may nullify the learning of Yesterday: therefore let us continue as seekers after Truth and always be willing to welcome new evidence.

Alcohol. Because it stealeth away the brains and character.

Hair-splitters. Because a man must not be heckled while he's pursuing his Destiny! Whether the i's are dotted or the t's are crossed does n't matter.

Child Labor in Mills. Because the Child represents all that we control of the Future of the Race—and to mistreat the child is to mistreat Humanity.

Censorship and the Higher Criticism. Because man is entitled to be mistaken, entitled to eat from the Tree of Knowledge even though the knowledge thus gained close the Gates of Eden behind him; and further, that no man is good enough to set himself up as a critic of other men and their works; that the right to select, to err, is a legitimate part of an Education.

Shams and Hypocrisies. Because self-convinced nuisances are bad enough—but when a hypocritical nuisance appears on the scene the situation becomes unbearable.

Certain " Secret " Orders. Only and particularly those that kept men apart, that attempted to divide and antagonize the race of humans and not those that brought men together in fraternity and fellowship.

Doctrines and Doctrinaires. Because Truth is a movable body: what is Truth today may not be Truth tomorrow; a doctrine set down as Truth becomes obsolete before the printer's ink is dry.

The Bible in Public Schools. Because he thought it unfair to support public schools with the money of all the taxpayers, and then to introduce the Holy Book of a particular group of tax payers: in a country where religious liberty is guaranteed, the Jews, Mohammedans, Buddhists and non-believers should have equal rights with the Christians.

Parasites and Coupon-clippers. Because irrespective of his bank balance, a man's self-respect should compel him to

ELBERT HUBBARD

do an honest day's work and not be a burden on society.

Yellow Newspapers. Because they pandered to the worst instincts of mankind, instead of cultivating the best ✠✠

The Closed Shop. Because it restricted Opportunity for boys and girls, and limited man's capacity for work, and attempted to enforce a dead level of production.

Academic Learning. Because it was too restricted and because it attempted to take men outside of life to teach them *theory,* when they should be incorporated into life and taught *facts.*

Unintelligent Wealth. Because it established bad standards and set a bad example.

Graft. Because it was simply a soft word for *theft.*

Consistency. Because to be consistent is to retrograde, to defy progress and to stick in the mud.

Intolerance. Because Pontius Pilate's question, " What is Truth? " has not yet been answered.

Idleness. Because it is the Original Sin.

Dirt. Because it is the by-product of idleness.

Casting Aside Worn-out Employees. Because when man loses his sense of gratitude—his sense of justice and fair play, he loses his soul.

In doors. Because there disease breeds.

Militarism. Because it perpetuates swash buckling, saluting, heel-clicking; because it is anti democratic, and there is no place for it in a democracy.

War. Because it is man at his worst.

Even so, most of his provocative preachments were positive ✠ ✠

The Confessional—fin de siecle!

The Contortionist. Fin de siécle!

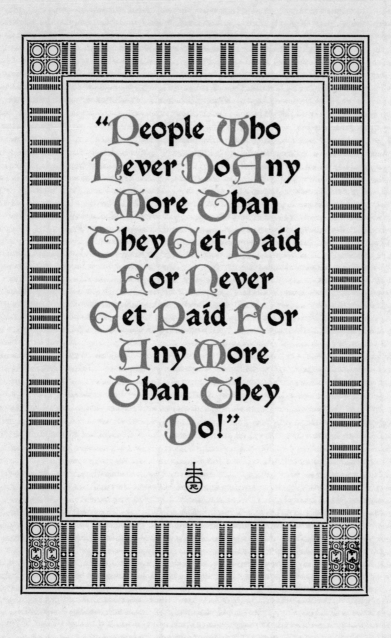

"People Who Never Do Any More Than They Get Paid For Never Get Paid For Any More Than They Do!"

Hubbard's Attitude Toward Money

THE falsest accusation ever aimed at Elbert Hubbard was that he was a money-grubber, a materialist, a mercenary. To the contrary, to the contrary ❧ ❧
I never knew a man who cared less for money as money, who saw less of it, who handled less of it, who carried less of it.
Elbert Hubbard II—Bert Hubbard —was the Financial Man at East Aurora ❧ He received the money, disbursed it, banked it, kept the records.
I have heard his father ask Bert, " Butch, what 's your bank balance this morning? "—and that invariably when he had some spending in mind and wanted to know whether the wherewithal was available to do it.
Apart from that infrequent "money" question, occasionally I have seen him scan the morning's mail to see the " color " of it, because we used a " color check " (colored order blanks) on most of the mail order offers, and so the amount of a certain kind of " color " told whether or not the plan was " going over."
Other than that his interest in the cash itself—in the stuff that clinks and sounds metallic—was nil.
I venture that any day of the year in East Aurora one could have rifled his pockets and the takings would not have averaged five dollars. Whenever I 've worn a reefer of his all that I ever found in the pockets was pencil stubs

and " notes." Whenever I 've helped him throw his clothes into a bag at a hotel, in a rush for a train after a lecture, and turned his pockets inside out, there were the same pencil stubs and nothing else.

Furthermore, I risk the accurate estimate that he did not spend more than one hundred dollars a year on clothes.

His suits cost him twenty-five dollars each—when they were not presented to him by Stein-Bloch or Hart, Schaffner and Marx—and a suit lasted a year.

His shoes were common coarse brogues.

His hats were broad-brimmed, wear-ever Stetsons.

His shirts were flannel or coarse cotton.

Over a period of ten years, I never knew him to buy a new overcoat. Probably this is why he said, " The glass of fashion and the mold of form are far from mine."

Bert is my authority for the statement that when E. H. went away on a trip he " drew " just fifty dollars. That carried him to the first stop, and after that the lecture honorariums supplied the necessary finance—and a surplus. Periodically this surplus was mailed home to be deposited to the account of the Roycrofters. I understood that he earned about Fifty Thousand Dollars a year " outside " the business, but my guess is not quite that much. But whatever he earned, after deducting his bare expenses, he turned it in to be credited to the Roycrofters.

" All the money I make by my pen, all that I get from my lectures or my books, goes to the fund of the Roycroft —the benefit goes to all. I want no better clothing, no better food, no better comforts than my fellow-workers have. I would be ashamed to monopolize a luxury."

Had he so elected he could have lived like a visiting Prince on what he earned personally, and let the Roycrofters take care of themsleves. Instead he gladly sacrificed self for the group, for the " community."

Remember, he wrote a daily column for the Hearst papers, which was syndicated; he wrote special articles and books; he wrote advertisements and advertising booklets; he lectured say one hundred times a year; and he appeared successfully in vaudeville at a fancy figure.

All this activity spells income, and a " mercenary " man would have held tight to it. Instead he put it into the pot and shared his good fortune with his people.

The salary he received from the Corporation was fifty dollars a week and he did not always draw that. When he did draw it I used to see him disbursing it to needy literary gazabos who wrote him touching notes. I used to see him tucking five-and-ten-dollar bills into envelopes and sealing and mailing them himself so that no one would be the wiser ❧ ❧

And this was the man who was supposed to be tight-fisted and grasping!

Show me a generous man and I will show you one who is not a materialist; show me a kind and thoughtful man and I 'll show you one not a money-lover. These sentiments are set down sincerely to attempt to do justice to the memory of one who was ofttimes unjustly criticized and much maligned by those who did not know him.

* * * * *

'T was this very unwillingness to think in terms of money for the individual that drew the criticism. He said, " The Reward for Good Work is More Work "—while most of us high-binders thought the reward for good work should be more money.

His idea of a top salary was fifty dollars a week—because

that was more than sufficient for the mode of living at
East Aurora.

There it was literally impossible to spend money, after
one's board was paid. Fifty dollars a year will equip one
with corduroys and reefers and flannel shirts—and we
escaped the tax for hats by not wearing any.

He said, " The business man is the one who produces the
business." And so I learned early in the game that the
way to make money with him was to take the fifty-dollar
salary without protest and then to fix up a commission
basis on business secured. He was always exceedingly
generous in arranging for these " splits " with me. He
was more than generous, in fact: because, to keep my
earnings out of the records, where they might make
others unhappy, he'd give me his personal checks signed
" E. G. Hubbard "—checks against his own modest bank
account ❧ ❧

❡ I know he thought I was earning too much for a young
man, but I was tending to business twelve hours a day,
and getting the orders, and saving eighty per cent of my
earnings. Even so, he gave me a gentle slam once in so often;
I hold in my hand a note of his which makes me smile. It
reads: " Felix: first in War, first in Peace, and first in the
Pockets of his Countrymen."

That was talking in code—but he knew, and I knew!

Ordinarily he took boys and girls out of the village school
and put them to work and paid them beginners' wages—
and they were not high wages. Neither was the work high-
pressure work—and there was advancement when deserved.

❡ More particularly he employed all who offered their
services—more than needed ofttimes.

He figured that enough money for a number was much
better than too much for a few. Primarily that was what

he meant when he said, " There is no wealth and no poverty in East Aurora."

But it was the low wages and numberless apprenticeships that drew the criticism of the Unions.

He simply worked a different system, that was all, and they could n't or would n't see merit in it. But after the years it 's clear to me that his system was responsible for the survival and prosperity of the Roycrofters; and looking back one can not help but realize that it was a splendid education in Work and Thrift for the average country boy and girl as well.

Moreover, please remember that each Saturday night he "looked a pay-roll in the eye "—a pay-roll for five hundred people, and that he was not endowed, and that the responsibility for having this pay-roll ready and waiting was strictly his responsibility.

* * * * * *

Recently I noted a certain famous editor who made a circle tour through Florida, and who was so much impressed with what he saw there that he devoted the entire next issue of his magazine to " Florida."

He waxed enthusiastic and gave Florida a beautiful boost. ⊄ Those Florida boys not being exactly stupid ordered one hundred thousand copies of that issue and dropped the same into the mails to inform the populace of the glories and grandeurs of their gorgeous State.

Apparently, let us assume, they paid the regular retail price for each copy less the news dealer's rake-off.

Does it seem to you there 's anything immoral in that transaction? ఎ ఎ

If so, let me call attention to this: Not so long ago a certain writer published a rather spectacular article in one of America's high-class magazines. When it was published he

ordered a couple of dozen copies plus—and was charged
the full retail price for each copy!

Is that immoral—that magazines containing articles are
bought and sold?

Well,'that was the " crime " Elbert Hubbard committed!
❦ He produced magazines and sold them!

In wending his way about the country on his lecture tours
he came in contact with men, concerns, controversies, and
events; he got his " copy " first hand, and he served this
copy hot off the press.

Is it any wonder that interested parties ordered ten, a
hundred, a thousand, ten thousand copies?

To like to read about one's self is the oldest instinct in
the world—emphasis on self is simply the law of self-
preservation. Hand a man a group photo and the first
thing he says is, " There *I* am! "

Hubbard wrote about live subjects—and he wrote sur-
passingly well—and live men appreciated him, and ordered
extra copies of *The Philistine* or *The Fra* for their friends
and enemies. They paid the regular retail price for them
less the regular quantity discount.

That 's not immorality—that 's Business!

They bought magazines—but the writer did n't sell his
opinions ✖ ✖

The opinion was already rendered whether they bought
or not ✖ ✖

* * * * *

That Hubbard was on the near side of Big Business was
no secret; he shouted it from the house tops.

You may remember that not so long ago there was such
a thing as an Era of Muck-raking and a tribe of Muck-
rakers in this country. They damned in print everything
capitalistic and everybody who was overly prosperous—

and pulled the Family Skeleton out of the closet by the
left hind leg! 'T was grand sport, and racy reading, but
it helped to bring about the Panic of Nineteen Hundred
Seven. And for a time they nearly ruined the country ∾
What good they did nobody knows!

Once there was a class of business men who said, " The
Public be damned! "

Then there came a class of publicists who said, " Business
be damned! " ∾ ∾

Between them we nearly were damned for sure!

Hubbard's policy of affirmation ended that Era—and even
though the muckers splattered him with a little mud it
was worth the price!

He said, " American business is not perfect, nor will mud-
slinging make it so. Let us overlook the bad and encourage
the good. Let us say the friendly word for men of *good
intent* even though they are not scoring One Hundred
Per Cent. Let us cheer for the fellow who is *trying* to do
the right thing. Let us praise the *Right*—instead of damning
the *Wrong.* " Deliberately he boosted the important men
—the Key Men of the Nation's Prosperity—and the domi-
nating corporations of America. He told all there was *good*
to tell about them. He brought them out in the open from
behind the guns and introduced the tired warriors as
Human Beings who would not shoot unless the snipers
continued to pot-shot them!

For a time he stood practically alone, and almost single-
handed he brought about a truce and helped start the
thinkers of this country thinking constructively—and thinking on the side of their bread and butter.

Reforms! Certainly Hubbard wanted reforms, but not
through *violence*, not through nasty, sensational mud-
slinging—not from *without,* but from *within.*

For the sake of this theory let us look at the magazine of twenty years ago, and read the scare heads:
" ON THE TRAIL OF THE CRIMINAL—BIG BUSI-NESS."
" THE CRIME OF THE CASH-BOX."
" THE RISING TIDE OF RESTLESSNESS."
Look again and see how the business man, the giver of Prosperity, is being glorified by similar publications today!
❦ Yet when Hubbard first boosted American Business the muck-rakers lifted their voices unto high heaven and cried, " He 's sold out! "
As a matter of record, I print his reply to an attack from an unexpected quarter—to illustrate how his mind worked on this subject—and to prove the prophetic character of his vision:

Norman Hapgood, Editor, Harper's Weekly,
New York City.
My dear Norman:
You and I both belong to the Illini.
We were disciplined in the same university.
We have fought together in the literary trenches, where the ink flowed like bilge.
I appreciate your worthy qualities of brain; I know your kindly heart—your generous nature.
Also, I recognize the military necessity of your marching your editorials across peaceful preserves, because " a man must live." ❧ ❧
The herculean task which confronts you is to galvanize the moribund Harper's into a semblance of life.
Upon doing this successfully your literary life depends, for you have already lost a few artistic argosies, and to lose another will, like the loss of two ships by a British commander, forfeit your captaincy. Hence, in view of all the ties that bind us, my heart is with you. And that muck-raking no longer pays, I, as a journalist, for your sake, much regret ❧ ❧

The times have changed; and that you can not change with them appeals to me almost as a personal sorrow I realize your horror of charity, and your well-founded fears of the bread-line, and therefore I do not blame you for trying to cash in by discovering to the world the alleged fact that I have sold my soul to Pluto.

I boost, and sell my products to my friends.

You knock, and sell your product to the enemies of enterprise and the foes of the human race—if you can.

I make no protest against your publishing certain letters that passed between myself and Mr. Rockefeller, and between Mr. Rockefeller and his Colorado Superintendent, Mr. Welborn, wherein I was concerned—such letters being a part of the record of the Federal Committee on Industrial Relations

Neither do I criticize your use of the phrase—repeated for three weeks—" Elbert Hubbard's Price! " your purpose being, of course, to make it appear that Elbert Hubbard has a price, and that you know what it is.

This on your part was advertising. And a chemical trace of piffle in publicity is allowable in a worthy pen-pusher sore pressed by the solicitors of the Hotel De Gink.

I do, however, regret your lack of logic when you come to your two final conclusions. These conclusions are:

First, that my opinions are for sale.

Second, that I wrote of the Colorado situation first, and investigated it afterward.

Both of these conclusions are gratuitous.

The fact that I speak well of Mr. Rockefeller and his business methods, and that he occasionally buys my products, does not carry any proof that if Mr. Rockefeller were a different kind of man I would still uphold his cause.

Second, the fact that I went to Colorado last August to investigate conditions did not justify your conclusion that I had never been there before.

The truth is, I have visited the Coal Regions of Colorado on various occasions during the last six years.

Conditions there were changing. Federal troops had replaced the militia—a new sentiment was said to prevail.

What the effect was of these changes I wished to ascertain.
❡ Hence, Mr. Rockefeller's letter to Mr. Welborn suggest-
ing that I be given every opportunity to study these new
conditions ❧ ❧

While it is within the range of possibilities that I have my
price, yet you have not discovered what it is.

On the other hand, in your endeavors to advertise my
price, you have revealed your own.

You have sold your birthright for a mess of perlmutter
potash ❧ ❧

Do I have to supply a blueprint? Very well, here it is:
You have succumbed to the temptation of trying to place
an old friend in a disgraceful light before the world, this
for the transient satisfaction of some undefined personal
whim, and a desire to secure the applause of people who
accept the philosophy of Mother Jones, Upton Sinclair
and Frank Tannenbaum as gospel truth, and who regard
the Constitution of the United States as an obsolete document ❧ ❧

You probably would consider it rude, crude, vulgar and
coarse to be bribed by money; but the bribers are abroad,
and the love of fame and the will-to-vengeance have taken
you captive, and the proof of this seduction you yourself
supply ❧ ❧

Nevertheless, I wish you well, and while I regret that
Harper's Weekly has few readers, and no advertising to
mention, I yet believe there is a place for your services
if you can but realize that today the world needs builders
and creators, not sappers and incendiaries.

With all kind wishes,

Your sincere,
ELBERT HUBBARD

As an average not one of ten " boost " articles that he
wrote ever brought him enough profit to pay for the scrap
paper on which they were written. For example, I remember
the *Little Journey to the Home of Andrew Carnegie* in the
Business Men series. Hubbard produced a masterpiece and
mailed it out to his subscription list, which approximated

one hundred thousand, at his own expense be sure. He
then sent an autographed copy to Carnegie who was a-
visiting at Skibo Castle, Scotland. While we awaited Little
Hoot Mon's verdict, there was some optimistic talk in
East Aurora about " Would n't it be nice if Mr. Carnegie
gave us a library! "
But a little while and another little while and Andy's
answer arrived:

> " I could not help bursting into laughter many times
> * * * You have a style of your own and it hits the
> nail in the most unexpected fashion. Several visitors
> in the house have enjoyed reading it, ' laughing con-
> sumedly.' * * * We shall, of course, want, say,
> one hundred copies."

Apparently the " laugh " was on Hubbard—and he laughed,
too ∾ ∾
My arithmetic says that at ten cents each one hundred
copies figures ten dollars.
And there were other incidents, many others!
You can't get rich thataway!
Another time Hubbard and I were in the office of a certain
well known national advertiser. The general manager
of the firm had just signed a contract for twenty-four
pages of advertising space and was about to pass it to me
when he thought to say, " But what guarantee have we
that when this advertising is printed there will not appear
immediately alongside of it an article like the X Article
of last month to which my president, Mr. Blank, seriously
objected? " ∾ ∾
When the G. M. opened up, Hubbard was looking out the
window—the remarks were really addressed to me—but
Hubbard turned and answered him:
" You have no guarantee—for the very simple reason that

Mr. Blank is not the editor of my publication, nor am I thinking of so engaging his services. When I wish to permit the advertisers to dictate the editorial policy of my magazines, we'll let you know—and meanwhile, Good Morning!" ఇ ఇ

Out we stalked and left my commissions on twenty-four pages resting, with the contract, there on the table.

No! You can't prove it by me that Hubbard loved money.

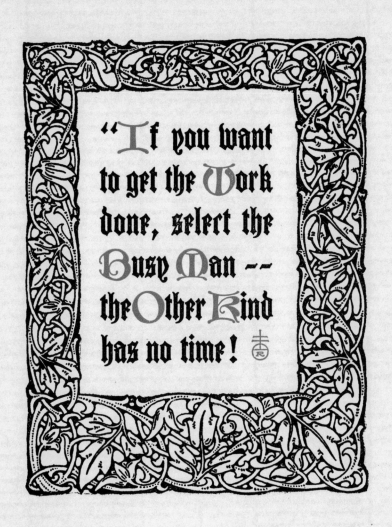

"If you want to get the Work done, select the Busy Man -- the Other Kind has no time!

Those Whom He Helped

HUBBARD was a champion of Progress, of New Ideas, of Fair Play and of the Strong Heart. Whenever he saw some one making a good fight against odds he gladly volunteered to lend a helpful hand.

Most of the articles he wrote were to help some person, or advance some cause—and from not one in a hundred did he ever make a cent either directly or indirectly ᘐ ᘐ It was easier for him to cheer than to criticize. He praised every book ever sent him, no matter who sent it and irrespective of how good or how bad was the book.

" What we all need in this World is more encouragement —not less." ᘐ ᘐ

So he 'd write, " I have read your book with both pleasure and profit. You have an insight on the heart of things that is very charming."

Not so very long ago I talked to a man who said:

" The trouble with Hubbard was that he was equipped to do a lot of harm! He had three magazines of national circulation, access to the lecture platform and newspaper syndicates: what he said could not be unsaid by an ordinary individual." ᘐ ᘐ

" The trouble with you, m'lad, is that you are full of negative thoughts instead of positive thoughts. What about his capacity to *do good!* "

I know of more than one instance where his national influence was thrown on the side of a struggling business or a struggling individual because his admiration was captured and he wanted to help—and without thought of self or pelf ✒ ✒

Consider the case of Carrie Jacobs Bond, the author of *A Perfect Day*. Twenty years and more ago Fame had not yet searched her out.

Hubbard discovered her—and her melodies!

He saw Genius in her work, and so he took his pen in hand and told the world. Moreover, he offered her the opportunity to give concerts at East Aurora.

Carrie Jacobs once confided to me that was the beginning of things for her!

Excerpt from The Philistine of January, Nineteen Hundred One: "Art at the last is a matter of Heart, not Head, and this fact was brought home to me strongly a few weeks ago on hearing Carrie Jacobs Bond. Here is a woman who writes poems, sets them to music, and sings them. Her performance is all so gentle, spontaneous, and unaffected that you think you could do the same thing yourself: simple pattering little child songs, set to tunes that sing themselves. But in some way they search out the corners of your soul and make you think of the robin that sings at Sunset."

To a person with sheet music to sell—and no money—that was very superior advertising when printed in *The Philistine*, with a one hundred twenty-five thousand circulation and say a million readers.

That article was the first that this nation as a whole had ever heard of Carrie Jacobs Bond—and today who has not heard of her?

Next time you pass the Mary Elizabeth candy establishment on Fifth Avenue, New York City, and some one remarks that just a year or so ago they refused more than a Million Dollars for their trade-mark and good will—please understand it was not always so.

Again let us go back twenty years and stage the scene in Syracuse, New York, and let the pen of Hubbard tell the story as he wrote it for the *Philistine:*

" Down at Syracuse where they take things *cum grano salis* is a concern that does business under the unique name of *Mary Elizabeth.* The head of the concern is Fanny Reigel Evans, a widow anywhere between thirty and fifty. Five years ago she had sorrow, bereavement, and a much tangled estate to fill up the void of leaden hours.

" The lawyers straightened out the estate—and kept it *so*.

" This simplified matters.

" The mother would have just lain down and died of a broken heart, for hearts are made to be broken, but she had a family of three girls and a boy just blooming into adult life, leaving childhood behind.

" It is easy to die: to bravely live and face each new day —that often takes courage, indeed.

" I think so.

" And so we find Mrs. Evans in dire extremity revolving in her mind what she could do and do well that she might earn a living for herself and brood. She thought she could not do anything but it came to her that years before she had made candy for her brothers and sisters, and then for neighbors and occasionally for fairs and bazaars.

" So she made some candy, and Mary Elizabeth, a bright slip of a girl, went out and sold it. The candy was wrapped, boxed, labeled and tied in a most tempting and appetizing way. Then Mary Elizabeth wrote her name with one hand on every package to show that the goods were genuine. People smiled and bought and would have patted Mary

Elizabeth on her flaxen head, but she was fourteen goin'
on fifteen ᔥ ᔥ

" Orders came in for the Mary Elizabeth candy—people
of taste and distinction liked it and liked the looks of it.
Then they liked the looks of Mary Elizabeth—she was
such a fine, strong, healthy youngster—so full of life and
cheer—so honest and genuine.

" The business grew.

" It continued to grow.

" It is growing still.

" It is managed by Mrs. Evans, her three daughters, and
her son.

" These five work together as one person.

" This earnest, honest, healthy, intelligent, active, alert
and loving little group, produce candy of a most superior
kind and quality. The candy they make is like themselves.

" That is all we can do anyway—reproduce ourselves.

" Your work is a broken-off piece of your spiritual estate.

" If there are sleazy strands in the warp and woof of
your character, they will reappear in the woven fabric ᔥ

" Everything we make we manufacture right out of our
hearts ᔥ ᔥ

" The name—' Mary Elizabeth '—stuck; it is still on the
package."

* * * * *

His interests were varied, diversified, and as broad as human
sympathy is broad. For example, I think of his contacts
with convicts. Not only did he employ them, and promote
them, and give them positions of trust, but he found time
to write those still in prison, and when on the road, to visit
prisons to talk to " The Boys."

I know that he spoke at Auburn, San Quentin, Florence,
Arizona, and that he visited Sing Sing and most of the

other larger prison establishments—not forgetting nor over-
looking insane asylums, at several of which he was an
expected and appreciated annual visitor.

Understand, please, that convicts and most insane people
are specialists: they are only dangerous to society when
working at their specialty. In all other directions they are
safe and sane enough.

He was vehemently opposed to the old style prison régime
of striped suits, cropped heads, lock-step, enforced silence,
damp and musty cells, solitary confinement, restricted use
of the mails.

That 's what he called the Crime against the Criminal. To
his mind the criminal was a sick person: sick either in body
or mind, or one afflicted with uncontrolled energy. The cure
for such a patient was not punishment, but treatment.

The purpose of prison was not to punish for a crime past
but to prepare the criminal for re-entrance into society ↝
If a person returned to society a felon full of hate and the
spirit of revenge—then the whole scheme of prison confinement was a failure. So he made friends with prisoners—
particularly Lifers. Many Lifers are young men paying for
a momentary act of violence (oftentimes when drunk) with
a life of shame and degradation behind bars.

He felt they needed consolation, friendship and help ↝
Each Christmas Time a letter would go out to a preferred
list of lifers in several different penitentiaries asking them
what particular little present would make them happy ↝
Back came the timid, hopeful, pathetic answers—most of
them asked for correspondence courses, so that they could
study! ↝ ↝

There came to East Aurora several years ago a letter from
Number 0000, Sing Sing, which told an extraordinary
story: ↝ ↝

" I am a convict—a first offender—a burglar—and guilty.
But if you believe that there is such a thing as a reformation
in jail, then I ask for another chance. I committed the crime
or tried to commit it, because I was out of a job—and crazy-
mad about a girl ✺ That temptation is past—and I have
served almost five years! The Pardon Board will let me
out of here some months ahead of time provided a reputable concern will guarantee me work."

Hubbard said, " Give him an advertisement in *The Fra*—
but let him write his own copy—he 's an educated man—
insist he tell the whole truth."

The advertisement appeared: " I Want a Show for my
White Alley; " and it told the tale of an educated Southern
boy who came to New York and met a girl and tried to
burn the candle at both ends—and got burned himself.
How one night being desperate and out of a job, he picked
up a carpenter's chisel in the hall of his boarding house,
left there by the Devil, and the idea came to him to try
to break into one of the curtained apartments up in the
Central Park district. The chisel had but snapped the lock
on the door, when up the stairs, the first flight, the second
flight, the third flight, came the occupant of the apartment.
❡ He brushed by the woman on the last flight of stairs,
and managed to reach the front door—when she threw
up a window and screamed, " Help! Murder! Police!"

The cop on the corner caught him.

The Judge gave him the maximum—five years—" for the
moral effect on others," even though he was a first offender.
❡ Since then he 'd been doing a tall amount of thinking:
he asked for another chance.

Actually, there came to him at Sing Sing several mail
sacks full of letters offering jobs with reputable, rated
concerns ✺ ✺

The Pardon Board were non plussed—they did n't know what had happened!

While he was still in prison I was instrumental in selling his " story " to the *Cosmopolitan*. They did the very decent thing of sending this convict a check for Five Hundred Dollars in advance—before they ever saw his manuscript. ⁋ The reader may remember the tale—'t was called *Four Years with the Grey Brotherhood*.

The last I heard of Sing Sing No. 0000 he was District Manager for a concern " down South," and doing well ✺

Once Hubbard visited Governor Hunt of Arizona to attempt to secure a pardon for Louis Victor Eytinge, an extraordinary man given a life-sentence on circumstantial evidence, and who instead of sulking and reviling went to work at the Florence Prison and through industry and intelligence earned the respect of the American business world—and say ten thousand dollars a year, selling the trinkets of horsehair and silver made by the prisoners. ⁋ 'T was an odd and unique mail order business which he conducted, that earned delicacies for the tubercular ward of the prison—and Freedom eventually for the Man. ⁋ I know Hubbard crossed the Arizona Desert in the company of a " trusty "—the hottest spot this side of Biloxi—to say to Eytinge, " Be of good cheer,"—and to speak to the other prisoners!

* * * * *

Not only does a hair divide the false from the true, but a hair line divides Success from Failure. Hubbard did not wait until a thing was " made," until Success was assured, until the establishment was a going concern, to praise and affirm it ✺ ✺

He said the necessary when it was most necessary for him to say it—and that was why so many of his friendships were firm, fast, never failing—and why his resources in friendships were so limitless.

Cynics to the contrary, the habit of gratitude is strong within us all: we never forget a good turn.

He helped men over the top of the hill—when they were not in position to pay for his services. Nor did he expect them to! ๑๛ ๑๛

But they remembered.

High and low, rich and poor, men appreciate such a service beyond price. That service is to *popularize* something that should be popular—but is n't.

I have gone a-visiting with him into the offices of Underwood of the Erie Railroad, Brown of the New York Central, Archbold of Standard Oil, Oliver of Oliver Plow, of " Uncle" Jim Studebaker, of Colonel Colt of United States Rubber, and dozens of others; as a rule 't was a meeting of friends, not of business acquaintances.

I have known Colonel Colt to dismiss a board meeting when Hubbard arrived, and to hold over the members of the board for a joking match with Hubbard.

I have known him to write on *Pan-Americanism* so effectively that John Barrett, the high commissioner, came to East Aurora in person to thank him.

I have known him to boost for more National Parks, for the Lincoln Highway when it was but a dream, for the potato fields of Maine, and the Children's Court of Ben Lindsey ๑๛ ๑๛

I have known him to boost the use of cement (anybody's cement), and paper coats as wind-breakers, and marble fountains and safety razors, and the Bergen Cut, and California, and Fred Harvey's Lunch Rooms, and Mother Child's (when we were doing printing for Hartford Lunch.)

I have known him to boost a New York department store

that could not find space for his Roycroft goods—and to keep on boosting it!

He was an odd man, with a catholicity of interests—and ofttimes a contradictory one. He approved, endorsed and praised—not for the immediate return but for the ultimate return. He believed sincerely that whatever helped American business was helpful to everybody.

Moreover, he had the *Success Habit*—seemingly almost everything he touched turned successful.

"Success is in the blood, there are men whom Fate can never keep down. They march jauntily forward and take by Divine Right the best of everything that Earth affords.

RESOLVED. THAT WE DON'T LIKE MEN WHO BUTTON THEIR COLLARS BEHIND AND HAVE SUNDAY SCHOOL IN-DOORS, WHERE DOGS ARE NOT WELCOME; THAT WE LIKE THE FRA, BECAUSE HE LOVES KIDDIES, KIDDEENS AND KIOODLES, AND STANDS FOR HEALTH AND HAPPINESS AND AGREES WITH TIGE THAT VIVISECTION IS WORSE THAN HYDROPHOBIA BECAUSE A DOG THAT BITES A MAN CAN'T HELP IT, BUT A MAN WHO STRAPS A DOG ON A TABLE, & CUTS INTO HIM WITH A KNIFE AND SCISSORS NEEDN'T IF HE DOESN'T WANT TO;
 THAT BOYS AND GIRLS DO NOT LIKE THE STUFFY IN-DOORS; THAT TO GET ACQUAINTED WITH BEES, BUGS, BIRDS AND BEETLES IS LOTS MORE FUN AND JUST AS MUCH BENEFIT AS READING ABOUT NICODEMUS & NEBUCHADNEZZAR WHO ARE DEAD ONES, BOTH ; THAT BAD CHILDREN ARE GOOD CHILDREN WHO HAVE ENERGY PLUS, AND THEIR PARENTS SAY, "QUIT THAT", "LET UP", "GET OUT";
 THAT DIRTY CLOTHES ARE PREFERABLE TO PALE CHEEKS, AND THAT WE SHOULD ALL LIVE IN HEAVEN HERE AND NOW, SO TO GET USED TO IT FOR BY AND BY   BUSTER BROWN.

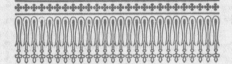

I KNOW OF NO RECIPE FOR SUCCESS IN AD-VERTISING ❧ IF I DID I WOULD KEEP IT TO MYSELF

Making Literature of Advertising

A T one time or other Elbert Hubbard wrote advertising for most of the important national advertisers— and it's only fair to assume that such intelligent gentlemen knew what they needed and wanted ᔑ For many of them he wrote advertising many times over a period of years. So that there may be no misconceptions I set down a few of the names: Armour, Burroughs Adding Machine,Ingersoll Watch,Wrigley's Chewing Gum, Burpee's Seeds, Cliquot Club Ginger Ale, Davey Tree Surgery, Equitable Life Insurance, Elgin Watches, Heinz' Fifty-seven Varieties, Hole-proof Hosiery, Jones' Sausages, Knox Hats, Lanston Monotype, Gillette Safety Razor, O'Sullivan Rubber Heels, Ostermoor Mattress, Prophylactic Tooth Brush, Parker Pen, Stein-Bloch Clothes, Globe-Wernicke, Van Camp's Beans,—*and more than a thousand others.*

For twenty years concerns of this type and character O.K.'d and O.K.'d his " Copy." Therefore there must have been something to the " Hubbard Style "—and just what it was is worth a look!

There must have been something to the Signed Advertisements, too—" An Advertisement by Elbert Hubbard "— which he introduced and established more than fifteen years ago; because I find that the very latest innovations of this year of Nineteen Hundred Twenty-six are advertise-

ments *signed* by Dr. Frank Crane, by Will Rogers, and
our old friend Irvin Cobb!

Of course the high-brow boys, the " merchandizers," turn
thumbs down on every advertisement that 's readable and
human, particularly those that are signed.

But they are not the ones with the bank balances, I wot!
❡ They are the technicians, and the advertisements they
produce are absolutely correct in all particulars—they do
everything but *sell goods.*

This year I have heard the Will Rogers "Bull Durham"
advertising criticized as the Hubbard advertisements were
criticized, because *seemingly* he does not stick to his
subject! ❧ ❧

Bosh! What is the subject?

The subject is *Buy Bull Durham*—and nothing else.

The interested parties want you to know that it 's on sale
everywhere, that it 's low-priced, that it 's good quality,
and that You 'll Like It.

They can tell their true *advertising* story in twelve words—
but ordinarily the prospective consumer is shy and wary,
and tobacco literature is not particularly a literature of
irresistible appeal—and that 's the point! An advertisement must be read—or it 's wasted!

Then comes along Will Rogers with a lot of gol darn non-
sense—intelligent and imaginative—and makes us smile,
and while we 're still smiling and full of Peace on Earth
Good Will toward Men, we find ourselves reading " On
Sale Everywhere—Low Price—Good Quality—You 'll Like
It—Bull Durham! "

Say, are we sold?

You just know it.

Sold *indirectly,* painlessly, pleasantly.

Whenever I see a Signed Advertisement my curiosity is

piqued, I am much more interested to know what Will Rogers thinks of Bull Durham—particularly when it's written slap-dash, slap-stick, without restriction—than to learn what Mr. Bull Durham thinks about himself.

I know in advance that *he 'll* make it unanimous!

But when some one else's pen is pushing the adjectives, there's always the hope that he'll say the thing is only Ninety-nine and Forty-four One Hundredths Pure, and that takes a strain off the reader!

So when it is used discreetly—particularly when it is not overworked—I am positive the *signed* advertisement as introduced and popularized by Elbert Hubbard is a legitimate part of the Science or Art of Advertising. I make this preamble in defense of the Signed Advertisements because certain of the boys in the back room did n't like them. And while their squak was not entirely altruistic, nor disinterested, I believe, nevertheless, the subject should be explained to them, so they can get on with their ink-slinging ✍ ✍

Back in Nineteen Hundred Eight began the general use of the Signed Advertisement—" By Elbert Hubbard "—and so far as the style itself is concerned the End is not yet—only the Beginning.

* * * * *

Hubbard dared to make advertising interesting.

Most publications offer preferred position " next to pure reading." Hubbard's advertising was just as " pure " as his text if not more so, and quite as readable.

The advertisements were never the Poor Relation in his publications ✍ ✍

He never apologized for the prominence he gave them ✍

Life to him was Advertising and Advertising was Life ✍

He held that the things that people bought to adorn or

beautify themselves or their homes or offices were just as
important to them as the things they bought to decorate
their minds.

Said he also: " The difference in our estimates of men lies
in the fact that one man is able to get his Goods in the
Show Window and the other is neither aware that he has
either Show Window or Goods."

Every act we perform is advertising of self.

Every movement we make advertises us for what we are.
What we eat, at what we laugh, the kind of clothes we
wear, the shows we attend, what we read, the stuff we buy
to please our fancy, *advertises* to the neighbors the facts
that will determine them in deciding whether or not they
will like us, or shun us!

The point is that *all* is advertising, and that ofttimes it
is the subtle kind of advertising, the kind that creates a
desirable atmosphere, that creates desire.

An association of ideas is the thing.

In advertising lard it is better to talk of cold Winter mornings and Hot Wheat Cakes, browned and delicious, than
it is to poke the reader's nose down into the pail and say,
" *smell it.*" ๛ ๛

Which is all the way round Robin Hood's barn to say that
Hubbard's " copy " introduced a catchy headline—a pleasant subject, an interesting idea; and while discussing it
in a free and easy and friendly sort of manner managed
somehow to *ease in* the true advertisement so naturally
that the reader reacted: " *Yes, yes: go on.*"

I say again, he dared make advertising interesting—he
dared to defy " Americanitis." (" Americanitis comes from
an awful desire to get thar.") He dared to take his time
in telling his advertising story, and not to arrive at the
crucial part of the story—where he 's asking the prospect

to " please sign here "—breathless from sucking wind ℘
The nonchalance of the man made the prospect his friend.
℀ His brains, his intelligence, his ideas, fixed the friendship ℘ ℘
Whether you bought or not, ultimately, you enjoyed reading his advertisement, and when you enjoy reading advertisements, ultimately you buy.
His instructions to copy writers were to find an attractive
idea that hooked up with the subject, that appealed and
convinced, and then write it so as to woo the prospect's
attention ℘ ℘
Said he, " Let a smile go into the ink bottle if it will. In
advertising you are dealing with very human men, and
you can not mistake by letting your copy be human."
℀ When one gets the prospect's favorable attention the
goods are half sold. Don't try to say it all in every advertisement. People are reasonably intelligent, leave something to their imagination.
A good sale is a little exercise in co-operation between
the seller and the buyer—so compliment the prospect by
showing that you know he too has brains!
" Say it," said Hubbard, " Say it and *stop!* "
                    * * * * *
They accused Hubbard of letting some one else write his
advertising—some satelite. They likewise accused Dumas
the Elder of letting some one else write his books. It is
said that he had seventy collaborators, but every book
bearing his name has the unmistakable touch of the master.
When a lady wrote to the great author to call his attention
to an obvious error in one volume of his Complete Works,
Dumas is supposed to have replied: " Dear Madam: I have
not read the book in question and damn me if I will "—
℀ What Hubbard said deponent sayeth not.

Obviously too much advertising was turned out at East
Aurora for one man to have produced it all. You need no
mathematical education to figure that. The fact was Hubbard usually had in training one clever young fellow—or
was it two?—who could lend a hand and help to carry
the piano up the stairs.

I assure you that it was much easier to need one than it
was to find one. To write the " Hubbard Style " true to
life was no incidental accomplishment—and after the me-
chanics of the style were acquired, there was still the little
problem of an inexhaustible supply of Ideas on which to
break one's head and one's heart!

Hubbard instructed: " In writing advertisements, first try
to have an Idea; then strive to put that Idea into a form
that may be easily read. Cut out every superfluous word.
Make what you say interesting Literature, and that means
that good Advertising need not be deadly dull."

Anon, and anon, it was necessary for Hubbard to give
the Hot Stuff (so called) produced by the Neophytes,
the " Immortal Touch "—and then maybe there was once
or twice when he did n't. But you may be sure that the
matter that passed his critical eye was all right and then
some ๑๏ ๑๏

Of the boys who struck thirteen occasionally, there was
Feland, and S. J. Kaufman, and Jimmy Wallen, Feussle,
and Freddie Bann.

Feland is now the vice-president of a substantial New
York City advertising agency. S. J. Kaufman writes the
"Round the Town Column" for the *New York Telegram.*
Wallen operates his own advertising studio and has made
a national reputation for fine copy.

Feussle was the creator of the much discussed Halitosis
copy! ๑๏ ๑๏

Freddie Bann is still the Major Domo at Roycroft. Which proves what Hubbard maintained that a man who really knows how to train, knows how to train on!

* * * * *

Hubbard insisted that all *A* Number One historians were advertising men and press agents, and nothing more nor less. They were the ones who invented the slogans and the battle crys, the headlines, the scare-heads.

Here's a sample of his quality:

" Horatius still stands at the bridge sword in hand because a poet placed him there. Paul Revere rides adown the night giving his warning cry at every village and farm because Longfellow set the meters in a gallop. Across the waste of waters the enemy calls upon Paul Jones to surrender and the voice of Paul Jones echoes back.' ' We have not yet begun to fight.'

In Brussels there is yet to be heard a sound of revelry by night, only because Byron told of it. Commodore Perry, that rash and impulsive youth of twenty-six, never sent the message, ' We have met the enemy and they are ours,' but a good reporter did and the reporter's words live.

" Lord Douglas never said, ' The hand of Douglas is his own, and never shall in friendship grasp the hand of such as Marion clasp.' Sir Walter Scott made that remark on white paper with an eagle's quill. Virginius lives in heroic mould not for what he said or did but for the words put into his mouth by a man who pushed what you call a virile pen and wrote such an ad for Virginius as he never could have written for himself. The Old Guard dies but never surrenders. Whipped, torn, muddy, bloody, and magnificent, Cambronne, the last survivor, stands with broken sword defiant and unsubdued. He, like Ney, might have shouted ' Come and see how a French Soldier dies!' The

English are awed by his courage and hesitate to again fire.
' Brave Frenchmen, surrender! ' an officer calls in pleading
accents. And Cambronne hurls back a word that can only
be printed in French—the most indecent and insulting word
that human lips can utter. The English fire and Cambronne
falls weltering in his blood. They kill the man—it is the
only thing to do.

I know it is a shame to say it, and I apologize on bended
knee, but this scene of the death of the last of the Old
Guard is an ad for the French written by Victor Hugo
who loved the French and hated the English.

All literature is advertising.

And all genuine advertisements are literature."

* * * * *

So is that clear?—A great deed does not live in history
because of the deed itself: rather it 's because of the advertisement of the deed written either by an eye-witness or
by one not born till a hundred years later—as the case may
be ❧ ❧

Nor is it the product that pleases: it 's what you are induced
to think of the product—after you read the attractive
advertisements—that creates all the excitement.

The desirable advertisement makes the product desirable.

❧ The unforgetable advertisement makes the Thing advertised unforgetable.

Mind is more than matter.

As Hubbard said about Mr. Wrigley's Spearmint Product:
" *Box Vobisgum*—Buy It by the Box! "

Lines to Pegasus and Stephen Crane

An Ounce
of Loyalty
is worth
a Pound of
Cleverness

His Friends and Fellow Citizens

ORDINARILY clever men are not friend-makers because they are *too* clever; it's the kind man who finds friends and holds them.

Therefore when some apostle observed, " I believe Fra Elbertus has more near, dear, personal, and loving friends than any living man in America," he guessed the truth, but only *half* the truth.

Hubbard's friendships were both numerous and variable.

He knew everybody and everybody knew him. Capitalists, actors, bankers, brokers, artists, inventors, engineers, business men, poets, prize fighters, professional base ball players, doctors, lawyers and preachers—they were all his friends—not casual friends but close friends. He was always glad to go more than half-way to meet a first-class man, a first-class performer, and once met he fastened them to his soul with hoops of steel by addressing to them periodically friendly little letters, and sending them gifts of beautiful books and things, and writing and publishing gracious sentiments about them and their work—and asking not a blessed thing in return but their friendship.

He was forever plaguing Bill Reedy and his other intimates for this or that—or spoofing Richard Harding Davis for carrying a valet around with him. " Suppose," he said, " I hired a man to curl my whiskers and put on my shoes and socks, and paid him fifteen dollars a week, would I be

a benefactor of mankind because I gave him work? Nix!
Nein! Aber Nitt! I would be pauperizing the Race to puff
up my own vanity! "

Once when Hubbard followed Davis into a hotel and found
" Richard Harding Davis and Man " on the Register, he
wrote down " Elbert Hubbard and Satchel."

Whenever and wherever Hubbard and his friends got
together there was much good swapping of yarns after the
manner of Lincoln—and much high good humor!

Uncle Joe Cannon told Hubbard this one: It seems that
the Ancient and Honorable Speaker of the House while
electioneering met a lady with a baby-carriage. The Political Gentleman gave a hasty glance into the basket and
said, " My, my, my! What a sweet child—the exact image
of his father! " * * The lady was returning from market
with nothing in the go-wagon but a head of cabbage ⚘
Uncle Joe said he did n't know whether he had lost two
votes or gained one! "

Golden Rule Jones, the famous Mayor of Toledo, told his
friend, Hubbard, that whenever he found a woman of the
streets in Court he fined each man present ten cents and
himself a dollar for living in a civilization that permitted
such things to be.

Hubbard admired Theodore P. Shonts, the Capitalist and
Builder, because he punched a husky Irish Labor Leader
in the nose when the Mick came into his office to threaten
him ⚘ ⚘

Hubbard liked John D. Rockefeller, not for what he got
out of him—because he says somewhere in print that he
found John D. quite a little *tight*—but because he somehow
managed to be a simple, sane and sensible man while at
the same time the wealthiest one in the world!

Once Hubbard sent John D. a black Persian lamb—a black

sheep—which he christened " Judge Landis " in honor of
the occasion of the huge fine inflicted by the Base ball
Mogul on Standard Oil—and the Ol' Gentleman chuckled.
While Elbert was spoofing and criticizing the *literati*, he
yet found time to say the kindly, friendly, appreciative
word for his less articulate friends.

Here is a fair sample of what Elbert Hubbard thought of
his contemporaries in various walks of life, and why:

Eugene Debs: Debs is a very superior man. He is more than
an agitator, for he has a generous swelling heart of love.
The years have tamed him, and educated him. His gradu-
ation from Unionism was a great stride in advance. The
Union is exclusive—it sets class against class. Debs knows
this. Now he would make us all free. Of the purity of his
motives there is not the shadow of a doubt. He is ninety-
nine one-hundredths fine.

John D. Rockefeller: Mr. Rockefeller is not the sanctimonious dogmatic joyless shrimp that we see pictured in the
comic section. The fact is he is a persistent joker and exudes
good nature. * * His success in the business world has
been no fluke. He is the greatest organizer the world has
ever seen; the greatest business general of the age—or any
age. And you find him today unspoiled, unaffected, kindly,
industrious, economical, practising the virtues with which
his mother endowed him.

Wu Ting Fang: Dr. Wu is the canniest Chink that ever
came over the cosmic pike. He has certain qualities that
make him akin to Benjamin Disraeli. He is clever, witty,
rapid, satirical, patient, ambitious, and possesses purpose
plus. He is a man who mystifies everybody and is deceived
by none ♒ ♒

John Burroughs: John Burroughs is the most Universal
man I can name. He is a piece of Elemental Nature. He

has no hate, no whim, no prejudice. He believes in the rich, the poor, the learned, the ignorant. He believes in the wrong-doer, the fallen, the sick, the weak, the defenseless. He loves children, animals, birds, insects, trees, and flowers. He is one who is afraid of no man and of whom no man is afraid ๑๑ ๑๑

Admiral Togo: Togo is five feet two inches high and weighs one hundred twenty pounds in the shade. He belongs to the Samurai caste, that is, the aristocratic fighting class. Bred for war, he is in fact the great original boy scout. The Samurai stand for the entire list of military virtues; that is to say, loyalty, truthfulness, honor, integrity, health, self-reliance, and the silent and prompt obedience of orders.

Joaquin Miller: He wrote the greatest poem ever written by an American. * * * He stood off and talked to us. He knew we were admiring him—how could he help it? His white beard fell to his waist while his wide sombrero was cocked carelessly to the northwest. * * * " And your books?" I ventured. "Books?" said the Poet. "Books? To hell with books! Books are for people who can not think! " ๑๑ ๑๑

Madame Montessori: " Happiness," says Dr. Montessori, " is the greatest asset in life." She never uses a negative except in cases of positive vice or present danger. She never rebukes a child. If the child is doing the wrong thing, she gently encourages it to do something else. If there is a band playing on the street, all of her children sit up to see the band and hear the music. The impulse to know what is being done, to be familiar with your surroundings, is one of the elements of power.

Leo Tolstoi: He was a man of sorrows. Like Buddha and Christ he believed he carried the burden of humanity. His mighty soul was gashed by the evils of the age. He saw that life and suffering were interchangeable terms; that man here below has been caught like a rat in a trap; that knavery, force and fraud ruled everywhere, especially in his own native land. He was a pessimist, if to see the Truth and speak it is pessimism.

Walt Mason: "One of these little—er—ah—poemettes, read on the trolley going down town in the morning, makes you smile all day." * * * They say that Walt is making a small barrel of money. My hope is that he will not make too much. As it is, he is a generous, human, charming and chummy gentleman, with baggy breeches besmeared with printers' ink, and all unconscious that he has done anything ⁊⁊

Ibsen: The man who treats life ruthlessly is the great man. Men, like races, survive because of their strength, not because of their goodness. Persistence of force is persistence of strength; the way to achieve Immortality is to deserve it. The strong full-blooded man has discovered Nature's meaning. Ibsen would not compromise with his Age. He lived up to his doctrine of heroic egoism.

James Bryce: His book *The American Commonwealth* is the best picture of the United States that has ever been presented. It is a book that no American could have written. It has the value of perspective. It told us some unpleasant truths—truths we should have known and that we did know, but which we tried to conceal. Great Britain should take a great and pardonable pride in this man's achievement. He will live in history.

Charles W. Eliot: Dr. Eliot, President Emeritus of Harvard, is the most conspicuous intellectual figure before the American people today. His position is one of singular dignity. Dr. Eliot has always been a conservative in the sense that he has conserved everything which is valuable,

never tearing down the scaffolding as long as it was needed.
He represents the established order. He keeps step with
the procession—but never ahead of it. He is a teacher ot
teachers ✍ ✍

Porfirio Diaz: It was Diaz who put Mexico on the map.
He lifted her out of the realm of Barbarism and made her
a front power. It is easy to criticize the powerful man,
but when we make an estimate of his character, in justice
we should set down on one side of the account a list of the
worthy things that he has brought about and accomplished;
then strike your balance.

Wilbur Wright: Wilbur Wright was the first man to solve
principles of aerial navigation. In speaking of his achieve-
ments Wilbur Wright never told of the things that he
himself had done. It was always the " Wright Brothers "
or " We." He left an unsullied name.

Ben Greet: In giving a play out of doors, or without complex scenic effects, Ben Greet has made a discovery. The
game is his; it is his idea, and those cheapen it or take it
away who can. Merry villagers, obtuse persons, drunk on
what the world calls Success may say, " Oh, it is naught!
It is naught! " His advertising manager may remark, " It
is I who hath made him, and not he himself! " The fact
remains that Ben Greet has done something never done
since William Shakespeare and Necessity demanded it.
I say that Ben Greet is not only a gentleman—business
man—but he is a very great actor.

Brann, the Iconoclast: Brann shook his cap, flourished his
bauble, gave a toss to that fine head of his, and with tongue
in cheek, asked questions and propounded conundrums that
stupid Hypocrisy could n't answer—so they killed Brann!

Elbert H. Gary: Well is Gary called the " Great Pacifi-
cator." His influence in the business world today is greater

than that of any other individual we can name. Gary is
modest, gentle, kindly, and has all the time there is. He
has the supreme ability to delegate, relegate, and supervise. Elbert H. Gary is a great Democrat. His days ot
poverty, obstacles and trials are still before him, unfor-
gotten ᴥ ᴥ

Samuel Pomeroy Colt: Colt realized that you could get
the best out of a man only when he was well paid, happy,
and made free. He liberated his men from the fear of the
alms house by giving them liberal salaries and permanent
positions. His was the far-seeing prophetic vision which
makes co-operation possible. As an economic factor today
Competition is as dead as Feudalism. Co-operation means
working with folks, instead of against them.

Henry Ford: Henry Ford's income is about steen million
dollars a year. This is more than Eva Tanguay gets; it is
more than I made in vaudeville. Also it is more than any
Vaudeville artist ever said he was offered. Nobody knows
how much twenty million dollars a year is, so I will have to
explain that it is sixty thousand dollars a day—and then
some. In two days, Henry Ford earns as much mazuma
as Arthur Brisbane does in a year. and then has enough
left so that he can go to a moving-picture show. Fifteen
years ago Henry Ford was on a salary; ten years ago he
was on his uppers. Henry Ford is the king of standardization
" This one thing I do."

Thomas Edison: Of course, Edison has gotten along pretty
well in a business way, but Edison has been more stolen
from than any other man in existence. Thousands of men
have appropriated his ideas, and attorneys without number
have sat up nights working out schemes to get around
his patents, and many of these schemes have succeeded.
Nevertheless, good to say, Edison is not on half-rations.

Judge Ben Lindsey: Judge Lindsey has done things that
have never been done before in the history of the world.
His beneficent influence is mighty and far-reaching. The
custom in most places when children are arrested, is to
put them in the pen with drunks, suspects, vagrants, and
hardened criminals. Lindsey was the first man in America
to provide a Detention School for children under arrest.
The next move was to investigate each case and find out
why the child did the thing. The child was regarded as
a victim of unkind conditions. Instead of bagging him
off to the Reform School, an earnest effort was put forth
to better his environment.

Luther Burbank: The next day I saw Burbank in his own
garden, there in Santa Rosa—a modest man with iron-
grey hair, furrowed face of tan, with blue eyes that would
be weary and sad were it not for the smiling mouth; a
gentleman—low-voiced, quiet, kindly. No matter how much
money he might possess, Luther Burbank's mode of living
would not change; he is wedded to his work. The finest
product of the life and work of Luther Burbank is Luther
Burbank so so

Henry L. Doherty: Everything that Doherty takes hold
of prospers, and his investors are educated into the idea
that anything Doherty recommends is a safe investment.
These investors are not speculators, bounders, or gamblers;
they are plain people who seek a safe investment and a fair
dividend. The intent of Doherty in every instance is to
increase the consumption of the current. He goes into
partnership with the public.

Fred Harvey: Fred Harvey? Do you know that name?
If not, then your education has been neglected! Where
the name " Fred Harvey " appears, the traveling public
expects much. It may be on the Desert of Arizona; but it

it is a Fred Harvey place, you get ice, fresh fruits, and everything that you get in the best places of New York and Chicago! How the miracle works out, you don't know —it is a Fred Harvey concern—that is enough!

Dr. Lorenz: I may have said in times past a few oblique things about doctors, but for all others let transverse atonement now be made. The finest specimen of physical and mental manhood I ever saw was a physician—and that man was Dr. Lorenz of Vienna. About his own performances he is very modest.

Pop Geers: Geers is just fifty, with a complexion like brick-dust, as a result of wind and weather. I make this explanation because the man never touches intoxicants in any form, and uses no tobacco. He is a trifle lame and a little hunched—who would n't be after being in a score of mix-ups, runaways, upsets, racers falling dead, and six horses and six sulkies piled as high as a haystack? Four times he has been carried from the track on a barn door for dead, but with nothing worse than a few broken bones sticking out through his clothes. Geers can not be bought, intimidated or turned aside when he thinks he is doing his duty.

Charles P. Steinmetz: Dr. Steinmetz is the last word in electrical development. Physically, he is sore stricken by the hand of unkind fate. When you meet him, your pity very soon runs off into admiration, as you catch a little of his enthusiasm, his hope, his bubbling wit, his courage, and his noble imagination. For what is an inventive genius save seeing with loving eyes? Steinmetz, next to Edison, is our great, modern, mechanical prophet.

Buffalo Jones: Buffalo Jones has done a few things that the world has never seen done before. He is a unique and peculiar figure in American history. If I can help it his fame shall not blush unseen. The particular thing that Buffalo Jones has recently done that merits our recognition is his going to Africa and lassooing wild animals, and doing it in the presence of a moving-picture machine. Above all, he is a naturalist, with rare ability.

Freddy Welsh: Freddy Welsh does not talk. Neither is his fighting done mostly on the typewriter. I never heard him say a purple word. The month that Freddy Welsh was with us, I never saw him lose his temper or give way to any fits of unpleasantness. He was always courteous, gentle and kindly in speech. He uses no tobacco, strong drink or strong language, and for the most part is a vegetarian! ♠ ♠

Purposely these brief appreciations and character outlines have been selected and excerpted at random from several hundred sketches of men of merit, to show both the scope of his interests and the breadth of his sympathy and understanding ♠ ♠

For choice I might have given you Clarence Darrow, Thomas B. Reed, John Hay, Eugene Grubb, Maude Adams, Nathan Straus, F. Hopkinson Smith, General Nelson A. Miles, Fighting Bob Evans, Edward Everett Hale, Ethelbert Nevin, Dr. Parkhurst, Arthur Brisbane, or Gentleman Jim Corbett—and others—but enough is enough!

Surely when he styled himself Fra Elbertus 't was no empty title—for he recognized himself as a Brother to Mankind.

I stood upon a High Place,
And saw, below, many Devils
Running, leaping,
And carousing in Sin.
One looked up, grinning,
And said, "Comrade! Brother!"

—*Stephen Crane*

℄ "Let's see! Let's see! What is it they pursue in Boston? Culture! That's it! In East Aurora we don't have to pursue Culture ⚜ She feels at home and abides with us!" ⚜

The World Visits East Aurora

THERE was the feeling in East Aurora among the Corner Grocery Philosophers that Stevie Crane was the Prince of the Great Men who had visited there.

To discover how truly great is a great man, don't take him to a city, take him to a village. There he feels superior, relaxed, so he lets down —and betrays himself.

There the Merry Villagers, with little to distract them, keep one eye on the stick they are whittling, and the other eye on him. They miss nothing and their judgments are shrewd judgments ๑ ๑

The Baba kept tabs, particularly on the personalities. He viewed them and interviewed them, aired his original views and garrulously swapped opinions with them.

Ask Ali Baba and offhand he'll give you more scandalous information about the Great and the Near Great than you'll ever find in *Who's Who.* Some day the Bab will write a monograph on " Great Men I Have Met " and tell the truth: and then the secret will be out of the box for sure ๑ ๑

Stephen Crane was young, a barbarian, a " varsity " ballplayer, an author of that amazing book *The Red Badge of Courage:* a genuine Roycrofter, not a visitor.

He earned his keep writing lurid philosophical sentiments full of " color " adjectives for the covers of *The Philistine:*

I saw a man tugging at his boot-straps.
" It is futile," I said,
" You can never lift yourself that way."
" You lie! " he cried,
And tugged on.

* * * *

I stood upon a high place,
And saw, below, many Devils
Running, leaping,
And carousing in sin.
One looked up, grinning,
And said, " Comrade! Brother!

* * * *

" You tell me this is God? "
I tell you it is a Printed List,
A Burning Candle and an Ass.

Once Hubbard announced another batch of such epigrams were contracted for, and would be printed irrespective of who cancelled their subscriptions.

Crane was a thin, ascetic, pathetic boy, with a fiery and indomitable will, a limitless imagination, and the sensitiveness of a girl.

He invented a " literary style," which supplied the newspaper paragraphers with inexhaustible material for their jibes and jeers—and so Stevie refused absolutely to read his press notices—they made him so unhappy!

Eventually Stevie cleared out of the country—went to live in England where he was appreciated the more, and where he escaped the petty persecution.

Said Hubbard, " Poe, Emerson, Whitman and Stevie Crane —America's four greatest writers—were first discovered

and lauded by the English, before their own countrymen
agreed to recognize their gifts! "

When he died—still a hopeful, despairing boy, under thirty
—Hubbard wrote these lines straight from the heart:
" I don't know where you are, Stevie, but when I die I
hope I will face Death as manfully as you did; and I hope,
too, that I shall then go where you are now. And so, Stevie,
good-bye and good-bye! "

Once I asked the Fra, " Why did Stevie leave East Aurora?"
" Ah—restlessness, that was all! I gave him a horse—a
big, fine, strong horse, and he rode away, over the horizon
and was gone! I never saw him again! "

*   *   *   *   *

I remember an incident connected with a visit Booker
T. Washington paid to East Aurora. Extra special arrangements were made for Dr. Washington to speak in the
grove on a Sunday afternoon to the Roycrofters and the
country people as well. I helped perfect the arrangements
and was rewarded with an invitation from Brother Elbertus
to lunch with Dr. Washington, Mrs. Hubbard and himself.

¶ Like the stupid young idiot I was—for obvious reasons
—I refused.

For a moment Hubbard was inclined to be exasperated,
and then he passed it off as a joke.

" I have another engagement."

" Ah, yes! I see you favor *blondes*."

There was a pause, and then he said, whimsically, " Well,
Mrs. Hubbard, I trust you 've locked up all your chickens? "

¶ She smiled her friendly, illuminating, understanding
smile—while he haw-haw'd!

*   *   *   *   *

When Edwin Markham, the author of *The Man with the
Hoe,* came to East Aurora, the Roycrofters in force met

him at the railroad station, each boy and girl in overalls—
with a hoe on the shoulder! They supplied the distinguished
poet with a hoe, and overalls, and the procession moved
on toward the farm in solid phalanx.

* * * * *

Dr. Horace Fletcher spent months with us—we all grew
to love the rotund, kindly, friendly old gentleman, with
enough degrees after his name to make an alphabet. He
was as human and approachable as a man may be. I 'll tell
you a story:

Once the X Safety Razor desired some testimonials, so they
made a proposition to give us so many pages of advertising
provided we 'd supply the testimonials from famous men.
⟨ I settled on Dr. Fletcher for one, and went to his room
to register my request.

Unfortunately I reported unshaven—and equally unfortunately (?) I had never used any other but an old style
blade razor in my life. So when I presented my proposition
Dr. Fletcher observed, " Felix, I notice you need a shave.
You say this instrument will save time: suppose you show
me how quickly you can shave yourself with it."

I was committed—convicted—sentenced!

I shaved and reported, " all finished," well under five
minutes; but I know how it feels to be a Spartan youth!
⟨ Another incident of that testimonial collection campaign
occurs to me—and while I think of it I 'll set it down ⤶
I sent a sample razor to Mr. Boldt, Manager of the Waldorf-
Astoria Hotel in New York, whom by chance I had never
met. I asked him to *use* the razor, and see how it improved
his appearance. " Just look in the glass, and then write
me your feeling of gratitude."

A day or so passed, and the answer came back: " While
I appreciate your suggestion, and feel that a marked im-

provement is entirely possible, nevertheless, and inasmuch,
as I have worn a *full beard* for more than twenty years,
I must beg to be excused! "

* * * * *

A London, England, newspaper is supposed to print this:
" On his way to Montreal, Mr. Hall Caine stopped off one
day at East Aurora, and reports that the crop of ginger
for next year is very promising."

That, of course, was Hubbard's own curious way of letting
the world know that the author of *The Deemster* and
The Manxman was a visitor in the Land of Immortality!

A certain famous—very famous—author of sentimental
stories, wherein the Heroine is usually taking desperate
chances with her Virtue, once visited us and engaged a
Roycroft girl in conversation. He was after " copy " and
he was trying his city-slicker-stuff on the beauteous young
thing ๛ ๛

" What size shoe do you wear? " he asked her, to make
the subject personal.

The blessed damosel, cognizant of his fell purpose and
nothing loath, bent over, unbuckled the single button of
each of her dusty sandals, took them off and plunked them
down in his lap, right in the middle of his lavender trousers.
" See for yourself! " quoth she.

Which incident was duly reported, properly fictionized,
with many an innuendo in America's most Respectable
Journal! ๛ ๛

But Ali Baba and the Bunch knew what it was all about!

* * * * *

Which suggests a story Ali Baba told me one day at the
barn when we were currying horses together:

A celebrated lady was scheduled to appear and perform
on the lawn at East Aurora. When the clock reached the

hour appointed, several hundred people were in their seats.
Only the lady herself was late! They waited and waited ৯⠶
Presently some one sent Ali Baba over to the Inn to dig
her out ৯⠶ ৯⠶

When Ali Baba turned the corner of the peristyle, the one
who is known across the country for her Sweet and Charming Nature and Philosophy of Gentleness—flew at him like
a fury! She called him all the names in the Catalog, the
Decalogue, and the Ship's Log! She found him and left
him speechless in wonder and admiration!

He said he heard cuss-words that day he never heard before!
❧ Seems she had engaged by telephone a Buffalo motion
picture man to come out and record her entrance, her
reception, her ovation and her exit—and Turn-the-crank
Jimmy had failed her!

Ali Baba, looking like a Suspicious Character, turned up
at an inauspicious moment and she thought he was Jimmy
—and so introduced him to her Vocabulary.

" By cracky," said the Old Man, " but when she let loose,
was n't she a cuckoo! "

                    *   *   *   *   *

Here 's a partial list of famous people who made the pil-
grimage to East Aurora: Theodore Roosevelt, Hon. James
J. Davis, Brand Whitlock, United States Senator Bourne,
Marshall P. Wilder, Booker T. Washington, Hall Caine,
Robert Barr, Stevie Crane, Robert Chambers, Harold
McGrath, Ellen Terry, Ben Greet, Henry Clay Barnabee,
William Muldoon, Joe Choyinski, Captain Jack Crawford,
Edwin Markham, Major Andrew Rowan (who carried the
Message to Garcia) Richard Le Gallienne, Clarence Dar-
row, Paul Bartlett, Dr. Algernon Crapsey, Winifred Sack-
ville Stoner, Carrie Jacobs Bond, Sophie Loeb, Helen Row-
land, Horace Fletcher, Alex Fournier, Hugh Pentacost,

E. H. Harriman, Fred Underwood, Henry Ford, William
Marion Reedy, Alfred Henry Lewis, Humphrey O'Sullivan,
Saunders Norvell, Scott Nearing, Harry Weinberger, David
Bispham, Minnie Maddern Fiske, Stevie Reynolds, George
Viereck, Dr. Tilden, J. C. Straus, Eugene Grubb, Mary
Elizabeth, Hudson Maxim, C. W. Post, Billy Van, Eva
Tanguay, William Sulzer, Marilla Ricker, Katherine Yates,
Elizabeth Towne, Mangassarian, Frank Keenan, Ed.Wynne
Rose Stahl, Crystal Herne, Michael Monahan, Gutzon
Borglum, etc.

* * * * *

Hubbard was a talker—when he wished to talk—and he
gave more than a full share of admiration and appreciation
to those who could talk interestingly, entertainingly. But
when he came up on a silent genius, when he happened to
be in a talkative mood himself—well, 't was not so good!
❧ I remember once Paul Bartlett presented him with a
replica of his famous Michael Angelo statue, in bronze;
the original of which stands in Washington, D. C. 'T was
to be mounted on the Roycroft lawn facing the East ❧
Bartlett was invited to East Aurora to select the spot
and to preside over the ceremonies.

He came: a silent, taciturn, undemonstrative man.

Hubbard, bubbling over with enthusiasm, could get only
" Yes," " No," and " I think so " out of the great sculptor.
❧ As a talker he was almost as silent as his famous " Mike."
After the ceremony was over, and affairs restored to
normal, the Fra and I stood in front of the huge bronze—
almost ten feet high, mounted on a great boulder. I noticed
at the base of the boulder, where the rock was bedded in
the cement, a bronze of a small turtle.

" What does the turtle signify? "

" Well, the statue of ' Mike ' is Bartlett's Statue to In-

spired Industry, and the figure of the turtle is Bartlett's
Statue to Inspired Oratory. You remember the Biblical
quotation, ' The voice of the turtle was heard in the land? '
You ought to read the Bible more and talk less—like a
Bartlett! " so so

* * * * *

" The mistake of monasticism seems to be in the assump-
tion that what is good is good all the time, and that if a
thing is good you can not get too much of it."
So sayeth the Sage of East Aurora.
Likewise the mistake one can make in living in a village
is to become a villager. While to keep house in a village
with the trees and the flowers and the birds for friends may
be Heaven—to think as the typical villager thinks is—
well, not exactly the same thing.
To live in a secluded spot may be all right and probably is,
provided and only provided the world makes a path to
your door, not to buy your mouse-traps, but to talk, to
inform, to inspire.
The fondest memories I have of the Roycroft are of soft,
warm Summer nights, with the sensible people of the world
sound asleep—and Talk, Talk, Talk—inspired, brilliant,
scintillating conversation to illumine the dark places of
Life and of the Night. Caught in the spell, held by the
magnetic presence of some famous visitor, many 's the time
I have not tucked in until the rattle of the milk-wagon
proclaimed the dawn!
You remember the old saw: "Early to bed and early to rise
and you 'll meet no Prominent People? " Well, I can con-
scientiously say that I learned my Who 's Who in America
by personal contacts long after hours in East Aurora,
and it was because of these nocturnal habits that E. H.
sometimes referred to the writer as "The late Mr. Felix."

With Apologies to Hippocampus Den.

What's the way?

With Apologies to Hippocampus Den.

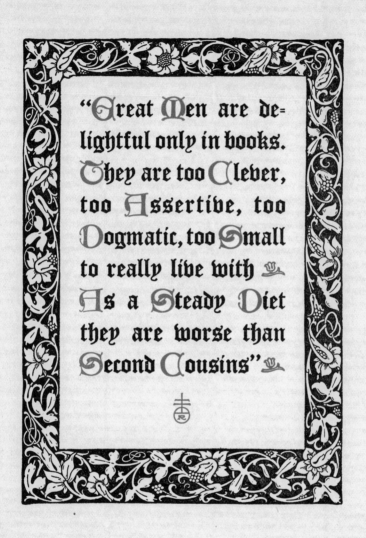

"Great Men are de=
lightful only in books.
They are too Clever,
too Assertive, too
Dogmatic, too Small
to really live with 🖐
As a Steady Diet
they are worse than
Second Cousins" 🖐

Some Historic Quarrels

FRED Gardner " owned " the advertising space in *The Philistine,* under contract with Elbert Hubbard ✦ Back in the beginning when *Philistine* space was not so much in demand, Gardner saw the possibilities, and signed up Hubbard to what the farmers call " a right smart " document.

He agreed to pay a sum—approximately five hundred dollars a month—for the privilege of selling *Philistine* advertising space. That is, he guaranteed Hubbard that sum monthly whether or not the space sold.

There was nothing to prevent either Gardner or Hubbard from selling space—but Gardner got a percentage on every advertisement printed.

When the magazine was little known, a newcomer struggling for recognition, that contract was fair, square and equitable.

But when *The Philistine* became a National Institution Mr. Gardner's substantial income from *Philistine* advertising was pretty nearly a free gift from the gods.

Moreover when the advertising patronage came rolling in it seemed to Hubbard that Gardner became satisfied, and rested on the income that Hubbard's work attracted.

He himself became dissatisfied, critical.

Finally there was a break.

The Fra's idea of a contract was, that it ceased to exist when it ceased to be mutual—when it became unilateral.

Unfortunately the law courts persistently disagreed with
him. They were dispensing Law, not Justice, I 've heard
him say ❧ ❧

Down through the years he learned his lesson in the courts
in blood and tears—provided he ever learned it, and I
doubt that he did!

To complicate matters the duration of his favorite contract
was for a period of " ninety-nine years." In the first fine
flush of his enthusiasm that 's the way he wrote them.
That 's the kind Fred Gardner held, and it was a perfectly
good and legal contract as events proved.

One day Hubbard sat himself down and wrote Mr. Gardner
something like this:

" Dear Freddie: I created the prestige for *Philistine* advertising space, I created the desire for it—I do the real work
and you take the profits. This arrangement is no longer
satisfactory to me, and I hereby recall it. With love and
blessings, Your sincere, etc."

For a while East Aurora solicited all advertising *direct*.
❡ Then Gardner sued—and collected, and collected!

I can not guarantee my memory but it seems to me that
Fred Gardner sued Hubbard about three times and collected a very large sum each time—a sum way up in the
thousands ❧ ❧

Stubborn as usual in such matters, nothing could convince
Hubbard that he was wrong. So he tried it again and again
—and each time paid straight through the nose!

In my own humble opinion Gardner was right all the way.
❡ He gambled his own money that *The Philistine* space
would eventually amount to something. He won. He insisted on receiving his winnings—which was as it should
have been! ❧ ❧

That much more advertising could have been carried in

The Philistine in the same period of time I have no doubt
—but that 's not the point. The point is, the case was fought
through the courts for years with much loss of time and
money and neglect of legitimate enterprise. In the end
Hubbard bought out Gardner's interest for a higher cash
price than it would have cost him in the *first place*.

* * * * *

His quarrel with Michael Monahan was another famous
one. Fact is, when Michael found himself ousted from
The Philistine, he hied himself down town to the center
of East Aurora and hired the local Opera House and played
a one night stand to standing room only. He told in no
uncertain terms just what he thought of East Aurora's
Leading Citizen—and why—much to the amusement of
the irrepressible yokels.

Monahan was given the freedom of the Village, but refused
the Roycroft premises!

What did they quarrel about?

I don't know.

I asked Hubbard and I asked Michael—neither seemed to
remember exactly. Michael intimated that the rumpus
started over whether there should be more or fewer Latin
quotations in a certain article! Or was it that one day
at the Three Mile Camp the scholarly Michael was lying
on his back in the sunshine liberally translating De Mau-
passant for the Bunch, when Hubbard rode up expecting
them all to be cutting wood—and said a few short and
ugly words?

I find in an old *Philistine* this testimony:

" Michael Monahan in puttees and a pith helmet blew in.
I was on the Farm when he arrived but when I returned
I found that he, Sammy the Artist, and Ali Baba had

interviewed the buffet. They were singing lustily ' When Ireland Will Be Free.' "

N. B.—Ali Baba has just read proof on the above item and declares it a malicious untruth. He said they were singing " Geraldine, My Geraldine."

Whatever the disagreement was it was a foolish one— because I have heard Hubbard on more than one occasion praise Monahan's style, and call him a classicist, and hold that he was a writer's writer and that his stuff could be studied advantageously by a certain nameless barbarian. ¶ Michael attended the first Memorial Services for Elbert and Alice Hubbard at East Aurora, in 1915. His speech at the Salon was a beautiful tribute to his erstwhile enemy. The gracious way in which he acknowledged the foolishness of their quarrel and the loss of energy in promoting it is evidence of the big heart of the somewhat impetuous Michael.

He said in part:

" I was unlucky enough to have been estranged from Elbert Hubbard some fourteen years ago by circumstances which need not now be recalled. The quarrel was actively served and diligently promoted by our common friends— I don't think the hearts of the principals were ever much in it. But it was a very pretty quarrel, eagerly ministered to by the creatures of envy, hatred and jealousy. There was bitter talk and counter-talk which the common friends alluded to traded back and forth with a quite incredible alacrity, never forgetting to dot and carry one in the process. And alas! there was too much bitter writing which I for my part would most gladly blot out. I can only hope that no ill-conditioned person may take it into his head to reprint any words of mine put forth long ago in anger and bitterness. I have no sort of fellowship with those who

will not let the dead rest and who would heap obloquy
and judgment upon the grave.

" Yes, Elbert Hubbard was a dreamer, and his dream
remains in the ' Little Journeys ' and a hundred essays
of a blended humor and pathos, tenderness and strength,
entirely his own.

" This man owed little to the schools and nothing to the
dead languages, but he was master of a vocabulary that
was most intensely alive and as copious as Mark Twain's.
He was one of the great workers of America, but not too
busy, and he never had time to whisper in his own left ear
that he was a genius."

Michael heartily agreed with Fra Elbertus about this thing
called " criticism "—as Hubbard stated it: " I have had
my share of adverse criticism, but I can truly say that it
has not embittered me, nor left me with any hard feeling
toward a living soul."

Had these two men met again under favorable conditions
they would have been friends instantly. Monahan's sin-
cerity would have appealed to Hubbard, and Hubbard's
spirit of brotherly love would have captured the latter.

Instead they stood a long way off and made faces and
strange sounds at each other—which to one who knew
them both intimately—and respected them both, was quite
a little absurd.

First Class men should not waste time on Second Class
disagreements.

                    *   *   *   *   *

One of the surprising things that Hubbard was wont to
do was to attack a friend in the wide open, in print, when
he thought that friend had erred or was doing harm. Not
venomously, not vindictively—and not meekly or modestly
either, but pertinently, pugnaciously.

There was no going round behind the offender's back to say his say! Oftentimes the attack came when the offender was relaxed in a complacent mood. It proved a surprise, and therefore doubly painful.

In the case of Jack London, for instance!

Once upon a time Jack got out a new Socialistic book. His publisher, to put the proper hurrah behind it, prevailed upon Jack to write a post card—or Jack prevailed upon himself—which read as follows:

" No quarter. We want all that you possess. We will be content with nothing less than you possess. We want in our hands the reins of power and the destiny of mankind. Here are our hands. They are strong hands. We are going to take your Governments, your Palaces and all your purpled ease away from you, and in that day you shall work for your bread even as the peasant in the field or the starved and runty clerk in your metropolis. Here are our hands. They are strong hands.

JACK LONDON "

'T was good press stuff, but imagine a property holder, a business man finding that on his desk in the morning mail! ℂ Fra Elbertus got hot, and in red ink he wrote not only what he thought of that doctrine, but what he thought of the man who would sign such rot:

" This threat of Jack's would be a tragic thing if Jack and his pals were really going to do all they say they are. But they are not going to do anything but talk. Those who can, do; those who can't, chin. Jack is a writing tramp who roams the world for thrills and copy. He is kindly, intelligent, amusing, indolent, and absolutely without the power to manage anything—even his own tongue! "

—And so on and so on.

Was this Hubbard's true opinion of Jack London?

Of course not ꝏ ꝏ

Was this Hubbard's opinion of Jack as a literary man?

No! ꝏ ꝏ

Elsewhere, and later he wrote, " *John Barleycorn* is a classic—a book upon which an author could safely found a literary reputation."

Of course Jack replied and words were said that were better left unsaid. Consequently they became enemies.

But in Nineteen Hundred Eighteen I stood with Charmion London alongside the mound of stones that marked my friend Jack's grave—out in California, out in the Valley of the Moon, and I thought of that other Good Man dead and gone—and of the benefits that both had brought to the world and I said to myself:

" Somewhere in some sunny corner of Valhalla they have surely talked it over, explained away their differences, and they are now friends."

* * * * *

Then there was the sham battle between Billy Sunday and Hubbard: but both were suspect, because they were such excellent showmen.

Even the newspapers refused to take them seriously ꝏ

One of them at least captiously observed, " It 's a sad time for America when Elbert Hubbard and Billy Sunday undertake to tell us what 's wrong with each other! "

What Billy said in his sermon was this:

" Elbert Hubbard is exactly the same kind of a man as Voltaire, David Hume, Thomas Paine, Thomas Huxley, and Robert Ingersoll. Hubbard stands for the same things that these men stood for."

Said Hubbard:

" Thanks for the compliment. Were it not for the men

mentioned by Mr. Sunday, religious liberty would be a thing unknown, superstition would still stalk rampant across the earth, and crouching fear would follow us in all our dreams."

When a critic says exactly what you want him to say, you can't make much of a quarrel out of that—rather a feeling of gratitude overcomes one!

* * * * *

For some reason not quite clear, Richard Le Gallienne was always a challenge to Hubbard. Their writings were not and never could be competitive, they were so essentially different. And yet, and yet, starting way back in an Eighteen Hundred Ninety-seven *Philistine* I find the Fra pricking Dicky with his pointed pen. Much of this criticism is co-incidental and indicative of favors to come.

For instance, Hubbard in *The Philistine* accuses Le Gallienne of plagairizing the theme of *The Quest of the Golden Girl* in Eighteen Hundred Ninety-seven—and later when the break came it was because Le Gallienne accused Hubbard of plagiarizing Le Gallienne.

" I like Richard Le Gallienne and I like *The Quest of the Golden Girl*" wrote Hubbard. " Yes, I like the book and I like it just as well as I did yesterday, before I read Chapter XXIV of *The Man of Feeling,* published in Edinburgh in Eighteen Hundred Eight. For by a strange coincidence Henry Mackenzie found that Golden Girl in the Venusburg of Piccadilly a hundred years before Richard Le Gallienne did. It 's the same fine tall girl, pure in heart, and starving to death, too. Both give her a square meal, and the story of her downfall gibes in both cases."

Again Hubbard digs Le Gallienne: At a banquet one man asks another:

" Who is that fellow? "

" Richard Le Galligan."

" Who? "

" Mr. Gallagher."

Again: " Richard Le Gallienne is warmly pursuing his quest of the Golden Dollar, (Lecturing). * * * He declares St. Louis girls are not so questionable as Chicago girls although all girls are nice."

Richard of the Quest was a queer, whimsical, lovable, poetical citizen.

In Nineteen Hundred Eight he spent the Summer in East Aurora, and he and I shared the Headquarters Tent out under the apple trees on the campus—Headquarters for all sorts of activities, including conversation long into the night.

Dicky was an acolyte of the Oscar Wilde group in London in the Glorious Nineties, when Wilde was the reigning sensation: and what tales he had to tell, and I was right there, wide-eyed to listen to them!

That Summer Dicky had trouble with asthma and found it almost impossible to sleep ❧ More than one night we watched the morning's sun redden the East before we called the session adjourned.

* * *

At breakfast one morning Dicky mentioned to Hubbard that some day when he got around to it he was going to write an Apology for Living—an apology to his wives, sweethearts, bailors, tailors, editors, creditors—all of them! ❡ The Fra, taking his copy the same place Kipling took his fun—where he found it—appropriated the idea, and ran it up into a nice article that filled a galley or two ❧ Dicky found it a little later in *The Philistine* on a day when the world was blue, when he was feeling morose, depressed, sinned against, took umbrage and promptly lost his temper. He said a few things. Then he went into Buffalo for the day, brooded on his sorrows, returned and said a few things more—most of them unpleasant.

He wanted to fight some one—the Editor of *The Philistine* preferred ᘑ ᘑ

Hubbard stood it till it became unbearable—and then suggested that Dicky pack up and leave, and go where he'd be happy.

Dicky presented him with the classical proposition: " Come outside and put me out! "

It was really quite absurd.

I think Hubbard felt that way about it too.

The Summer was over—a village in Winter is really no inspiration for a cosmopolite, so the next day I helped Dicky get his duffle together and on to the train for New York ᘑ ᘑ

Which only goes to prove what it goes to prove, which is that one little village is not large enough for two big men, even when both are of good intent.

Ah, me; how Time flies!

Just recently I smiled when I read in an article about Oscar Wilde by Le Gallienne, in one of the current magazines, this sentiment:

" Wilde was under no necessity of borrowing from Whistler or any one else, though like every one he would now and again elaborate on ideas which he rather made his own than originated."

As Hubbard once pertinaciously remarked, " Rightly understood and accepted all experiences are good, and the bitter ones best of all."

Obsolete

**"In Useful Work
there is no Degree.
That which is
Necessary
is Sacred
and
nothing else is!"**

His Philosophy of Work

AID Cassiodorus, a monk of the Fifth Century: "Idleness is the enemy of the soul; hence brethren should at certain hours work at manual labor, and at other times engage in holy reading, then in silent reverie and prayer—these things are God's will, for they bring good results."

Hubbard knew his Cassiodorous and likewise his Leo Tolstoi—and there was more than a little of the Ecclesiast and of the Philosopher of the Soil in the Sage of East Aurora ❧ ❧

He believed salvation came through Work, Manual Labor—and he welcomed the association of the man with calloused hands. There was no pose in this—it was an essential part of his nature.

I have the feeling Hubbard would have found the company of the Galilean Fisherman most acceptable—and had he lived in the time of Christ would have found it easy to have given away all he possessed and followed The Leader. When he was perturbed, there was surcease in work ❧ ❧ When he was happy—he expressed his happiness in work.

❡ He drew his strength directly from the soil.

To him there was a dignity and a divinity in Labor.

To him Culture and Useful Work were much the same thing ❧ ❧

The Apostles were hand-laborers.

Jesus was a carpenter—but something more, something
more ৯০ ৯০

* * * * *

Round about East Aurora were located Roycroft Parks,
Roycroft Farms, Roycroft Camps—and there was always
plenty of hard work to be done.

I 've cut brush with Hubbard till I raised blood-blisters.
The man who commended himself to Fra Elbertus was the
one who could turn his hand to the Arts or Crafts in the
morning and to pitching hay in the afternoon, with equal
ease and zest!

Whenever he praised, he praised a man's versatility ৯০ ৯০
But certainly the physical man came in for more than a
full share ৯০ ৯০

When a youth, Sanford, Hubbard's second son, was an
almost perfect physical specimen—and Hubbard took
especial delight in the feats of strength of this youthful
Apollo ৯০ ৯০

When he wanted to show off the boys around the place
he did not particularly invite them to do their " parlor
stunts; " rather he called them out on the Green to exhibit
their strength and agility.

He was proud of the Roycroft Baseball Team, and enthusiastic when it won! * * * Wally Schang, one of Our
Boys, became the famous catcher of the Athletics!

Whenever a group of " tired business men " came to Roycroft for a Convention, to enliven the proceedings, they
were challenged to play ball against the Roycroft Girls
(for the Boys it would have been No Contest) and the
Girls invariably turned in a victory.

They played real ball, too.

When he spoke of St. Jerome (Jerome Connors, the Sculptor)
it was not so much to commend his work as it was to call

attention to the fact that he had the arms and shoulders,
and torso of a blacksmith.

His admiration for Ali Baba turned on the fact that the
Bab was a worker and a first-class Physical Man!

At East Aurora many pleasant and profitable hours were
spent in the fields, on the Woodpile, at the barn.

" No one ever suffers from insomnia or loss of appetite
who does his daily stint of hard labor! "

* * * * *

Half the so-called jokes at East Aurora were rough jokes
befitting a farmer-like community. I remember once, somebody bought a new horse, an unknown, shipped direct
from Kentucky, and supposedly spirited. After he was
taken from the cars and properly rested, there was an
attempt made to ride him—with fear and trepidation ✍
Then we discovered the horse was a plug.

Life was not in him—an honest horse, but dull.

Yet there were the possibilities for a joke.

So we trussed up the horse with ropes as though he were
a man-killer, arranged a twitch for his nose to hold him
down, scattered rigging around to make the place look
like an arena—and then called the Shop and asked Cy
Rosen to send down to the barn at once Nick Faber, our
best " horse jockey," to ride a bad 'un.

Nick arrived, self-conscious—excited—determined.

No horse had ever unseated him—and he was not going
to let this one establish a precedent.

A half dozen of us, looking as though we had been thrown,
advised Nick not to try it—'t was dangerous.

" Nick, that horse is *dynamite!* "

But Nick was obdurate—no horse could bluff *him.*

Great preparations were made.

Another horse was saddled and brought out. The head of

the Kentuckian was held snug across the saddle of the
first one; on a signal Nick was to mount, and the outlaw
was to be turned loose.

Up into the saddle with a free swing—" Let 'im go! "
shouted Nick.

The gentle Roycroft horse wheeled away on its hind legs,
and left Nick sitting there, tense, expectant—and nothing
happened—and nothing continued to happen!

I hope never to forget the quizzical look on Faber's face!
Most of us just rolled around on the ground, and howled.
That was the kind of a harmless joke Hubbard enjoyed.

* * * * *

Here 's a little yarn Hubbard told about some workers.
I give it because it illustrates a strange favoritism and
mental inversion; I really believe he figured the Laborer
fundamentally superior to the Cultural Worker.

" It so happened that one fine day Uncle Billy Bushnell,
Ali Baba and a hoodlum kid known as Odds Bodkins were
laying a new sidewalk in front of the Shop. I was quite
particular that the job should be done right. That is, I
wanted sand under the walk instead of earth, and I wished
the walk to line up properly with the roadway and adjacent
walks. Therefore I went out and told ' the boys ' (all are
boys in East Aurora) to tamp the sand down well and make
sure the grade was right. I also availed myself of the opportunity to rub a little good advice and admonition into
them while I was at it, as to doing one's tasks well and
working for the highest so as to receive the approbation
of your Other Self.

" As I told them how to do the job I took up a shovel
and exemplified my meaning with a few object lessons ⚹
" ' There! ' said I, ' d' ye see that? There! that 's the way
to do it—see? '

" ' Hain't you got nothin' to do inside, sonny? ' asked Uncle Billy in a tobacco-chewer's voice. ' 'Cause if you have you better climb right along and do it—we air layin' this 'ere walk, we air! '

" Then Ali Baba took it up, increasing the tone volume and disposing of the subject by saying, ' That 's all right, John, you better go right along now and 'tend to your own business, an' we will 'tend to ourn! '

" And all the time Odds Bodkins stood by giving me the smile audible.

" Diplomatic relations were getting a trifle strained, and I resolved to break off communications at once. I made a hasty run for cover.

" That night I went out with a lantern and inspected the new sidewalk. It seemed exactly right, in fact the boys did a better job than I could have done.

" Possibly it is just as well not to bother and badger men who are doing their work, nor confuse them with too many instructions. Anyway, that is the opinion Uncle Billy Bushnell seems to hold."

* * * * *

While the Young Bloods around the place were willing to feed hogs, pitch manure, split logs, plow a furrow, or scrape down a horse, 't was for diversion only—or excitement or recreation—and *not* because they participated in his philosophy or felt themselves no better than farm hands ✺ ✺

To feel superior is inherent—or not, as the case may be ✺ That Utopia is not yet here, when men through choice prefer to do " the dirty work of the world."

With him 't was a serious matter.

With the College Boys who came to stay for a month or a year, the " personal equality " was a pose, a phase.

Many a time I 've heard him talk the wisdom of his own
conduct: " To subjugate another is to subjugate yourself.
The way to gain freedom is to give it. The Superior Class
is always a menace, sometimes a curse. The distinguishing
feature is to exclude—it is ossified selfishness as opposed
to enlightened self-interest."

To argue against his principle, I 'd say: " Well, where
does ' ossified selfishness ' leave off and ' enlightened self-
interest ' begin? Does n't that Law of Self-preservation
cover them both like a blanket?   *   *   I want to know! "

❡ This will I say, that at home or away, his conduct was
always consistent.

When on a journey he always carried his own bag to and
from trains and in and out of hotels. When by chance
he came face to face with a porter burdened with luggage
he 'd hold the door or gate open to " give the right of way
to the Worker."

Whenever on a city street he saw a drayman trying to
lift up into his dray a packing case beyond his strength
Hubbard would stop, and without any fol de rol lend a
hand! ❧ ❧

" Work is for the Worker."

*   *   *   *   *

" Since Eighteen Hundred Seventy-five, when I landed in
Buffalo, till the Tenth of May, Nineteen Hundred Fourteen (when this was written), I have never been sick a day,
never consulted a physician, never missed a meal, and life
on the whole has been one delightful Little Journey." ❧
So wrote the Fra.

This desirable condition he credited to the commandment:
" Give us this day our daily work "—and work to him
meant work with his hands.

I 've heard him caution, " When it comes to a pinch the

world can get along without everybody but the worker:
therefore be sure you know a hand-trade."

He glorified the Laborer.

But of course the Laborer he pictured was a glorified
Laborer. He endowed that useful personage with his own
brains, with his own imagination, with his own high intent.
❦ That a laborer could be dirty, disloyal, greedy, selfish,
stupid—well, while he admitted it—while circumstances
ofttimes forced him to admit it—nevertheless he held that
such was the exception and not the rule.

He has written that " One who criticizes must be very right
or else he 's bound to be very wrong," and so I know the
pitfalls of criticism!

Yet it always seemed to me that the emphasis he put on
the Common Man was unfair and unjust—that the Common Man did not deserve the honors.

At the last, the common man is common, *not* because he
wishes to be, but because he *is*.

That 's poor Democracy, but good Biology, as I understand
it ❧ ❧

This is not said in any snobbish sense—but inasmuch as
mankind is trying to work up and away from common
things—from sweat and swill and muck—to those who
have achieved the heights belongs the glorification.

Otherwise, why strive? Why not sink into a condition of
innocuous desuetude—or worse—and let the higher things
of life go hang!

Life is a struggle.

Life is a competition.

Why, then, should those who have fought their way up
half a flight of stairs voluntarily go back to claim fellowship with those who have made no effort?

Is n't Heaven one of the Provinces of the *Mind*—and is n't

Hell a place to put those who have no imagination, and
no character?

* * * * *

Here is Hubbard's Philosophy on Work:

" Work is for the worker. Can you afford to do slip shod
evasive work? Can you afford to shirk or make believe or
practise pretense in any act of life? No, because what the
world thinks and says about you is really no matter, but
what you think and what you do are questions vital as
Fate." ⮞ ⮞

And finally his Credo:

I believe in the Motherhood of God.

I believe in the blessed Trinity of Father, Mother and
Child ⮞ ⮞

I believe that God is here, and that we are as near Him
now as we ever shall be. I do not believe He started this
world a-going and went away and left it to run itself ⮞ ⮞

I believe in the sacredness of the human body, this transient
dwelling place of a living soul, and so I deem it the duty
of every man and every woman to keep his or her body
beautiful through right thinking and right living.

I believe that the love of man for woman, and the love
of woman for man, is holy; and that this love in all of its
promptings is as much an emanation of the Divine Spirit
as man's love for God, or the most daring hazards of human
mind ⮞ ⮞

I believe in salvation through economic, social and spiritual
freedom.

I believe John Ruskin, William Morris, Henry Thoreau,
Walt Whitman and Leo Tolstoi to be Prophets of God
and they should rank in mental reach and spiritual insight
with Elijah, Hosea, Ezekiel and Isaiah.

I believe we are now living in Eternity as much as we
ever shall.

I believe that the best way to prepare for a Future Life
is to live one day at a time, and do the work you can do
the best, doing it as well as you can.

I believe in Manual Labor.
I believe there is no devil but fear.
I believe that no one can harm you but yourself.
I believe that we are all sons of God and it doth not yet
appear what we shall be.
I believe in freedom—social, economic, domestic, political,
mental, spiritual.
I believe in every man minding his own business.
I believe that men are inspired today as much as they
ever were.
I believe in sunshine, fresh air, friendship, calm sleep,
beautiful thoughts, and the paradox of success through
failure *so so*
I believe in the purifying process of Sorrow; and I believe
that Death is a manifestation of Life.
I believe the Universe is planned for good.

The
Higher
Education

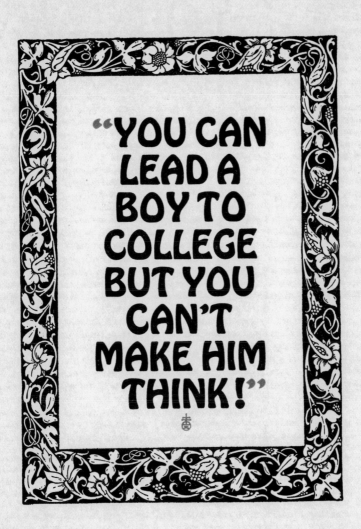

"YOU CAN LEAD A BOY TO COLLEGE BUT YOU CAN'T MAKE HIM THINK!"

Education and Schools

HUBBARD used to say: "The Millenium will arrive when parents will refuse to send their children to any school, college, or university where the curriculum does not provide that at least one-half the school day shall be spent in work."

He had a low opinion of schools which cultivated the mind only—or attempted to. Education should be a preparation for life—and life resents over-specialization.

Those dear aristocratic girls, North and South, East and West, who boast they have " never done a tap of work in their lives "—who don't even know " how to boil a potato " —were not aristocratic to him. They were not even civilized. An educated person is one who is Master of his Environment ◆ ◆

An educated person is one who knows how to produce more than he consumes.

An educated person is one who is qualified to take care of himself under a variety of conditions and circumstances.

An educated person is one who has endeavored to develop *all* his faculties and latent powers.

Of the American universities, he thought Tuskeegee—or rather the plan behind Tuskeegee—the best. There each student works his way and is self-supportlng. There the day is divided between the manual and the mental. There each day's effort is a little bit of Life itself—and in consequence Tuskeegee turns out self-respecting, respectful, self-reliant men. To learn how to earn a living is much more important than to learn how to parse the Greek Verb, or how to enter and leave a room. As a choice between the " purely academic " university and the University of Hard Knocks, he preferred the latter and its alumni—every time. ❡ I have heard him say: " I can hire the graduates of any college or university in America at $10 a week " (that was ten years ago.)

More to the point, he did.

'T was a poor season at Roycroft when we were unable to muster an Intercollegiate Glee Club on the Green, by the light of the silvery moon—and the starting salary at Roycroft for bright young men was Ten Dollars a week —don't I know!

These college boys were first-class theorists—taught by first-class theorists, and when they went up against the practical phases of life at first they were nonplussed.

They discovered they knew so many things that were n't so. ❡ They had so much to unlearn.

Their first six months in business was little more or less than permission to test themselves and their theories at the expense of their employer.

They were a liability, not an asset.

Education ought to be training in self-expression—but under the Lecture System in most colleges the thing boils down to this: " Shut up and listen."

An ordinarily receptive boy can store up more stuff and nonsense in four years at the ordinary " academic " college than he can unload in four years more.

That 's one of his handicaps.

Moreover, after four years of exam-cramming, cigaret-sucking, and prom-hopping—when he first attempts to

really synchronize his mind and muscles to accomplish a
definite result, he's like a beginner on a bicycle—he wob-
bles and, unless he's fortunate, falls!

The fault is not the boy's!

Some of the brightest boys that ever breathed—who came
to Roycroft direct from college—were helpless to be of
service until they got themselves adjusted. Certain of their
faculties were almost atrophied—and at the beginning it
was necessary to manipulate them, and massage them to
restore circulation and to bring them under their will ॐ
They lacked practise in self-determination.

They had been taught to lean instead of to stand upright.

❡ Dr. Hadley once said, " The boy who gets the most
out of college is the boy who works his way through."

The Fra gave him nine Yale " Rahs " for that.

But he also took the trouble to call attention to the fact
that the wealthiest country in the world makes scant pro-
vision for the youth who wants to work his way through
college: he must wait on tables, clean dormitories, drive
jitneys, tend furnaces, mow lawns, usher in theaters; which
kind of work disciplines a boy and teaches him the work
habit but very little else.

Why not a guaranteed job doing constructive work in an
auxiliary industry for the boy with the will to want to
earn a college education?

Why not an endowment or two for that kind of prospective
citizen? ॐ ॐ

This is a practical nation, and a practical era!

Let's make education practical!

* * * * *

The Roycroft was a kind of school—a practical work-a-day
school, and what we were trying to do there excited the

curiosity of savants and investigators. Many times we were " inspected," and this is the record of one such visit:

A live Count came to see us the other day—a real live Count. He is in this country studying sociology, with intent to make a report to his Home Government. Some one in Buffalo told him he should visit the Roycroft Shop, and he came here with a Secretary, a Valet and Preconceived Ideas. He thought(and still thinks) we are running a Reform School.

I showed him a room where forty or more girls were at work—bright, fine, healthy country girls, girls who never have been more than twenty miles from home, and are innocent as lambs before they are sheared, or calves at weaning time. The Count adjusted his monocle, and after a little pause, said to me in a royal whisper:

" Ah! how vot you call sad to see ze mark of sin zat can neffer be vash avay—I vould know zey vas ba-a-a-d! "

¶ I looked at the man and saw that he was in fond memory running down the dim and misty vista of his past and congratulating himself that experience had given him insight. So I let him pat himself upon his back. He thought he knew—he chattered like a Chinese when you have lost your laundry ticket and want your washing. He explained everything to me, compared our Shop with other similar institutions(?) in France and Austria, and then told me ot these in pigeon English.   *   *   *   *

No, I did not explain anything to him, because language does not explain anything. The Count could not comprehend a Roycroft Idea, because he brought no Roycroft Ideas with him.

He was a " Nobleman." I laughed aloud and then sighed to think of this joke of Dame Nature, in allowing men to take a dub and by legal enactment call it " Noble."

¶ " How long vas it dot you hold your office—four years, yes? " he asked.

" During good behavior," I answered.

" Oh," he replied, " ze Tammany Boss vill haf you out, and a new Superintendent vill be here soon—zere vas no

permanent in Amerique," and his Secretary standing at
his elbow took down his words in Pitman shorthand.

This man spoke four languages and had no ideas to express
in any. He and his forefathers for many generations have
lived off other men's labor—the law of his land makes him
a nobleman.

God makes the noble Man.

The fine irony of an entailed nobility is so obvious one
marvels to think it still endures.

This Count walked around one of our big, lusty, silent
carpenters—an honest man—a man of power, with no
pretense in his composition—nothing to conceal.

I looked at the two and said: God made the Carpenter;
Man made the Count.

There's a long article in Elbert Hubbard's *Selected Writings* which begins on page 397 of Vol. I and runs almost
10,000 words, the subject of which is that a college education
(in the purely " academic " college) is something worse than
a waste of four years of time at a critical period in a boy's
life and five thousand dollars of money.

His arguments are most emphatic ones:

Says he: " The college gives honor where there is no merit;
position without character; rewards the unworthy; inflates
the foolish; makes mention of the mediocre and advertises
nullity. As Robert Ingersoll said, ' It polishes pebbles and
dims diamonds.' It imparts to a nobody the standing of
a somebody, and as such supplies a service which will long
be in demand."

He deprecated 'varsity football teams, glee clubs, frats
and university clubs. He observes that " a football game
bears the same relation to education that a bull-fight does
to agriculture."

He pitied the college undergraduates and college graduates
who were Remittance Men. " The first essential is that
the individual shall earn his own living. No man can be

called educated who is a parasite on the community, a
care to other people, a burden to his relatives."

He believed that in the doubtful years of seventeen to
twenty-one it was very essential that a boy be kept busy,
worked hard, so there would not be too much time for
foolishness—and self-destruction.

Besides, the youth who starts early in business gets an
early start, and given character and ambition and the
proper incentive, he's not likely to surrender his lead to
the college fellow who starts four years later.

Not a department head or executive in the Roycrofters'
organization was a college graduate (whatever that suggests) though there were lots of college men about the
place ❧ ❧

Hubbard balked at the idea that a college education was
necessary to success and that a man who really wanted an
education could surely accomplish it while at work. He
pointed to Edison and Ford, and John D. Rockefeller, and
Andrew Carnegie—and scores of others who never attended college—to prove his point.

All educated men are not college graduates, nor are all
college graduates educated men.

"An educated man," said he, "is one who is *useful* to
Humanity and to Himself."

He wanted to get away from the old monastic idea of education which was to educate men away from the world of
work ❧ ❧

He wanted to do away with the "educated classes" by
educating all the classes at a self-help, self-supporting State
University under a compulsory system, where the best of
education—and work—would be had by all and none
would have any better!

"The division of the world into ignorant and educated,

literate and illiterate, bond and free, saved and lost, all tends towards tyranny, hate, strife, separation, dissolution, death."

Make it possible for a girl or a youth to *earn* an education, make manual labor respectable, make it an Ideal and this will be a happier, healthier and more satisfactory world in which to live.

" If a college education is a good thing then let 's *all* have one."

* * * * *

A truly educated man is a natural man.

A true education is a natural development.

That was why he gave full and complete admiration to Friedrich Froebel, and why he thought the Kindergarten Idea should be incorporated into the School Idea, and into the College Idea.

Education should be play; work should be play.

Play is more important than athletics and quite as important as work ﹏ ﹏

When the teacher is the right sort—when the pupils are inspired—then school becomes a joy unconfined.

" We are all children in the Kindergarten of God."

He thought the profession of *teacher* the highest in the land ﹏ ﹏

When you deal with children you are dealing with soul stuff. They are the People of the Future.

Through them one anticipates and prepares for Tomorrow!

❡ Boys and girls by correct ratio were ten times as important to him as those whom the world called Important Men and Women!

Tomorrow is more potent—more attractive—than yesterday! ﹏ ﹏

That was why he fought for better salaries for teachers—
and more respect and co-operation for them, too!

They should be the inspired Leaders of Civilization ✿ ✿
That was why he preferred public schools to private schools
—because he estimated the public-school teachers to be
more self-sacrificing, more sincere, and the public schools
more democratic, more self-reliant,—less pampered.

I well remember the indignation with which he greeted a
picture of a student at a private military academy astride
of three horses:

" What that boy needs is not to be put on the backs of
three horses—but behind two—and a plow! To learn to
ride three horses is a preparation for nothing—except how
to be a damphool! But to learn how to plow—that 's Life! "

❡ Though Hubbard very apparently admired Girard College and the University of Valparaiso and certain Indian
Reservation Schools where the young Indian is held with
the tribe, one particular school captured his enthusiasm,
and that was the Farm School in Doylestown, Pennsylvania, conducted by Rabbi Joseph Krauskopf.

This school especially appealed to him because it combined
all that he thought a school should be, plus a very special
purpose and that purpose to teach the Jew agriculture, and
put Jewish boys " back on the land." It is now more than
twenty-five years since Rabbi Krauskopf started this school,
and invested in it thirty-five hundred dollars, which he
had earned and saved himself. Since then the school has
prospered, and is going forward! The boys taken in as
students are preferably poor boys from the lower East
Side of New York and other congested districts. Originally
it was exclusively a Jewish school, but later developments
have made it undenominational and non-sectarian.

These boys are given the ordinary high school course with

half a day at books and the other half at work on the Farm.
They are taught to take care of themselves, their clothes,
their rooms, the farm tools, and to look after their stock
with a solicitous care.

Originally, the Jews were a pastoral people. Of the same
blood as the Arab, originally they were horsemen.

Almost two thousand years in the restricted quarters of
European cities have made them forget—though not all,
not entirely. Soon they become good horsemen again, good
dairymen. They grow large and husky, hardy and brown.

⁋ To give a boy a practical education, to let him earn that
education approaches the ideal.

At the Bucks County School each boy is encouraged to
hold on to his self-respect; he is charged with his board
and clothes, and given credit for his labor.

Besides, city boys are taught the love of country—and
that 's a school for any one's admiration.

Whenever Fra Elbertus spoke of a private school he called
to mind the ancient English boarding school—" that
atrocious relic of a barbaric past." To his mind, one was
the inheritor of the other.

He believed and advocated that education should be the
freest thing in a Free Land; that there should be only
public schools and public colleges, both of which should
offer the best; and that no private educational ventures
should be countenanced.

He believed that half of every school day should be spent
outdoors at work, and half of it indoors at books—and that
all of it should be play, and all of it self-expression.

" We learn only by doing."

half a day at books and the other half at work on the Farm.
They are taught to take care of themselves, their clothes,
their rooms, the farm tools, and to look after their stock
with a solicitous care.

Originally the Jews were a pastoral people. Of the same
blood as the Arab, originally they were horsemen.

Almost two thousand years in the "tailored quarters" of
European cities have made them forget—though not all
for activity. Soon they become good horsemen again, good
dairymen. They grow large and husky, lanky and brown.

¶ To give a boy a practical education, to let him earn that
education, approaches the ideal.

At the Roebe County School each boy is encouraged to
hold on to his self-respect. He is charged with his board
and clothes, and given credit for his labor.

Besides, the boys are taught the love of country—and
that "a school for any one" admit it on.

Whenever Fra Elbertus spoke of a private school he called
to mind the ancient English boarding-school—that
atrocious relic of a barbaric past." To his mind, one was
the opposite of the other.

He believed and advocated that education should be the
freest thing in a Free Land, that there should be only
public schools and public colleges, both of which should
offer the best, and that no private educational ventures
should be countenanced.

He believed that half of every school day should be spent
outdoors at work, and half of it indoors at books; and that
all of it should be play, and all of it self-expression.

" We learn only by doing."

THE JUGGLER!

THE JUGGLER!

"I believe that no one can harm us but ourselves..that sin is misdirected energy...that there is no devil but fear ...and that the Universe is ever good!"

Religion: Organized and Otherwise

WAS Hubbard an unbeliever, a skeptic, a free thinker, an iconoclast, an atheist, an agnostic, a Christian, a Mohammedan, or a Buddhist? What was he?

Whatever Faith he discussed, he always found something to praise about it—and the praise and the blame usually were so equally distributed that he left an unprejudiced person guessing as to his personal religion; sure only of his toleration.

¶ Nevertheless he distrusted orthodox faiths—because he saw them as the most disquieting and disorganizing influence in history, a constant cause of trouble. And he gravely doubted that the help they rendered was wholesome help. He doubted they helped advance civilization.

A priest or a minister hired to speak and teach a *doctrine* can not search for truth and expound it. Should he do so he 'll lose his job. Such conditions and limitations immediately disqualify him to serve as an inspired teacher because inevitably there comes a day when a conflict is forced between what he himself sincerely *believes* and what he is employed to *teach*. Then he must either unfrock himself —or become a hypocrite. The choice is not an easy one ✺ Of course there are thousands of sincere men of the Cloth who never take the trouble to think—and the choice for them is no choice at all. They simply *believe* and teach what they are taught to believe and teach. The whole

" system " of organized religion is against producing strong
men or freedom of inquiry—and without strong men and
intellectual curiosity and investigation there can be no
progress and the world comes to an end forthwith.

He balked at the " professional " preacher, the man who
preached The Word because it was his Duty. He believed
the ideal preacher was the amateur who only spoke when
he was inspired and when he had something to say. He
believed that the preacher who earned his living in other
pursuits was perpetually free to speak his mind, and not
restricted by the fixed opinions of the gentry who occupy
the front pews, and demand that they be taught only what
they already know.

He wanted the pulpit made *free,* by putting *free* Men in it!

℄ Here 's another phase that he thought ridiculous: In
East Aurora, a village of less than four thousand, there
were nine to a dozen preachers, earning from Six Hundred
to Nine Hundred Dollars a year—all Christian preachers,
all worshipping the same God, all working toward the same
Heaven—and because of unwillingness to co-operate going
on short rations Here Below—and having a desperate time
trying to preach a full religion on an empty stomach.

Once Hubbard offered to employ every minister and
priest in the village at the same salaries they then received
with a chance for advancement, provided the Church
organizations would turn their pulpits over to volunteer
preachers—and so eliminate the economic waste of a dozen
non-producers.

Of course nothing came of it.

Another time there was some agitation to combine all the
Protestant congregations and all the salaries paid to the
(say) ten Protestant ministers—and then go out and call
one first-class man, write him a contract that would leave

him *free,* and so participate in some real genuine *uplift.*
¶ Nothing came of that either.

All villages are alike—not excepting East Aurora. The villagers like the petty honors and the petty politics that go with maintaining a dozen different Church organizations. Each man chooses to think he is " different " from his neighbor, and in some subtle way, superior!

Hubbard was no extremist. He was not trying to reform the world overnight. But he did think that before the *Church* was entitled to set out to reform the world, it ought to put its own house in order—and that a combination of all the Protestant churches in America was Good Religion, Good Economics, and Good Sense, he never hesitated to set forth.
¶ He was willing that orthodox churches, orthodox religions should exist (for a certain class of people) provided they were set free and made progressive—so that they might stop being a drag on Civilization!

*   *   *   *   *

Understand these were his *opinions,* I might almost say his confidential opinions, on this subject, because he recognized that a religious belief is a fundamental belief and that it is easier to improve a man than it is to improve his religion.

" Improve Man—and ultimately Man will improve and advance his religious conceptions. * * * He always has! * * * One World at a time—and one Man at a time! " ﹏ ﹏

So religion as such was not emphasized either affirmatively or negatively at the Roycroft. We employed Christians and Unbelievers, Jews and Gentiles, Protestants and Catholics—and all were given an equal chance.

There was no prejudice, no discrimination.

The fact is we never knew what a man's religion was till

we chanced to meet him on a Sunday morning walking to
church self-consciously in squeaky boots.

Once in so often Charley Rosen, Superintendent of Printing,
used to take me to the Methodist prayer meeting for the
good of my soul—and certainly Hubbard never objected.
On occasion Charley would gently rebuke some boy for
using profanity—and that was all right with Hubbard
too. Whether or not he cultivated the orthodox religions
personally—he was always on the side of the *good*.

Fra Elbertus and the old German priest of the R. C. Church
were firm friends. Every now and then one would see them
closeted in executive session. Quite obviously the Father
was telling the Brother that he was a little short on cash
—and finances were being equalized.

Once when the Roycrofters were to play a ball game against
somebody or other the holy Father re-arranged his Sunday
Schedule so that his congregation would be able to attend
the game ᔈᕀ ᔈᕀ

You see Reciprocity begets Reciprocity.

Only once in a decade did Hubbard become involved with
the village people. Marilla Ricker, that rare old agnostic,
was the cause. Marilla was a flaming disciple of Ingersoll,
as well as a famous woman lawyer. Many Summers she
spent at East Aurora and really became " one of the family."
One Spring she decided to present to the village library the
Complete Works of Robert G. Ingersoll.

Hubbard encouraged her (perhaps he suggested the gift
in the first place).

The offer was made—and declined.

The village Board of Education took the time and trouble
to mention that Ingersoll was a " celebrated atheist,"
and that " Mr. Ingersoll's writings on religious subjects
can accomplish no good purpose."

Right there Hubbard stepped into the breach. He offered the village library *his own* Complete Works.

But he warned them—" Personally I lay no claim to being a better man nor a greater writer than Robert G. Ingersoll." ✌ ✌

He also took time to mention that "At the present writing I receive about three-fourths of the mail that comes to the village, and am the largest tax payer in town," etc.

❡ The Village Fathers advised him that they would accept his Complete Works but that some of his books would probably be relegated to a Department of Objectionable Literature—which they were about to inaugurate.

Naturally he refused the honor.

Hubbard indulged himself to the extent of having the First Word and the Last; his last letter, he announced, remained unanswered.

Eventually he published the entire correspondence in *The Philistine:* and labeled it ironically, " A Tempest in a Village Teapot."

I am quite sure Hubbard initiated this controversy. I am positive he wanted to prove either one thing or several things, not the least of which was that a Prophet is still without honor in his own village.

Even so, he was shocked!

For quite a little while, he was ashamed for East Aurora —ashamed for its lack of appreciation and gratitude ✌ ✌

You see, he had expected the worst and hoped for the best. But at the last, it probably dawned on him that, well— a village is a village and nothing more!

* * * * *

Stripped of all verbiage his Belief was a simple one: " One World at a time—One Day at a time—Do your Work as well as you can and be Kind: I don't believe in governing by force, or threat, or any other form of coercion. I would not arouse in the heart of any of God's creatures the thought of fear, hate, or revenge."

Those were his essential Commandments.

I remember a Protestant layman, a critic, once wrote in to condemn the Editor of *The Philistine* because his teachings " took away and did not give back "—that he was destructive, negative.

Instantly Hubbard called his attention to the fact that *eight* of the Ten Commandments were negative—Thou Shalt Not's! "And so," he chortled, "this pleasant Protestant who leans heavily on the Ten Commandments protests *The Philistine* is Protestant! "

Of course, the Fra had no panacea to sell, and therefore was a disappointment to those who are accustomed to spiritual Cure-alls. There was no Ritual to follow, no Doctrine to observe, no set of Rules and Regulations— and the defect of that sort of a " religion " is that it presupposes that the communicant has brains—which must always remain a supposititious proposition.

He was a Dealer in Intelligence, a Vendor of Ideas.

That he was an Atheist—No!

It was not in him to say, " There is *no* God! "

He was not that kind of a man.

He wanted to believe *all* that was *Good* and Beautiful.

He was glad of the opportunity to help chase the Devil out of Hell, and to help chase Hell out of existence. But to him God was still in his Heaven and all was well with the World! ॐ ॐ

He was not an Iconoclast—an Image Breaker—because he was not concerned with symbols of Ideas—he was concerned only with the Ideas themselves.

He was not an Unbeliever—an Infidel—a Skeptic.

His *Faith* was his distinguishing feature. Always he believed in the Best, hoped for the Best, wished for the Best, worked for the Best.

There was no intolerance in him, nor in his speech, nor action, nor life.

His Faith (religiously and scientifically speaking) was the same as Herbert Spencer's: " Affirming the existence of an Unknowable."

Said he, " Every man is a Child of God and the best man who ever lived was nothing more."

To his mind there was not too much genuine Religion in this world, but too little; too many Cults and Creeds and not enough of Faith and Hope and Charity.

That it was necessary, or possible, for a finite man to solve all the problems of the Infinite, he doubted. Was that desirable or needful, then the Supreme Intelligence would have opened the Door, shed the Light and shown the Way.

❡ Obviously the Divine Plan was not to divulge all and for us *not* to know all. That was to be our Test by Faith.

❡ Life was an enfoldment, a turning of pages: some day we would reach the End of the Book of Life, and then the dénouement ❧ ❧

When the proper time came we would pass through the Door to which there was no Key—and then we would know whatever it was that we should know! And meanwhile, and meanwhile, let us labor while we wait, let us get on with the Day's Work, and live this life so creditably that it must surely be a preparation for the next.

* * * * *

Years ago Fra Elbertus lectured in Philadelphia on a Sun·day night. There was a Blue Law operating in that ancient and honorable city forbidding Entertainments, Theaters and such, on Sunday.

That's why the Philadelphia hotels are deserted three
nights a week, by the commercial travelers and others of
their ilk, from Friday afternoon to Monday morning—
while the Boys journey over to Broadway where they
hold " Sacred Concerts " on Sunday nights, in the vaudeville establishments.

But no matter!

The lecture was delivered, and the Elect of the City of
Brotherly Love filled every seat, and the Standing Room
Only sign went up in the lobby.

Obviously *some one* was breaking a Law!

Who it was, was not long left in doubt. Shortly after the
lecture, a citizen in broad-toed shoes stepped up to Fra
Elbertus, tapped him on the shoulder, and said, " The
Captain wants to see you."

He was arrested!

At the police station there were hurry-up telephone calls
for friendly lawyers. When Number One came hurrying in,
he said, " They can't arrest you for this! "

" I know they can't," Hubbard observed, " but they have."

Soon bail was arranged.

The trial was set for the next morning.

Next morning, when Court was called, it was observed
by the party of the first part, that the Judge, the Prose-
cuting Attorney, and the Attorney for the Defense were
all gentlemen who had occupied reserved seats the night
before—and laughed immoderately at some jokes about
lawyers that the Sage of East Aurora was always obliged
to tell! &o &o

That was one time that he thanked God that most lawyers
(unlike most preachers) have a sense of humor!

" What is the charge? "

" *Giving an Entertainment,* your Honor."

" That 's just the point, your Honor," moved the Attorney
for the Defense: " I was there in person and I was *not*
entertained; and I noted that the Attorney for the Prose-
cution was there, and I would like to ask him was he entertained! " ๑๑ ๑๑

" Certainly I was not," testified Sheepskin, Sr.

" And, your Honor, I noticed you were there—were you by
chance entertained? "

" Not a bit," said the Woolsack.

" That being the case," observed Marks, of Marks & Marks,
" there is no case! If the lecture did not entertain, it could
not have been an entertainment: Therefore no Law was
broken. I move the case dismissed."

" Dismissed—and Court adjourned."

Though this is not an exact interpretation of the events
as they transpired, nevertheless, it is approximately correct; and what is more, I learned from a Reliable Authority
that at Noon that day Hubbard purchased four lunches
and consumed only one of them himself!

We Have With Us Tonight

We Have With Us Tonight

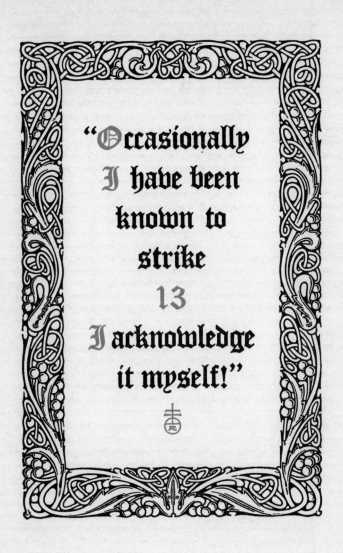

"Occasionally
I have been
known to
strike
13
I acknowledge
it myself!"

We Have With Us Tonight

LBERT HUBBARD'S first (and I may almost say his last) Lecture-Impressario was Major James B. Pond. 'T was a short relationship but a merry one, and a profitable one for both parties to the agreement. The Orator of the Evening describes Major Pond thus: " He was big, brusque, quibbling, insulting, dictatorial, painstaking, considerate and kind. He was the most exasperating and lovable man I ever knew. He was despotically kind."

Pond, the Universal Impressario, speaking of his East Aurora Star, said that of all the Greats and the Near-Greats whom he had escorted round about the country, Hubbard was the most desirable man for New Territory. For Return Engagements he preferred Henry Ward Beecher —but for a first-time appearance he gave the preference to the Man from East Aurora.

Here is a sketch of the Pond-Hubbard combination on the road together:

" At a hotel, Pond always got a room with two beds if possible, or connecting rooms. I was his prisoner. He regulated my hours of sleep, my meals, my exercise. He would throw intruding visitors down stairs as average men shoo chickens or scare cats. He was a bundle of profanity and unrest until after the lecture. Then we would go to our rooms and he would talk like a windmill. He would crawl

into his bed and I into mine, and he would continue telling
Beecher stories half the night, comparing me with Beecher
to my great disadvantage."

The first time Major Pond booked Elbert Hubbard for
the Waldorf-Astoria, Fra Elbertus was refused admission
when he attempted to register for a room. He and Ali
Baba turned up there in hickory shirts and brogans. The
Clerk said, " Very sorry, sir, we 're all full."

Not by any chance would Hubbard miss an opportunity
like that, so he turned on his heel and made for the door.
He was almost outside when Mine Host Boldt effected
a rescue ᔕ➤ ᔕ➤

Of course the smart and snappy reporters got hold of the
item and it made spicy reading (and good advance publicity
for the lecture) in the New York newspapers: " Apostle
of Simplicity Refused Admittance to Waldorf-Astoria! "
Hurrah! ᔕ➤ ᔕ➤

There were only six hundred seats in the Astor Gallery.
They were quickly sold out at one dollar each.

Hubbard said, " When Major Pond saw this capacity
audience, he fell upon my neck and rained Pond's Extract
down my back and cried, ' My God, my God! Why did
we not charge them a Dollar and a Half a seat? ' "

Once when Hubbard was out on a tour with Pond, the
Major distributed a circular which made the Orator out
to be the Greatest Thing ever. E. H. went to Pond and
declaimed that if this Themistocles thing was true—and
that he had no doubt it was—then he wanted at least
one hundred dollars more a week. Pond fell into a swoon
and awoke swearing. He swore the circular was merely
kabojolism, hokus-pokus.

He remarked pointedly, " You are really a considerable
chump." ᔕ➤ ᔕ➤

They both got a lot of incidental pleasure out of this oratorical partnership.

For twenty years or more Elbert Hubbard went up and down the land—speaking, lecturing, making friends.

Back in the Spring of Nineteen Hundred Fifteen, planning some lecture dates for the following season, I submitted a list of the One Thousand Largest Towns and Cities, and asked him to please " check " it and tell me where he had spoken (previously) and where he had not spoken.

Much to my surprise—and to his surprise, too—we learned that he had spoken in *every one* of the thousand largest towns and cities in the United States.

From Nineteen Hundred to Nineteen Fifteen, there was no more sought-after lecturer than Hubbard and none that gave keener pleasure to his audience, or that was received with more appreciation, more applause.

I have heard him speak a hundred times, and never the same lecture twice. I never failed to be surprised and entertained at some odd quip or quirk, never failed to enjoy his performance, and never saw him leave a disappointed audience! ❧ ❧

Major Pond introduced him to the American audience all right, but he fastened them to himself with hoops of that fine-spun steel called loyalty!

* * * * *

Any man who addressed a fashionable audience of two thousand or three thousand while wearing his work-a-day clothes—including his well-known flannel shirt—must have been a rarely natural man. Hubbard was so natural that he was a disappointment to the Professors of Oratory who sadly missed the wind-up and the peroration. Each sentence of his was a peroration, and 't was wise to give attention, else you might miss a couple of fast ones.

The last time I heard him speak to a paid audience he opened with this statement, " Silence is the College Yell of Experience," and a certain Captain of Industry in the stage box, all keyed up for the expected—unexpectedly exploded a chuckle!

The audience joined in.

After that 't was easy going—really a family affair!

But as to naturalness—when he talked he was so relaxed that for a moment or two first-time audiences, expecting the usual oratorical attitude, were disappointed—until they caught the tempo.

He had a contempt for artifice, the studied gesture, and the " bishop's " voice! He did not orate, he talked! Soon the distance between the speaker and the audience dwindled, the Talk became more and more intimate until each person in that audience gathered the impression that Hubbard was confiding the Message to him alone.

'T was an ordinary occurrence to have a member of the audience come up afterwards and whisper to him, " I got that particular joke all right, all right—that the others missed! " ๑๑ ๑๑

And the speaker would laugh and reply, " I knew you would! " ๑๑ ๑๑

To make the Message personal—that was the thing!

In his heart of hearts he believed he had a *message* for America, and he intended that no stage mannerisms, no false attitudes should break the contact between him and his audience ๑๑ ๑๑

Here he describes one orator to his liking—one who held *his* attention:

" I have seen a coatless laborer, speaking from a wagon in Hyde Park, reach the very height of oratory in his impassioned appeal. The inspiration for his oratory lay

in the fact that he had a message—he forgot self, and
mounted to sublimity on the wings of spirit. He had pathos,
with logic, entreaty, reason in his employ."

So I repeat, Hubbard was natural, and extraordinarily
popular ᴓ ᴓ

There was substance to his talk.

Nevertheless he deplored the fact that the lyceum of
Wendell Phillips, and Ralph Waldo Emerson, and Henry
Ward Beecher was passing from our national life, to be
replaced by minstrel monologues.

The Speech that marks an epoch, the Lecture that thunders
down the ages is not a one-man performance—it's a co-
operative affair. The speaker supplies but half and the
audience the other half. Audiences must go into training
too or they lose their appreciation and understanding of
the finer sentiments of life.

Said Hubbard: " Some time possibly a man will come out
of the great silence, and we will go and hear his Message
and our hearts will warm within us for days thereafter
as we ponder on the things we heard when in that potent
presence. * * * And our work will be lightened, and
our companions nobler and some way God will seem nearer
because we have seen and heard one of His Messengers."

Though his lecture work was a strain, though it entailed
late hours and three a. m. train connections, and accom-
modations at impossible hotels, he never seemed to tire;
I never heard him complain.

There was no artistic temperament about Hubbard. He
was always accessible ᴓ Whether in Pullmans or day-
coaches, passengers would go by him, stop and return,
" Don't I know you? "

" Well, sir, my name is Hubbard."

Before long the two-man conversation would turn into a *meeting*—a group would gather.

Walk down Broadway or Michigan Boulevard with him and he 'd be stopped forty times to a block by friends who wanted to say " Hello " and to ask him, " Have you heard this one? " *so so*

That was how he found much of his " copy "—through casual contacts.

That was why his " copy " was so alive!

One Sunday afternoon at the Grand Central Station in New York, we discovered we had two hours to wait between trains. From his bag he brought out a soft ball *so*

" Let 's go out and get a little exercise while we wait."

❡ The bags were checked and we retired to the open place between Forty-fifth and Forty-sixth Streets and Park Avenue. Before we 'd tossed the ball back and forth many times some chauffeurs showed interest and were invited to play the game *so so*

A couple of business acquaintances came along, shouted a greeting, and received the ball direct. They took off their coats, and joined us. Then three gentlemen in top hats arrived, returning from church, and they doffed their silk lids, and played first, second and third base, respectively.

❡ A boy found a barrel stave and we had a rousing game of " one ol' cat." A cop arrived on the scene, but some one spoke to him and he sidled away smiling out of the corner of his mouth.

'T was a great game, good exercise, everybody enjoyed it, Democracy was served—and we caught the train when it was due, on the minute.

* * * * *

I have previously mentioned that he sometimes rode in day-coaches, even on all-day trips; rode in day-coaches

and bought his lunch in a paper bag at a railroad lunch
room. I have shared the dubious pleasure of this sort of
journey. The less I enjoyed it, the more fun it was for him.
❡ 'T was n't a matter of economy, because when we 'd
reached journey's end and we had pried the cinders out of
ourselves, perhaps at dinner he 'd tip the waitress a bill ᔕᵒ
I 've seen him do that, too.

He was a contrary citizen!

I have tried to reason out why he liked this sort of travel
and I have come to the conclusion that by avoiding the
Pullmans, by secluding himself in the day-coaches, (perhaps!), he got more work done.

On these all-day journeys he wrote incessantly, and many
a *Philistine* was produced between the raucous announcements of Bill the Brakeman, " The next stop will be ' So-
andthus! ' " ᔕᵒ ᔕᵒ

The conductors and the colored porters on all the through
trains, East and West, knew him by name ᔕᵒ He was a
distinctive sort of a passenger; a journey with him always
was sure to prove an event.

Once when Coach Two developed a hot-box and there
was a delay for a couple of hours, instead of letting the
passengers annoy the crew with the usual assortment of
damphool questions, he organized a game of " one ol' cat "
in a nearby clearing and most of the crowd so enjoyed
themselves they were real sorry when the train tooted
" Let 's go! " ᔕᵒ ᔕᵒ

In New York it was the Waldorf-Astoria to sleep, and
Mother Childs' for breakfast; in Chicago the Auditorium-
annex to sleep and Thompson's for breakfast.

Mention of the Auditorium-annex reminds me that he
and his son Bert, on a return trip from California, were
refused admittance there. They attempted to register and

found the house " all full." They were on their way toward
the street, when Pat Sheedy, the Chicago politician, col-
lared them and took them back to the desk, and said to
the Clerk, " You This and That, are you trying to make
a monkey out of yourself or out of this hotel?—This man
owns a whole damn town down East. You 'll be lucky if
you 're not fired! Just tell him what you want *Fray,* and
you 'll get it."

Strange, is n't it, how some sort of people judge by super-
ficial externals!

* * * * *

I had a minor adventure with him in Chicago, once on a
time:

That year he was super-enthused about Mangasarian,
the Orator of Orchestra Hall: a man who to my way of
thinking lacked humor!

It came to pass that in a certain issue of *The Fra* Hubbard
wrote a rousing laudatory article about Mangasarian ∾
This particular issue of the magazine came off the press
just as he was leaving for Chicago to fill a lecture engagement at the Studebaker Theater. Instantly he decided to
take a thousand or more copies along, as a surprise gift
for each member of Mangasarian Sunday Morning Free-
thinking Congregation.

From the cellars of Roycroft were excavated some very
antique trunks—with ragged tin edges—mark that! Into
these trunks were piled the thousand copies of *The Fra*
and checked through to Chicago.

When we reached Chicago on a Sunday morning, Hubbard
balked at the prices asked by Parmelee or whoever operated
the regular delivery service, and went outside the gate and
hired a weazened old man with a three-legged horse and
a three-wheeled wagon.

This impossible combination he wished on to me and then hurried off to Orchestra Hall to announce the glad tidings of great joy that I was coming up the Avenue " riding the baggage! " ✍ ✍

But first I had to lift those trunks aboard the rickety wagon because the old driver was superannuated (and of course none of the regulars would lend a hand)—and when I reached Orchestra Hall at the very hour of the Sunday Morning Parade, I had to lift them down again—and in my Sunday Best clothes!

Imagine my thoughts *in re* Mr. Mangasarian!

Meanwhile the Sage of East Aurora had arrived and presented an inscribed copy to Mangasarian off stage. Then he busied himself with the ushers arranging for the proper distribution of *The Fras.*

About the time I dumped the full trunks on the side walk, Mangasarian came out of his brown study feeling blue and talking red! It seems that Hubbard had made a technical error (if I remember correctly) in tracing the learned gentleman's Family Tree! O Gosh!

He 'd have none of it—none!

Hubbard said one or two things himself!

What happened to the trunks, or the magazines, I don't know to this date—I left them there on the side walk!

But I have a hunch they were not passed out to the congregation that morning!

* * * * *

There were always gay spirits to volunteer to help make Hubbard's Annual Visit to Their Town an Event, and various and devious were the ways they went about it ✍

He joshed them, and they joshed him.

In the preliminary correspondence he rarely failed to mention that his fee for lecturing was, say, two hundred

dollars—but to lecture and to be a guest at a private
house was two hundred fifty dollars ❧ He charged fifty
dollars extra when obliged to receive " entertainment "
—or so he said.

That opened the way for the jokers.

Invariably the cleverest man in town was selected to introduce him, and frequently these bright minds would evolve
some little masterpieces of Ballyhoo calculated to put the
Speaker of the Evening in a " hole."

Herewith one such is quoted. After perusing it, the gentle
reader may declare a ten-minute recess to determine just
what *he* would say (in Hubbard's place) to wipe out the
impression of such a star-spangled prelude:

" The gentleman who is about to address you this evening
is a Jack of all trades, and the master of each one. He is
the Grand Past Master, High Mogul, Lord Exalted Ruler
of everything he undertakes. He does not merely one thing
at a time, but twenty things, and each of them better than
his neighbors, than you or I, could do them.

" As an author, he has written stories that have sold literally by the millions and that have made the highly vaunted,
much advertised Six Best Sellers retire precipitately to the
tall timber behind, there to hide their diminished heads.

" As a biographer, his Little Journeys to the Homes of
Good Men and Great have combined a depth of research
with a brilliancy of style that is the wonder and amaze-
ment of all who have read them.

" As a manufacturer of furniture and other useful articles
in his Roycroft Shops, he was the Moses who led a horde
of barbarians out of the Desert of these plush-covered,
spindle-legged atrocities, which used to desecrate most of
our parlors but a few short years ago, into the Promised
Land of those simple, dignified, artistic styles which now,
thanks to him, have become so common in the home of
the average cultured American citizen.

" He is the editor of two magazines of wide circulation,

practically the entire contents of which, including the advertisements and items about himself, he himself writes. And it is not the least of his accomplishments that many of us regard the advertisements as even more interesting than the alleged pure reading matter interlarded amongst them ა✻ ა✻

" Lately he has essayed to become a purveyor of amusement upon the vaudeville stage; and there, a well-known critic informs me, he has snatched the laurel wreath from those famous Iowa products, the Cherry Sisters, and with it adorned his own classic brow.

" As to his merits as an orator, you yourselves shall be the judges a short time hence. Having never heard him speak, I am unable to deliver an opinion, ex-cathedra, but I understand that his silvery tongue makes Demosthenes look like a Four-flusher, Cicero a Back Number and Wendell Phillips a Never Was.

" Ladies and Gentlemen, it gives me great pleasure to introduce to you a man with the vocabulary of a Shakespeare, the strenuosity of a certain mighty Lion-hunter, and the persistence of the Devil himself, Mr. Elbert Hubbard, otherwise known as Fra Elbertus, who will speak to you, for a few moments, if you will permit him, a few hours, if you insist, upon *The March of the Centuries* ა✻

William Allen White, in writing up Hubbard's talk in Emporia, Kansas, said: " He gave his lecture on one leg." ℭ And Hubbard promptly retorted that most of Will Allen White's stories " crawled around on all fours."

Once in Pittsburgh he missed a familiar quotation, reached for it and missed again—and a deep voice from the audience called " Strike Two! " followed by a wild burst of applause. ℭ The self-appointed umpire had saved the evening!

When he visited New York the honorable editors capitulated after this fashion:

Fra Elbertus, editor of *The Philistine*, the author of Little Journeys, and the Master of the Roycroft Shop, visited

New York last Friday, and by order of the King of Bohemia
was welcomed with princely state. As the special train from
East Aurora, personally conducted by General Agent Daniels, entered the Grand Central Station, the city was bril-
liantly illuminated, a line of fire flashing from the Torch
of Liberty to the Brooklyn Bridge, and along the Harlem
to Grant's Tomb. The streets were crowded. Mr. Hubbard
was conducted by Major, the Honorable J. B. Pond, to
regal apartments in the Everett House and Union Square
opposite was adorned with the statues of Washington,
Lincoln and Lafayette. In the evening Mr. Hubbard lectured at the Waldorf-Astoria on the " Work of the Roycrofters." The Astor Gallery was overcrowded, and as the
lecture proceeded the audience overflowed into the whole
hotel, the parlors and sitting rooms being utilized as private
boxes. Mr. Hubbard is as handsome as Membrino Prince
—handsomer than his published pictures. He looks like Lord
Byron, and talks like a combination of Artemus Ward
and Mark Twain. His hearers were alternately amused
and thrilled. After the lecture Mr. Hubbard held a reception, the Honorable Clark Bell acting as Master of Ceremonies. Customs differ when celebrities meet, and he greeted
his titular sovereign with " Hello, Steve! " ✒ The town
was painted a royal purple in his honor, and refreshments
were served at the wide open houses until daylight did
appear. On his next visit Mr. Hubbard will lecture in a
larger hall—Carnegie or Chickering—and the Lotus Club
will give him a congratulatory dinner. On Saturday he
returned to East Aurora with five hundred dollars in gold,
the freedom of New York City, and a broad-brimmed
hat a little too small.

Came a season when the Clover Club invited him to Philadelphia to shout him down—but they miscalculated their
man. Be it known that the Clover Club pays nice fat fees
to Prominent Gentlemen for the sole and only pleasure of
not listening to them. They talk them down, sing them
down, shout them down, or get up and leave the room
while the speaker is still spieling.

This, I understand, is called Humor. Only two men have
scored off the Clover Club in all its history, so the saying
goes so Only two men were heard through to the finish
—and one was Elbert Hubbard!

When he started to speak to them, the audience rose and
sang, *Johnny Get Your Hair Cut—Hair Cut—Hair Cut.*

That caused some delay so When he began again a
large red-haired man arose and in a thunderous voice re-
cited *Old Mother Hubbard*—and all about her trip to the
empty Cupboard—and the Poor Dog, and the Bone that
was n't there! When he finished there was a tear in every
eye. Some in fact wept aloud, sobbed! Hubbard tried his
soft wheedling tones for a third time. Just then a spruce,
energetic and somewhat irate individual arose and pointedly
asked the Chairman, " Who is this Actor-like person who is
perpetually interrupting us? "

After that it was a free-for-all!

Hubbard smiled, and smiled!

They could not ruffle or annoy him.

" Will you give me a chance to tell a couple of stories? "
They replied, " Yes, but make 'em brief."

With his eye on the Large Red-headed Man, he told the
story of the Day the Truce was declared between the Birds
and the Beasts. Two geese stood talking by the roadside
when they saw a red fox coming down the road.

Said one goose, " Goodbye old fellow, I must be going."
Said the other, " You 're not afraid, are you? Remember
today is the Day of the Truce! "

" Ah, yes! Quite so! But just the same it looks to me as
though that red-headed son-of-a-gun has n't heard about
it yet! " so so

And then another:

When North fought South, along the Border brother con-

tested brother, and father faced son. In one engagement
an old man crouched behind a rail fence, was being shot at
by a Johnny Reb concealed behind the stump of a tree.
The grey-coat shot, and missed. Again, he shot and missed.
The third time he shot, and missed! And the old man
peeking up over the fence recognized his own son ◦❧ He
opened up his yawp and called, "Zeke, I'll give you one
more shot and if you miss me this time I'll take a fence
rail and come over and beat Hell out of you!"
That fetched them and they subsided.
He continued, uninterrupted to the finish.
But just the same, his true opinion of the Clover Club was
unprintable.

* * * * *

"Oratory?" queried Hubbard, "You must give your
audience more than Oratory. Always the impressive orator's
theme must be a Plea for Humanity."

Madam, you have an incurable disease!

Madam, you have an incurable disease!

A Vaudeville Artist
has Three Salaries
❧ ❧ the First, the
one which he tells his
friends he gets ❧ the
Second, the one which
he thinks he ought to
get ❧ the Third, what
he actually receives ❧

Vaudeville, Before and After

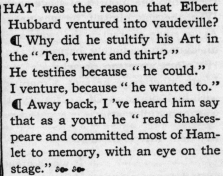

HAT was the reason that Elbert Hubbard ventured into vaudeville? ¶ Why did he stultify his Art in the " Ten, twent and thirt? " He testifies because " he could." I venture, because " he wanted to." ¶ Away back, I 've heard him say that as a youth he " read Shakespeare and committed most of Hamlet to memory, with an eye on the stage." ✺ ✺

As he grew older, he looked like an old line actor of the Classical Period, with his finely chiseled profile, his large luminous eyes, long hair and sensitive, expressive hands.

He was an actor at heart, with something of the histrion's psychology—a master of make-believe: a showman.

In conversation and in all the little acts that go to make up one's daily life, his dramatic sense was very keen. He always wanted the right thing to happen at the right time, and keener still, to have the right thing said at the right time ✺ ✺

Always there was the lure of the foot-lights.

Always the stage beckoned him.

Twice, at least, I have known him to write plays; but in my humble judgment, he was an essayist, a moralist, a publicist; not by any chance a playwright.

'T was a curious contradiction that the dramatic skill apparent in every movement and in every word of con-

versation was lost when the curtain rolled up on his manuscript play! The sparkling witticisms, the brilliant conversation, the keen remarks, the odd and curious turns
of expression all deserted him when he attempted to put
them into the mouths of stage-characters.

When he was himself, he was natural.

As a stage-character, he was artificial—and the stilted
dialogue immediately betrayed the difference in style ✒
His plays were too preachy.

I remember once he sent a manuscript to Maude Adams
with high hopes ✒ Of a certainty, the answer she returned
was most diplomatic:

My dear Mr. Hubbard:

It was a great disappointment to me
to feel I was not suited to the part in your play. In the
theater I fancy I am better fitted to deal with pleasant
things that might be, than with unpleasant realities. In
other words it 's easier to expose good than evil. With the
one we say how delightful, and try for it—With the other,
we say this is wrong and should be changed, but HOW?
Of course this applies no more to your play than to many
others—it 's just a different point of view. I did not read
the play at once, we were traveling all the time and I saved
it to read in Dublin. It did not occur to me that I had the
only copy or I should not have dreamed of taking it out
of the country for fear of some accident. I hope it has reached
you safely.

If you were less sincere I should not be so anxious to tell you my heart feeling and of course this is not
at all a criticism of the play. I should not presume to criticize it for I am not a good judge of plays. It is only my
feeling of unfitness for the part.

Believe me with many thanks for having considered me,

Faithfully,

Maude Adams.

But as a Vaude-Villian he scored. He was what the Twice-
Day'rs call a " Scream "—a " Knockout "—a " Wow! "

* * * * *

Hubbard appeared on the Orpheum Circuit.

He opened in Chicago.

There he received an ovation.

He was obliged on one occasion to give an extra noon-time
Matinée all by himself for a full house of business men *o*
There, when a Sunday Evening Benefit was held for the
Actors' Fund—in listing the Talent to appear they printed
Hubbard's name at the very head of the list—followed by
many of the truly great names in the Profession.

So I presume, Terese, he made a hit—eh, what?

That was the start, and the finish came in Cincinnati!

But to get back to the beginning.

After much correspondence, Fra Martin Beck sent Dapper
Dan, the contract man, along to East Aurora to sign 'em
up. To soften the solicitation to allow plenty of time, he
arranged to stay over a Sunday with us.

'T was a nice balmy day in Spring when the primroses and
violets by the river brim were appearing exactly as advertised *o* *o*

We invited our Vaudeville Friend to accompany the Bunch
on a cross-country walk, though he was dressed for the
sunny side of Broadway.

He was a Good Sport and came along.

All went well until in crossing a small stream he slipped
on the slimy stepping-stones—and sat down in eight inches

of water—and rolled over. Brown derby, pearl panties, spats, spit-curls, patent-leathers an' everything were ruined. ⟨ To refit him each man present contributed a garment, and in this motley and grotesque costume he appeared the rest of the day while Mother Grant, the Housekeeper, was a-drying his wardrobe on the line over the kitchen range ↞ He suffered a loss in dignity, but a gain in fellowship ↞ Hubbard signed up for ten weeks at two thousand five hundred a week—or that 's my recollection.

He opened in Chicago and, I believe, made the Western Loop—out through Minneapolis, Omaha, Denver, Spokane, Seattle, Portland, San Francisco, to Los Angeles—and thence back toward the East to close his contract and take the train for home at Cincinnati.

The Third Gallery hissed him in Cincinnati.

They wanted jazz—snappy stuff, and he made the technical error of trying to appeal to their minds (?).

When he boarded the train for home, he 'd had enough of Vaudeville ↞ ↞

Speaking of the Hissing Incident he says, " The precedent still survives in Cincinnati and some of the River Towns."

⟨ Surely he felt no bitterness toward the intelligent people of Cincinnati.

He simply refused to again risk the approval or disapproval of the hoodlums in the Third Gallery.

He explained, " The ' hoodlum ' can't be controlled, because he can't be anticipated. No one knows when he is going to break loose! Why, in a certain Pennsylvania town not long ago some one broke out in a loud Ha! ha! in one of the quiet and effective parts of the ' Music Master.' Others took up the howl, and David Warfield, the gentle, the generous, and the kindly, was obliged to retire from the stage and the curtain was run down."

After ten weeks of Vaudeville he was *tired*—weary—that was the real reason for quitting. He had operated under an unusual strain, because obviously he took the Two-a-Day seriously—much more so than he took Platform Speaking. His was not the temperament for the daily grind!

As for the Orpheum Circuit itself, and the men behind it, he felt only admiration and gratitude. Hear what he says: "The tendency of Orpheum Vaudeville is up, not down; more and more does it appeal to men and women of worth. It supplies the laugh in which there is no bitterness. It amuses without degrading. It relaxes tired nerves. Incidentally it instructs. Always it rests and refreshes. It furnishes fit preparation for the work of tomorrow—more work and better work."

When he opened up in Vaudeville, and while he was in the midst of the hurly-burly, the excitement, he was enthusiastic: "I am glad I can mix with many people and influence them. I am glad I can laugh with them and I am glad I can laugh at myself."

But when it was all over and there was time to measure and weigh, to consider and reconsider, he said, "My advice to anyone about to enter Vaudeville would be this: *Don't*." ❧ ❧

"You live in this narrow world of the mime, and your little life is bounded by the boards—the footlights to the South, the wings to the East and West, and North of you is the olio. Above, in the clouds, partially overhanging you, with grim set faces, sometimes pickled in alcohol, crouches that thousand-headed thing called the gallery.

"When you get one thousand, or two thousand, or three thousand dollars a week you are then not only doing the work but supplying the usufruct, or the cumulative good name and good will of a life that has done big. Life insurance

actuaries tell me that actors are the most hazardous risk
they are called upon to carry."
The reaction against Vaudeville (from the performer's
angle)—that, too, was only a passing phase!
He grew to love and admire the Actor Folk—their devotion,
their self-sacrifice.
Incidentally he made a host of new friends.
Before many moons had passed over following his return
to East Aurora there arrived a letter, to wit:

Dear Mr. Hubbard:

Will arrive in Buffalo Friday night and
I will find a way to get to East Aurora and rest there
Saturday and Sunday before opening September First in
Buffalo. Am as happy over the idea of going as a child
would be. Have a girl friend and my dog—Please reserve
two rooms. I hope now you will have a chance to know me
as I am, not as others would make me.

Eva Tanguay.

Then there was Billy Van, and Marsh Wilder, and Harry
Lauder, Ed Wynne, Sarah Bernhardt and Frank Keenan,
and the Great Raymond, and many, many others of the
far-flung Fraternity whom he called " friends," and about
whom he told stories. Ellen Terry, Sir Herbert Tree, and
Richard Mansfield were old friends—
I remember a story about Mansfield—who, it appears,
did not like *music* with his meals:
Mansfield walked into the Grand Central Hotel at Oshkosh.
Behind him was his valet, carrying two big grips.
The tragedian took four strides from the door to the desk,
and leaning over in one of those half-confidential stage-

voice asides that reach to the topmost gallery, said " Ah,
have you music at meals? "

And the clerk adjusted the glittering glass on his bosom,
smiled serenely, and said, " Oh, yes, surely so; yes, we
have music at all meals."

And Mansfield turned to his valet, who was resting from
labor with the heavy valises, and said, " Oho, oho, James!
Look you to our luggage! To our luggage! " And four more
strides took him to the door, and the actor and valet disappeared ✺ ✺

When Hubbard and Jim Corbett and Harry Lauder went
to call on Sarah Bernhardt, Madame was graciousness
itself—but she mistook Hubbard for Lauder:

" Not that I was peeved because she took me for Monsieur
Ladaiere, for the Little Hoot Mon, after all, is a man of
brains—an individual. Lauder prizes truth, hates a trifler,
has all the Scottish virtues, knows how to keep his health,
and is master of himself every moment. I just imagine that
in order to be a great comedian, a man must be something
else besides one. In Harry Lauder's work there is a touch
of the pathetic—just a bare chemical trace—which gives
a hint of power and deepens the comedy. You see that his
fun is born of sensitiveness."

Continued Hubbard:

" Madame is tall, trim, slim, or reasonably so, and has a
flat back. She is not as slim as when I saw her in Eighteen
Hundred Seventy-six, when her gloves wrinkled over her
skinny arms, and she set the world a fashion. I was a cub
reporter on a Chicago paper, and launched a story, which
has since gone clattering down the corridors. It is that
wheeze about a marble cutter who carved on the base of
a monument the legend, ' Lord, she was Thine,' and acci-
dentally left off the ' e ' on the word ' Thine. ' "

He told me this one on Lauder that may or may not be
new:

It seems that Messrs. Corbett, Hubbard and Lauder retired
to a corner Drug Store for a Malted Milk and Egg—when
it came to pass that three separate and distinct flies alighted
in their three separate and distinct glasses—at one and the
same time. Corbett *blew* his off into space—Hubbard
daintily inserted his thumb and *dipped out* the fly, and let
it go at that—while Harry took up his fly and *wrung it out.*
❡ Here 's another one—on himself.

In Saint Louis something happened which was not down
on the official program.

He was booked to speak for twenty minutes, but had discovered that twenty minutes, straight off the reel, was a
little too much, and so he divided his " time " up into a
first appearance of twelve minutes—when he would fire
off a final skyrocket and bow himself off the stage under
cover of the " smoke."

Usually there would be a burst of applause; although on
this occasion the applause was not there, and when he
came out to respond to the encore he appeared embalmed
like black beetles in an amber silence.

" The silence engulfed me; and right at my elbow in a box
three feet away, I heard a lady's shrill voice shoot up above
the orchestra, and the words she said were these: ' Is that
all that man does? ' "

                    * * * * *

One day I asked him, " What *was* your Subject in Vaudeville? " ﹏ ﹏

" Felix—the *title* of my Talk is like a Mother Hubbard
wrapper—it covers the subject without restricting it! I
talked about various things! "

Then he went on to tell me how the Management insisted

he wear exactly the same suit of clothes at each performance—tell exactly the same stories. For example, usually
he told the Horseshoe Story, but one day being inspired
in another direction he omitted it.

Immediately the House Manager raised a protest: " People
expect you to be the same. They talk about you outside
the theater. Their friends come expecting to hear certain
stories, and you must not disappoint them! "

That lack of variety *in Variety,* was one of the heartbreakers
for the Fra.

One day a Song-and-dance man came to him off stage and
perked up thus: " Say, fellah! You 're a Scream! An' they
tell me you write your own stuff. Write me a Knock-out
Speakin' Act—an' I 'll slip you a thousand—see! "

Here 's the Horseshoe Story, without the trimmings:

A man driving along a country road finds a horseshoe on
the roadside.

" Ah, that 's Good Luck," he exclaims, stops his horse,
picks up the horseshoe and drives on.

A little farther along he finds another—he 's elated ❧ ❧
" Ah-ha! My luck is doubled! "

He stops, picks up the horseshoe and drives on.

Then sad to say he comes upon a third, and a fourth, and
then a *heap* of horseshoes—and then he overtakes an
Italian junk man who had lost the tail-board out of his cart!

❡ The Moral is: One Horseshoe is Good Luck—but a
load of Horseshoes is *junk.*"

* * * * *

From his Venture into Vaudeville, much good " copy "
resulted, and this sample seems to be amusing—so here
it is:

James J. Morton, the Boy Comic, weight two hundred
and forty ❧ ❧

I met Jim first, going over that long Sunday ride from Spokane to Seattle.

He is a Harvard man with generous culture and a fine appreciation of every beautiful thing. He is as impressive as Judge Smith. But to see him off the stage no one could ever possibly imagine what sort of a performance he would give ✺ ✺

In the troupe with Morton was a girl who also played kid parts; but while Morton is a giant, this girl looks the genuine thing. I suppose she weighed about ninety pounds, but seeing her around in the waiting-room I thought that of course she was a chee-ild, until Jim pointed her out and introduced me to her.

Her hair was bobbed and tied with an enormous pink ribbon that flopped as she danced and jumped around over the seats. She wore red patent-leather shoes with black tops, and socks instead of stockings. Her dress barely came to her knees, and her belt was one of those loose things that dangled around her hips. She was a most amusing and entertaining kidlet.

" How old do you think she is? " said Jim to me; and I answered, " Oh, nine or ten, but big for her age! "

" She is twenty-eight," said Jim, " and there is a bet on that she can not ride to Seattle on a half-rate ticket. These duds you see her in are simply her stage-clothes. I bet that she will make the journey all right unchallenged. Joe Jenny over there in the corner put up twenty-five dollars and said she would not."

The girl bought her half-rate ticket, crouching down and putting her retrousse nose up above the window at the ticket-seller. He looked at her big pink flopping bow, and handed out the half-rate without question.

She went through the gate all right and entered the Pullman. She gave her ticket to Ollie Mack, and then lay down with her head in Mack's lap and her feet up in the window, with her bare legs, Scotch fashion, toward the end in view.

❡ The conductor came through, took the tickets, glanced at the " kid " and did not say a word. The car was full of acts, and we were all on, because it takes only a little thing to interest the genus actor. This was a sure-enough play. There were quiet side bets made that the conductor would pinch her when he came back.

When he returned, however, she was sitting up, and he merely reached over and chucked her under the chin, and gave a sort of paternal love slap at her big pink bow ᴈᴐ ᴈᴐ In an hour or two the conductor came back and took the only vacant seat, with his little green tin box in front of him. He began to count up his tickets. Then it was that Jim Morton went over and dared Joe Jenny to put up five more that the girl would not go and sit on the conductor's lap and help him count the tickets. The money was put up, and the facts explained to the girl. She took an orange and went dancing up and down the aisle, jumping from one side to the other. Finally she stopped and stared at the conductor, and asked him what game he was playing. He smiled, of course, and then went on to explain the matter to her. She went up closer, she looked at the tickets, she examined some of them, she leaned over on the conductor's shoulder, and—so God help me!—in a minute she was seated on his knee with one arm around his neck.

And so they had a very jolly time of it—this beautiful, innocent child of twenty-eight and the fatherly conductor of forty ᴈᴐ ᴈᴐ

The day wore on, as the days do. We reached Seattle, and Joe Jenny was thirty plunks to the bad. The next evening, in the dining-room of the hotel, Jim Morton, Joe Jenny and I sat quietly Fletcherizing on a modest lunch; when who should come in but the conductor and this girl, now transformed into a full-grown woman by a wonderful fifty-dollar hair effect and a clinging gown.

They seated themselves over in one corner.

" Would n't that give you the gumwillies! " exclaimed Joe Jenny in a stage whisper.

" Oh, I don't know," yawned Jim; " I saw them dining together every evening last week over at Davenport's! "

" Then he knew she was twenty-eight all the time! "

" Certainly; that is why he passed her at half-rate! "

"Stung! " said Joe.

One On Plutarch

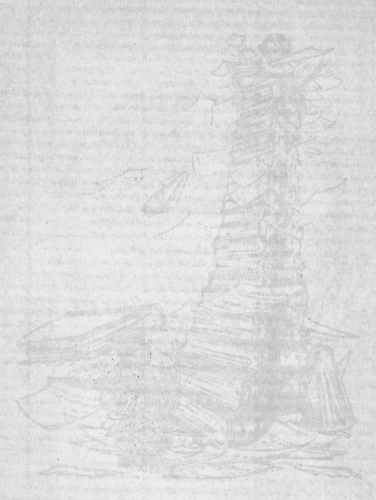

"Mine is the
Experimental
Life; all we
do things
for anyway
is just for
the Exercise
of our
Faculties"

The Philistine, The Fra and Little Journeys

THE *Little Journeys* were a search for an education.

The Philistine was a whim, a gesture *so so*

The Fra was a purpose.

The three together were a highly profitable business.

Hubbard was founder, perpetrator and the principal performer.

" Blessed is that man who has found his work."

Years agone when Hubbard went to Harvard Professor Bumble-Bumble haled him in on the carpet one day to tell him that his literary work was " totally lacking in *tout ensemble,* you know."

" You will never make a writer; you should be a tiller of the soil, an agrarian, an agriculturist, a buckwheat, a farmer." *so so*

After the amenities were properly amended the something less-than-meek aspirant managed to get in one edgewise, thus:

" Emerson, you are aware, says ' I would have every man rich that he might know the worthlessness of riches.' I am convinced of the logic of the remark and have come to college to find out how little a college education is really worth. I do not take my literary aspirations seriously—nor yours—it is just an attempt at expression, for all life is expression. So I pray you waive the advice as to occupation, and criticize my theme."

I cite that incident because it proves how much the judgment of a Professor of Literature is worth. It proves how impossible it is for mortal man to look into the future and make his prophecies prove up. The student who was sentenced to become a farmer by the Harvard Professor became a farmer. He likewise became the most prolific writer of his time, produced the *Message to Garcia* which received the largest circulation of any piece of literature extant (the Bible excepted), and by himself (only and alone) held the attention of a larger class audience, and for a longer period of years, than any writer of his era.

Of a certainty this man did not learn about Life, nor learn how to write, at Harvard. For him the Harvard experience was a fizzle.

Nor was he educated there.

He came away very soon!

His real education he plotted, planned, and worked out for himself.

Empirically he decided that the World of Events revolved around *Men*. Therefore to know *men* was to know History, Geography, Sociology, Adventure, Art, Science, Literature and Romance *so so*

That was a primal discovery.

Like Alexander Pope, he came to the conclusion that " The proper study of Mankind is Man."

Out of that line of one-two-three-four reasoning evolved the decision to study the Good and Great Men of all centuries, of all countries *on the spot*—and so to acquire an education from original sources.

Next he discovered that the way to *learn* a thing best is to *teach* it, and that the way to perfect a literary style is to put it to work. Henceforth not only would he write *Little Journeys* to the Homes of the Good and the Great—

but that while there he would set down what he found
true and what untrue, what inspired him and what failed
to inspire him, with a check-up of the chit-chat of the
biographers—and then to tell in plain, simple English
where he felt them to be weak and where strong.

That was the plan, and well did he consummate it.

Elbert Hubbard's *Little Journeys* are read by intelligent
people wherever the English Language is understood, and
they have been translated into several foreign languages.
℃ Over a period of twenty years, millions of people have
read them.

For why?

Are n't there biographies a-plenty?

Yes! But these were written by a man who knew what
he was talking about, who was intensely human, extremely
sympathetic—and unafraid. They were written out of the
Heart as well as the Mind and the Imagination of one who
had a Heart. No pedant annoys you with his profound
aphorisms, no learned Doctor struts his learning to con-
found you, or tries religiously to make it difficult for the
uninitiated to understand.

There 's not a foot-note to one of them.

But set down, word after word, page after page, is a story
told for the American temperament by an American—the
heart-story of a Great Man who succeeded or failed, or
failed or succeeded—or who did both.

The Man lives again for you.

You understand his feelings—his emotions.

When he 's in love, you 're a little bit in love yourself *.*
When the tides of life go against him, within your sub-
conscious mind you struggle, you reach out to help him.
℃ Through these *Little Journeys* you can forget yourself
and for an hour *be another man.*

Through the magic of Hubbard's sympathy you can for an hour or hours march down the centuries, the flesh and blood image of the man you are reading about.

My years in East Aurora I read all these *Little Journeys;* I read them for an hour or so each night after I went to bed and before I turned out the light.

'T was n't study—Lord, no!

Not as Hubbard wrote them!

Call them Romance, call them Adventure! Call them History! Call them *fiction*—what matters it!

I only care to know that they introduced me to an Unknown World peopled with charming beings. Those nights through my dreams and across the dark of my room, promenaded Great Poets, Great Musicians, Great Orators !

Half an hour with a *Little Journey* and the story of a Great Personality was mine forever!

You who know envy—or you who know not these delightful little Romances of Men—please envy me this experience! ❡ Turn the pages of a *Little Journey* and you feel yourself in the presence of *two* of the World Great's—the one trying to understand the other: like listening-in on a brilliant conversation ➤ ➤

Critics who are supposed to know say that *Little Journeys* are Elbert Hubbard's best bid for immortality.

Critics (like myself) who are neither too critical nor too knowable simply recognize that Hubbard performed the extraordinary service of making the Great Dead live again.

*   *   *   *   *

The year he died Hubbard himself had this to say:

" There are one hundred and seventy *Little Journeys,* each a biography in miniature, giving the brief facts in the evolution of some great man who has lived or is now living. If you know *Little Journeys,* you know all history.

" To know the Little Journeys is to be an educated person.
" I think I can forget my own part in this Little Journey
business, get out of sight, fade into the landscape, and view
the matter without prejudice. And I again repeat, Hezekiah,
that if you know *Little Journeys* you are an evolved individual ❧ ❧
" And if you are not on good, easy, friendly, chummy
terms with the men and women written of in *Little
Journeys*—no matter about your college degrees—you do
not know humanity.
" The biggest thing in the world at the last is humanity,
and to chart the tides that play through the human heart
is to understand your own nature."

* * * * *

The Fra was a successful attempt to formulate a National
Forum in print.
What 's that old quotation?—

> One man's word is no man's word,
> Both sides in Justice must be heard.

To publish a magazine that gave the leading contenders
of each side of an argument of importance a chance to
state their case before a representative audience was a
departure indeed!
Except for grammatical errors and printers' errors, the
contents of *The Fra* was not edited—and for the one who
favored an opinionated magazine, you may realize what
a treat this very beautifully printed periodical proved to
be ❧ ❧
Of course *The Fra* would not appeal to those who like their
reading matter " edited," " expurgated," " toned down "—
but then it was never intended for them!
From a printer's standpoint *The Fra* was well named,
" The most beautiful magazine in America "—with pages

almost fourteen inches tall, and wide in proportion—printed in red and black, bold type easy to read, wide margins and bold sentiments.

It was a delight to the eye of the one who appreciated the artistic, and to the eye of the one who depreciated propaganda ๛ ๛

The Fra was Elbert Hubbard's serious-minded contribution to the Intelligencia of America—and "contribution" it was too, because, though it commanded and interested a large and growing clientele, nevertheless, because of its printed excellence and high cost, it lost money (purposely) every year of the eight or so of its existence.

* * * * *

I say *The Philistine* was a whim, a gesture, an accident! Take testimony from Hubbard himself: "There was no intention at first of issuing more than one number of the pamphlet, but to get it through the mails at magazine rates we made up a little subscription list and asked that it be entered at the Post Office of East Aurora as second-class matter. The Post Master adjusted his brass-rimmed spectacles, read the pamphlet, and decided that it surely was second-class matter!"

Note—*The Philistine* was a pamphlet, and Elbert Hubbard was a pamphleteer—a lineal descendant of Dean Swift, Thomas Paine, and Ben Franklin. His *Philistine* pamphlet was "One man's opinion worth just that much and no more." ๛ ๛

His subject was *That Which Will Benefit Mankind* ๛ ๛ He waged war on Ignorance and the Tyranny of the Past.

❡ Of course his serious purpose ofttimes masqueraded behind the grotesque mask of comedy—but the knowing knew!

❡ When he wrote: *A Doctor's bill will give you a thrill that his pill never will*—it was a little sermonette—if that was your inclination or preference. If you preferred to laugh and forget it—well, go ahead and laugh!

Maybe next time you 'd *think*.

When he told how the Oberammergau Players were invited to come to East Aurora (a hoax) and the Religious Press of America got excited and stood on its head in protest, he may or may not have sought to expose the unchristian spirit of the modern church.

When he told the story about the Peanut Vendor, who put in Pop-corn and got nervous prostration because of the strain of too much business—there may or there may not have been a two-hour sermon concealed in that foolish story for the American business man.

The Philistine was an awakening of the Spirit—of the Mind.

* * * * *

Elbert Hubbard was a Pamphleteer; he was also an Epigramatist

Into a single sentence he could pack a world of meaning

Because *The Philistine* was famous for its smart sayings, a few samples are set down here for your divertisement:

It 's getting so that it is harder to find a gentleman than a genius.

It 's a wise guy who does not monkey with his destiny

Hike for Respectability, and cuddle safely under the Paisley, and it 's you for a Mollycoddle. Get weaned—in God's name, get weaned!

Hot air is all right, but see that it is well compressed before you use it.

A college degree does not lessen the length of your ears; it only conceals it.

To civilize mankind: Make marriage difficult and divorce easy

Writers seldom write the things they think. They simply write the things they think other folks think they think ✍

Now, owls are not really wise—they only look that way. The owl is a sort of college professor.

He who admits that he, himself, is a worm ought not to complain when he is trodden on.

" No man is a hero to his valet." Heroes never have valets. It is perfectly safe to say that ninety-nine men out of a hundred, in civilized countries, are opposed to war. We recognize that life is short and the night cometh. Leave us alone!

I doubt me much that the time will ever come when two pigs, meeting at the trough, will hesitate before jumping into the swill, and the bigger one say to the other, " After you, my dear Alphonse."

How sharper than a serpent's tooth is a thankless parent!

" You say," said the Reno Judge, " that your client was true to one woman? "
" Yes, your Honor; not only was he true to one woman, but more than that—he was true to five, as I can prove."

No man should be pitied except the one who wears his future for a bustle.

The greatest mistake you can make in this life is to be continually fearing you will make one.

You are what you think, and not what you think you are.

We can stop a Chinaman from coming to the United States; but we can not stop a Chinaman from going to Heaven! When we get across the River Styx, the first thing we will do is to go behind the ferry-house, and roar us like cooing doves to think that we were born red and died bald and always took the thing so seriously.

Chickens always come home to roost, which is right and natural; but when they come to cackle and crow, that is another matter.

In parsing the word, " doormat," it is well to remember that it may be either male or female.

The author who has not made warm friends and then lost them in an hour by writing things that did not agree with the preconceived ideas of those friends, has either not written well or not been read.

You must not only bury your dead, but you must forget where, smoothing every grave—else you are not safe from ghosts—ghosts, my fine sir!

You can't get away from yourself by going to a booze-bazaar ఈ ఈ

Don't sit down in the meadow and wait for the cow to back up and be milked—go after the cow.

Expectancy is an exciting interval between rounds.

Pushing to the front is very bad. You had better get in line and wait your turn, then you won't evolve a rhino spiritual rind and grow a crop of bristles up and down your back.

Women are all alike in this: they are all different, and most of them are different every hour.

To go fast, go slow.

* * * * *

" If you would be a successful publisher," said he, " get the best printing ink and the press built by Mr. Hoe that will print one million magazines a minute. The rest does n't matter. Never mind about the literature: Mr. Munsey does n't and he ought to know! "

When one reads the careful, cautious, prudent, self-conscious cash-conscious twaddle that is passed out these days for " Editorial Opinion " one longs again for the fine free matter of Elbert Hubbard's " One-man magazine "—wherein Hubbard dared to embrace an Idea and an Ideal, dared to have an opinion—and dared to *lead* subscribers instead of cringing after them!

Health, Wealth and Happiness was *his* theme.

Head, Heart and Hand, *his* approved method.

He talked and wrote perpetually for Life, for Liberty, the pursuit of Happiness—and for Freedom!

For Life in the Fullest, and Here and Now!

For the widest possible Liberty for Individual Genius;

For Happiness through Self-realization!

For Freedom from the festishes of the Past!

And for Fraternity: the Brotherhood of Man!

This is the Life! I don't know of anybody I'd trade iobs with!

"Men who Learn
to Write before they
have anything to say
have No Style ⸴
they merely have
Mannerisms"

The Writer

CERTAIN visitor at the Roycroft once asked Ali Baba questions as to the alleged greatness of a certain author. " Is he really a great writer? " " Is he? " said Baba in scorn. " Why, he can write things so smart that you nor he, nor nobody, can make head or tail out of it." That was Hubbard's little joke on himself. Of a certainty his style was clear, understandable—even when he was using manufactured and unpronounceable words, his *meaning* was clear! On occasion he was most direct by being indirect.

He left the interpretation to the intelligence of the reader, and so paid the reader a compliment—and acquired a partner

All good writing is a partnership between the writer and the reader. Yet he has said, " Good writing never comes from the effort to be clear or forceful or elegant. Clear to whom, forsooth? And as for force, it has no more place in writing than has speed! Let the writer have a clear conception, then express it so that at the moment it is clear to his other self—that self that looks over the shoulder of every man."

Be that so or be it not so, the fact remains his writings were clear and forceful to a variety of intelligences. Not one grade of intellect read Hubbard, but many grades

and all found companionship and comfort in his stuff ✖
That was the amazing fact.

Never was there a writer with a more cosmopolitan reading
public ✖ ✖

When I think back, and remember a score of totally different individuals, high and low, rich and poor, educated
and uneducated, who called him " brother "—I wonder!

❡ He thought little of the writer who was a writer and
nothing more!

"To make a business of an art is to degrade it. Letters should
not be a profession in itself. Literature should be a product
of the ripened mind, the mind which knows the world of
men and which has grappled with earth's problems."

" Have a trade or a profession and make literature a side-
show. If the side-show becomes more money-making than
the circus, you can abandon the circus."

Like all epigrammatic utterances that's a half truth—
the other half is to put all your eggs in one basket and then
watch the basket!

Not to write until one had accumulated sufficient experiences to draw on would be to deprive the world of some
first-class literature. * * * Did n't Will Shakespeare
write one or two things pretty well in his youth—and did n't
Stevie Crane (one of Hubbard's particular heroes) write
The Red Badge of Courage, the greatest war story ever
told, in his early twenties?

Ah, but let 's agree that such are the exceptions that prove
the rule! So let it stand—one writes best when he writes
from the accumulation of his own experience.

Certainly Hubbard did. He was thirty-nine the year he
started *The Philistine,* and a business success as this world
judges success; so it follows naturally that the work that

the world will remember was but a by-product of his life
and living—or was it?

Was it that he did not start to live until he was forty?
❡ These complex problems are too difficult for settlement
here ✺ ✺

" How did I learn to write? Hush, Hezekiah! Don't be
silly. I learned to write by writing. The Cadmean game is
a great one: just the arrangement of twenty-six letters
which compose the alphabet, and the juggling of punctu-
ation marks and there you are.

" The great writer is he who eliminates self-consciousness
and writes himself down as he is!

" The recipe for good writing is this: Write as you feel,
but be sure you feel right.

" And even though the author has lived and experienced,
and enjoyed and suffered, he must serve his apprenticeship
at the writing trade, otherwise he can not write save for
the surprise, delectation, divertisement and ravishment of
his relatives."

* * * * *

Many people have asked, " How in the world did this man
write so much? What was his method in writing? What
was his system, his habit? "

There was no set schedule for Hubbard's writing. He wrote
whenever he felt like it. That meant at all sorts of queer
times in all sorts of strange places. He 'd interrupt his own
conversation to make a note or write an epigram. Usually
it was not the " note " he jotted down but the phrase
itself. Much of his copy did not require correction.

Always he carried a supply of " canary yellow " in his
pockets; always his pockets were stocked with stubs of
lead pencils. Actually he did not interrupt himself to write,
rather it was an interruption when he was not writing ✺

Writing was his favorite pastime, diversion and occupation. Out on a walk when a thought came he 'd rest by the side of the road and write steadily for five minutes. Horseback riding, he 'd climb down from his horse, prop his paper against the saddle-top and make a memorandum. Such was his power of concentration he could and did write steadily on trains—in Pullmans and in day-coaches—hour after hour. That, to a certain extent, explained why his copy always seemed so fresh and new. Most of it was inspirational.

❡ Victor Hugo and Jack London, for example, wrote so many hours each day, each and every day, regular hours. Each locked himself up in a room and went to it.

Interruptions were out of order.

Not so with Hubbard: to him interruptions were a legitimate part of the day's work.

Abruptly he would walk away from a group at the fire place of the Inn, and retire to his little study off the main room and write steadily for any hour—" putting salt on the tail of an Idea." I have known him to write before eight a. m. and after ten p. m. and at all hours in between.

He spent full days at the Three Mile Camp turning out *Little Journeys*—and I have seen him take advantage of a half hour's rest between trains in a railroad station, take out his pencil and go to work. Always he wrote on the same " canary yellow " and always with a lead pencil.

In one particular Hubbard had the special advantage of his contemporaries: no editor ever pawed over or blue-penciled his stuff.

He was his own editor and his own publisher.

Imagine that!

Imagine the *freedom!*

This writer printed what he wanted to print—all he wanted

to print—and no one to say him " nay," no one to order
him to " please cut out a thousand words."
No one to buy an article from him by the yard!
No one to expurgate or annoy!
Just recently William Griffith, sometime editor of *Current
Opinion* magazine, told me a story about Oscar Wilde to
illustrate this point: An editor returned an article to Wilde
with the verdict that he " liked it "—but at the same time
he asked the author to " please cut two thousand words
out of the manuscript so that it will fit the allotted space."
❦ Wilde's retort was more curt than curteous: " Who am
I to mutilate a masterpiece! "
That which makes Hubbard himself, and which is a delight
to the reader was the very stuff that a high-powered editor
would have omitted. That daring which was a surprise and
joy, would have shocked and made timorous any bespecta-
cled editor who ever drew down a salary and the Big Boss'
condemnation ❧ ❧
Hubbard, like Fuzzy Wuzzy, did n't care a damn!
He did not have to.
That made for *style* in his writing.
That and his brains and his erudition and his humor
and his infinite scope in subjects and sympathy.
When he wished to write a political editorial he wrote it
like this:
" The Bull Moose is all right till milking time comes round."
When he wished to exchange compliments with a neighbor
this was the method:
" On my barn-door I found written in chalk the word
' rascal.' Evidently some gentleman had called and having
forgotten his card case left his name! "
When he wished to answer a critic he observed:

" Once a flea lived on a lion and boasted, ' I have in me
the blood of the King of Beasts.' "

That 's getting to them by the right oblique, is it not,
Terese? All his self-answered questions he addressed
to " Terese," or " Clotilde "—two imaginary charmers—
when he did n't bring the discussion to an abrupt close
with that immortal phrase of Chimmie Fadden the Bowery
Boy—" Wot t' ell! "

'T is said he used more words than Shakespeare—but what
astounds me is that Shakespeare's vocabulary is that of
a learned, scholarly man, a playwright, an actor, a country-
man—while Hubbard's choice of words runs the gamut
of all classes of society, (up and down), of all professions,
of all subjects, of all specialties.

There was no Farthest North or Farthest South to his
interests! He discussed everything under the Sun, Horatio,
—with a flow of words that would have done honor to a
savant on the subject!

When no proper word was available he invented one ✺
His manufactured expressions carry the meaning in a
most smile-provoking fashion.

Off hand I think of one: Said he, " I smole a smile."

And another: a " gabbyjack "—an over zealous talker ✺
And another: " kabojolism "—meant to credit to some one
something that person did not say, but wished he had.
❡ Along this same line a " cabthought" was the bright
thing you thought of on your way home from the party
—the thing you neglected to say.

The prize " kabojolism" of all time was the " Mouse-trap "
quotation which reads: " If a man preach a better sermon,
write a better book, make a better mouse-trap than his
neighbor...," etc.

Elbert Hubbard wrote that, and no one else wrote it—but

he practised " kabojolism " and credited it to Ralph Waldo
Emerson. Eventually when some learned cuss failed to
find it in Emerson's writings, he raised the question *so*
Then the discussion started that will not be stilled.

Hubbard refused to take the matter seriously. "What
difference—that mouse-trap guff is n't true anyway. The
world will never make a path to your door unless you
advertise. It may also be well to have an automobile meet
all trains and a free lunch served on the front porch! "

* * * * *

I have said that Elbert Hubbard was never required to
submit his stuff to an editor. There were three exceptions
to that statement. At the beginning of his career the
editors sneered and scoffed and pooh poohed and rejected,
because he was something different. They did n't understand what he was driving at! I 've heard him say, " I 've
received enough rejection slips to paper a bathroom."
❡ After success crowned him the editors were glad to
take what they could get and no suggestions made and
no questions asked. There were always more literary orders
on hand than he could fill. Rather, these latter-day editors
" submitted " to him!

The third exception was John T. Hoyle.

For a round dozen years, Hoyle was the Man-behind-the-
scenes. He was the " technical editor " for the three Roycroft publications: *The Philistine, The Fra,* and *Little
Journeys*—or whatever you care to call him. Hubbard
leaned on him, depended on him, had faith in him. Hoyle
was the Human Encyclopedia. He knew everything: and
what he did n't know he knew how to find out.

Hubbard was a rapid, voluminous writer. Most of his
copy was written in lead pencil, with interlines, and marginal notes, corrected and re-corrected. Much of it was

turned over to Hoyle as-is, to be prepared for the press. Many's the time Hubbard never saw his stuff from the time he released the manuscript until the printed page was placed in his hands.

To follow after Hubbard, to understand every historical reference, to grasp his thought and his meaning perfectly, to know exactly when he was serious and when he was joking, to sense the odd manner in which certain words were to be spelled or misspelled, required a fine feeling of fellowship, and extra-special brains. (To wit: " I will arise," said the famished Prodigal, " and go to my fodder.") ∾ Hoyle had both, together with devotion to the task. He was not one of the most conspicuous members at the Roycroft, but he was one of the most necessary.

He abominated an error, and there were few of them—few! 'T was a job for a smart and learned and a loyal man— and I am glad for the opportunity to pay him this tribute. Where and how did Hubbard acquire his " style? "

My guess is this: Victor Hugo for the short sentences, Shakespeare for the use of words, and the Bible for clarity. ❡ Hubbard knew the Bible as he knew his right hand ∾ The first book the Roycrofters ever printed was Solomon's *Song of Songs*. Later they printed the *Book of Job,* and the *Book of Ecclesiastes*.

That showed his leanings.

The influence of the Bible was clear in his writings: " Arise and go thee hence," " A little while and another little while," " Thus endeth the first lesson."

There's no mistaking the analogy.

He was an omniverous but a discriminating reader, and the Bible was surely not the least of his books, and he approached it with reverence particularly because of its literary content.

While the influence of Shakespeare and Hugo and the Bible are reflected in his style, that does not explain the half of it.

His effects were unique, peculiar, different.

His descent from the sublime to the ridiculous, his flight from the ridiculous to the sublime, between the beginning and the ending of a sentence was essentially Hubbard *

The sureness of his touch, the authority he gave a statement, his confidence, his picturesqueness, his learning, his references, his clearness, his quips and quirks, his satires and jibes, his odd endings and unusual words, his inspiration and sympathy—all tend to make a composite man that is like no other in the writing world.

Hubbard is read *five* times as much today as he was ten years ago—the year he died. That is the true test of greatness. I venture ten years hence his readers again will have multiplied themselves by ten!

That's Progress—and the World doth progress.

A little while and another little while and perhaps the Thought of the Times will have caught up with him *

As it is he is still the shining leader.

He was no perpetrator of sweet nothings to idle away a Summer Afternoon in a hammock—no author of Best Sellers that live for an hour and die the death forever.

He struck out and strove for permanency.

There's the temptation to attempt to value, to review some dozen or more of his hundred books, but I desist when I remember that he recommended the reading of his " amusing rot " (as he styled it) " for those over thirty —and under." And if that's a hint—well, like the primrose by the river brim, it is nothing more.

* * * * *

When I think of literary praise for Hubbard, I yield to

Stephen Crane—dear, lovable, explosive Stevie! I recall
the surprise note he sent to East Aurora from far-away
England, after perusing an inspired Hubbard paragraph:
" Your flowers on the water—Good God, that is magnificent!—a thing that I felt in the roots of my hair. Hell and
Blazes, but I do envy you that paragraph! * * * The
book strengthened me and uplifted me."

A SEARCHER AFTER TRUTH

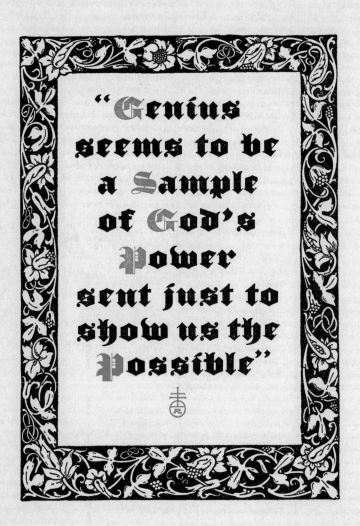

"Genius seems to be a Sample of God's Power sent just to show us the Possible"

Specimens of Hubbard's "Style"

Here follow some excerpts from Hubbard:

THE TITANIC

It is a night of a thousand stars. The date, Sunday, April
Fourteenth, Nineteen Hundred Twelve.
The time, eleven-twenty p. m.
The place, off Cape Race—that Cemetery of the Sea ❧
Suddenly a silence comes—the engines have stopped—
the great iron heart of the ship has ceased to beat.
Such a silence is always ominous to those who go down
to the sea in ships.
" The engines have stopped! "
Eyes peer; ears listen; startled minds wait!
A half-minute goes by.
Then the great ship groans, as her keel grates and grinds.
She reels, rocks, struggles as if to free herself from a Titanic
grasp, and as she rights herself, people standing lose their
center of gravity.
Not a shock—only about the same sensation that one
feels when the ferryboat slides into her landing-slip, with
a somewhat hasty hand at the wheel.
On board the ferry we know what has happened—here we
do not ❧ ❧
" An iceberg! " some one cries.
The word is passed along.
" Only an iceberg! Barely grated it—side-swiped it—that
is all! Ah, ha! "
The few on deck, and some of those in cabins peering out
of portholes, see a great white mass go gliding by.
A shower of broken ice has covered the decks. Passengers
pick up specimens " for souvenirs to carry home," they
laughingly say.
Five minutes pass—the engines start again—but only for
an instant.

Again the steam is shut off. Then the siren-whistles cleave and saw the frosty air.

Silence and the sirens! Alarm, but no tumult—but why blow the whistles when there is no fog!

The cold is piercing. Some who have come up on deck return to their cabins for wraps and overcoats.

The men laugh—and a few nervously smoke.

It is a cold, clear night of stars. There is no moon. The sea is smooth as a Summer pond.

The great towering iceberg that loomed above the topmost mast has done its work, gone on, disappeared, piloted by its partners, the darkness and the night.

" There was no iceberg—you only imagined it," a man declares ๑๑ ๑๑

" Go back to bed—there is no danger—this ship can not sink anyway! " says the Managing Director of the Company.

❧ In a lull of the screaming siren, a hoarse voice is heard calling through a megaphone from the bridge—" Man the lifeboats! Women and children first! ! "

" It sounds just like a play," says Henry Harris to Major Butt ๑๑ ๑๑

Stewards and waiters are giving out life-preservers and showing passengers how to put them on.

There is laughter—a little hysteric. " I want my clothes made to order," a woman protests. " An outrageous fit! Give me a man's size! "

The order of the Captain on the bridge is repeated by other officers—" Man the lifeboats! Women and children first ! ! "

" It 's a boat drill—that 's all! "

" A precautionary measure—we 'll be going ahead soon," says George Widener to his wife, in reassuring tones as he holds her hand.

Women are loath to get into the boats. Officers, not over-gently, seize them, and half lift and push them in. Children, crying, and some half asleep, are passed over into the boats.

❧ Mother arms reach out and take the little ones. Parent-age and ownership are lost sight of.

Some boats are only half filled, so slow are the women to believe that rescue is necessary.

The boats are lowered, awkwardly, for there has never been a boat drill, and assignments are being made haphazard ∾ ∾

A sudden little tilt of the deck hastens the proceeding. The bows of the ship are settling—there is a very perceptible list to starboard.

An Englishman, tired and blasé, comes out of the smoking-room, having just ceased a card game. He very deliberately approaches an officer who is loading women and children into a lifeboat.

The globe-trotting Briton is filling his pipe. " I si, orficer, you know; what seems to be the matter with this bloomin' craft, you know? "

" Fool," roars the officer, " the ship is sinking! "

" Well," says the Englishman, as he strikes a match on the rail, " Well, you know, if she is sinking, just let 'er down a little easy, you know."

John Jacob Astor half forces his wife into the boat. She submits, but much against her will. He climbs over and takes a seat beside her in the lifeboat. It is a ruse to get her in—he kisses her tenderly—stands up, steps lightly out and gives his place to a woman.

" Lower away! " calls the officer.

" Wait—here is a boy—his mother is in there! "

" Lower away! " calls the officer—" there is no more room."

Colonel Astor steps back. George Widener tosses him a woman's hat, picked up from the deck. Colonel Astor jams the hat on the boy's head, takes the lad up in his arms, runs to the rail and calls, " You won't leave this little girl, will you? "

" Drop her into the boat," shouts the officer. The child drops into friendly hands as the boat is lowered.

Astor turns to Widener and laughingly says, " Well, we put one over on 'em that time."

" I 'll meet you in New York," calls Colonel Astor to his wife as the boat pulls off. He lights a cigarette and passes the silver case and a match box along to the other men ∾

A man runs back to his cabin to get a box of money and jewels. The box is worth three hundred thousand dollars.

The man changes his mind and gets three oranges and gives one orange each to three children as they are lifted into safety ᔭ ᔭ

As a lifeboat is being lowered, Mr. and Mrs. Isador Straus come running with arms full of blankets, brought from their stateroom. They throw the bedding to the people in the boat.

"Help that woman in!" shouts an officer. Two sailors seize Mrs. Straus. She struggles, frees herself, and proudly says, "Not I—I will not leave my husband." Mr. Straus insists, quietly and gently, that she shall go. He will follow later. But Mrs. Straus is firm. "All these years we have traveled together, and shall we part now? No, our fate is one." She smiles a quiet smile, and pushes aside the hand of Major Butt, who has ordered the sailors to leave her alone. "We will help you—Mr. Straus and I—come! It is the law of the sea—women and children first—come!" said Major Butt.

"No, Major; you do not understand. I remain with my husband—we are one, no matter what comes—you do not understand!"

"See" she cried as if to change the subject, "there is a woman getting in the lifeboat with her baby; she has no wraps!"

Mrs. Straus tears off her fur-lined robe and places it tenderly around the woman and the innocently sleeping babe ᔭ

William T. Stead, grim, hatless, with furrowed face, stands with an iron bar in hand as a lifeboat is lowered. "Those men in the steerage, I fear, will make a rush—they will swamp the boats."

Major Butt draws his revolver. He looks toward the crowded steerage. Then he puts his revolver back into his pocket, smiles, "No, they know we will save their women and children as quickly as we will our own."

Mr. Stead tosses the iron bar into the sea.

He goes to the people crowding the afterdeck. They speak a polyglot language. They cry, they pray, they supplicate, they kiss each other in frenzied grief.

John B. Thayer, George Widener, Henry Harris, Benjamin

Guggenheim, Charles B. Hays, Mr. and Mrs. Straus, move among these people, talk to them and try to reassure them ✒ ✒

There are other women besides Mrs. Straus who will not leave their husbands. These women clasp each other's hands. They smile—they understand!

Mr. Guggenheim and his secretary are in full dress. " If we are going to call on Neptune, we will go dressed as gentlemen," they laughingly say.

The ship is slowly settling by the head.

The forward deck is below the water.

The decks are at a vicious angle.

The icy waters are full of struggling people.

Those still on the ship climb up from deck to deck.

The dark waters follow them, angry, jealous, savage, relentless ✒ ✒

The decks are almost perpendicular. The people hang by the rails.

A terrific explosion occurs—the ship's boilers have burst ✒

The last lights go out.

The great iron monster slips, slides, gently slides, surely, down, down, down into the sea.

Where once the great ship proudly floated, there is now a mass of wreckage, the dead, the dying, and the great black all-enfolding night.

Overhead, the thousand stars shine with a brightness unaccustomed ✒ ✒

* * * * *

The Strauses, Stead, Astor, Butt, Harris, Thayer, Widener, Guggenheim, Hays—I thought I knew you, just because I had seen you, realized somewhat of your able qualities, looked into your eyes and pressed your hands, but I did not guess your greatness.

You are now beyond the reach of praise—flattery touches you not—words for you are vain.

Medals for heroism—how cheap the gilt, how paltry the pewter! ✒ ✒

You are beyond our praise or blame ✒ We reach out,

we do not touch you. We call, but you do not hear.
Words unkind, ill-considered, were sometimes flung at you,
Colonel Astor, in your lifetime. We admit your handicap
of wealth—perhaps pity you for the accident of birth—
but we congratulate you that as your mouth was stopped
with the brine of the sea, so you stopped the mouths of
the carpers and critics with the dust of the tomb. If they
think unkindly of you now, be he priest or plebeian, let
it be with finger to his lips, and a look of shame into his
own dark heart.

Also, shall we not write a postscript to that booklet on
cigarettes?

Charles M. Hays—you who made life safe for travelers
on shore, yet you were caught in a sea-trap, which had
you been manager of that Transatlantic Line, would never
have been set, baited as it was with human lives.

You placed safety above speed. You fastened your faith
to utilities, not futilities. You and John B. Thayer would
have had a searchlight and used it in the danger-zone, so
as to have located an iceberg five miles away. You would
have filled the space occupied by that silly plunge-bath
(how ironic the thing) with a hundred collapsible boats,
and nests of dories.

You, Hays and Thayer, believed in other men—you trusted
them—this time they failed you ๑ We pity them, not
you ๑ ๑

And Mr. and Mrs. Straus, I envy you that legacy of
love and loyalty left to your children and grandchildren.
The calm courage that was yours all your long and useful
career was your possession in death. You knew how to
do three great things—you knew how to live, how to love,
and how to die.

Archie Butt, the gloss and glitter on your spangled uniform
were pure gold. I always suspected it.

You tucked the ladies into the lifeboats, as if they were
going for an automobile ride. " Give my regards to the
folks at home! " you gaily called as you lifted your hat
and stepped back on the doomed deck. You died the gallant
gentleman that you were. You helped preserve the old

English tradition, " Women and children first." All America
is proud of you.

Guggenheim, Widener and Harris, you were unfortunate
in life having more money than we had. That is why we
wrote things about you, and printed them in black and
red. If you were sports, you were game to the last, cheerful
losers, and all such are winners.

As you souls play hide-and-seek with sirens and dance
with the naiades, you have lost interest in us. But our hearts
are with you still. You showed us how death and danger
put all on a parity. The women in the steerage were your
sisters—the men your brothers; and on the tablets of love
and memory we have 'graved your names.

William T. Stead, you were a writer, a thinker, a speaker,
a doer of the word. You proved your case; sealed the brief
with your heart's blood; and as your bearded face looked
in admiration for the last time up at the twinkling, shining
stars, God in pardonable pride said to Gabriel, " Here comes
a man! "

And so all you I knew, and all that thousand and half a
thousand more, I did not know, passed out of this earth-
life into the Unknown upon the unforgetting tide. You
were sacrificed to the greedy Goddess of Luxury and her
consort the Demon of Speed.

Was it worth the while? Who shall say? The great lessons
of life are learned only in blood and tears. Fate decreed
that you should die for us. Happily, the world has passed
forever from a time when it feels a sorrow for the dead.
The dead are at rest, their work is ended, they have drunk
of the waters of Lethe, and these are rocked in the cradle
of the deep. We kiss our hands to them and cry, " Hail
and Farewell—until we meet again! "

But for the living who wait for a footstep that will never
come, and all those who listen for a voice that will never
more be heard, our hearts go out in tenderness, love and
sympathy ✍ ✍

These dead have not lived and died in vain. They have
brought us all a little nearer together—we think better
of our kind.

One thing sure, there are just two respectable ways to die.
One is of old age, and the other is by accident.

All disease is indecent.

Suicide is atrocious.

But to pass out as did Mr. and Mrs. Isador Straus is glorious. Few have such a privilege. Happy lovers, both. In
life they were never separated, and in death they are not
divided ✒ ✒

INITIATIVE

The world bestows its big prizes, both in money and honors,
for but one thing.

And that is Initiative.

What is Initiative?

I 'll tell you: It is doing the right thing without being told.

❡ But next to doing the thing without being told is to do
it when you are told once. That is to say, carry the Message
to Garcia: those who can carry a message get high honors,
but their pay is not always in proportion.

Next, there are those who never do a thing until they are
told twice: such get no honors and small pay.

Next, there are those who do the right thing only when
necessity kicks them from behind, and these get indifference
instead of honors, and a pittance for pay. This kind spends
most of its time polishing a bench with a hard-luck story.

❡ Then, still lower down in the scale than this, we have
the fellow who will not do the right thing even when some
one goes along to show him how and stays to see that he
does it: he is always out of a job, and receives the contempt
he deserves, unless he happens to have a rich Pa, in which
case Destiny patiently awaits around the corner with a
stuffed club.

To which class do you belong?

THE ELK'S CREED

I'm not a jiner, but if I ever jine the jiners I will begin with the Elks—and probably end there. Without any special written code or creed the Elks stand for a certain standard of intellect and ethics. The man with an elk's tooth on his watch chain, or the antlers in his buttonhole, has no quarrel with God. He accepts life, and finds it good. He may not be so very wise, nor so very good, but since he knows he is not wise, and is ready to admit he is not so very good, he is wiser than he knows and better than he will acknowledge ❧ ❧

The true Elk does not condemn, disparage nor rip reputations up the back. Realizing his own limitations, he is lenient in his judgment toward those who have been tempted by fate beyond their power to resist. This quality of mercy, I have noticed, is strongly implanted in the Elk nature. Your Elk never weeps over his own troubles, but for the stricken souls of earth his tears of pity are near the surface. The Elk loves children, respects old age, and so far as I have seen does n't incline especially toward indifference to feminine charms. In many instances I have imagined the Elk revealed a just appreciation of the elevated spheroid. Yet in all your life you never saw one of those horny sons of Elkdom going off alone and cutting into the grape— irrigation is all in the line of good fellowship. And his worst fault lies right here—in this matter of conviviality; he sometimes slightly overdoes it.

But I believe this will hold: no little pismire apology for a man ever joined the Elks—he would not feel at home among them. To be an Elk you must have faith in other men, faith in yourself, and faith in the Universe.

The Elks all look alike, and are all of one age. Just what that age is, I have not yet made out, but it lies somewhere between thirty and fifty. No Elk ever is over fifty, no matter how long he has lived, and none weigh over two hundred pounds. They all have the joyous, boyish, bubbling heart of youth, and no whiskers. Lilacs are out of their line, and Galways are tabu.

I never saw an Elk who was very rich, excepting in kindness and good cheer, nor did I ever see one circumnavigating on his uppers. They all have all the money they need, even if not all they want. They make money, and they spend it, and the more they spend the more they seem to make. "Keep the change," is a remark the Elk always has in electrotype.

I have been occasionally pained by hearing Elks relate stories that were slightly gamboge—tinted on the edges—but although these tales of persiflage had a Neufchatel flavor, yet there was always enough Attic salt supplied to redeem the mass from mortifying microbes.

The Elk is not troubled about saving his soul—in fact, he is not troubled about anything. Perhaps that is his one distinguishing feature—he does not worry, nor shake the red rag of wordy theological warfare ✒ He believes that everything is all right—or nearly so—and that his task is to do his work, and not bother other folks any more than he has to. When Ali Baba said, "Blessed is that man who does not bellyache," he had a sixteen-pronged antlered Elk in mind.

An Elk takes his medicine—sometimes with a wry face—but he always takes his medicine. Often he overcomes temptation by succumbing to it; and if he trips and falls he is up and joins in the laugh of the bystanders. You can not down a man who can laugh at himself. The Elk stays right in the game; I never heard of one retiring from business; when death calls for an Elk, the Elk is apt first to sell him a bill of goods and then they shake the dice to see who shall pay Charon's toll. The Elk does not seek to pry into the future, for he realizes perfectly well that if he waits, he 'll know all about it. And for a similar reason he does not chase after women, for he knows that if he does n't women will chase after him.

And they do.

There seems to be little danger that this Fraternity will evolve into a religion. Most religious people take their religion seriously, but the Elk takes his with seltzer. He knows that truth is a point of view, that all is relative, that

nothing is final nor absolute, nor can it be in a world where
nothing is permanent but change. So the Elk's religion is
now and here; to partake of all good things in moderation;
to give out love and kindness because these things come
back; and to supply a scrap only to the man who repeatedly
asks for it, and will accept nothing else—this as a matter
of accommodation. To do good is the first prong in an Elk's
creed. And he realizes, being wise, that the best way to
benefit yourself is to benefit others.

As for myself, I am strictly on the hose-cart, so I do not
affiliate very closely with the boys, but if I were flying light
and wanted to borrow ten or twenty maybe, I'd tackle
the first Elk I met, without apology or explanation. And
my needs would be to him a command, for he is not clannish
and he knows no higher joy than to give the other fellow
a lift ♥ ♥

And all these things I have here recorded are set down as
a matter of truth, forgetting the fact that once at Flint,
Michigan, I suffered the deep humiliation of being arrested
by the Elks, and fined two seventy-five for advertising
Quaker Oats without a license.

nothing is final; nor absolute; not can it be in a world where nothing is permanent; but change. So the Kib is enjoined to now and how; to be tender of all good things in moderation; to give out love and kindness because the—; things come is—; and to supply a scrap only to the man who honestly asks for it—and will accept nothing else—unless a matter of accommodation. To do good to the first person on Kib's queer. And for realizes, being none, that the best way—to be its—; is to be right there.

As for myself, I am already on the down-hill; so I do not shrink very close—so with the boys, but if I love those left who wanted to become Fine Twenty; nay, I'd rather that if all the Fine—they suppose others of cabin—with you, and I know no higher joy than to live the other fellow—

And all these things I too have reported are set down as a matter of truth together the fact that once at Fin1, while Michigan, I mustered the deep humiliation of being arrested by the Feds, and shot two seventy-five for advertising Quaker Oats without a license.

S M A C K :
A crude, rude, vulgar and unsatisfactory substitute for a kiss

SMACK;
A crude, rude, vulgar and unsatisfactory substitute for a kiss

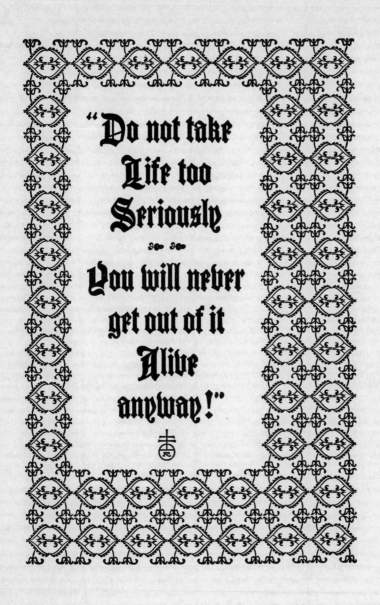

"Do not take
Life too
Seriously

You will never
get out of it
Alive
anyway!"

The Stories He Told

IS humor was strictly bucolic ✎ ✎ I cheerfully admit that some of his Jokes, Yarns, Stories, were rude, crude, farm-hand stuff—but then he was no delicatessen himself. Said he, " There are only six original stories in the world—and four of these are unfit for ladies' ears." Even so, there was little in his Humor to bring the blush of shame to the cheek of any happy, healthy normal individual, and this of course does not include the purists, for has it not been very well said that, " To the pure all things are impure? "

Besides this is a coarse world—more's the pity—and the psychologists are inclined to agree with what the physiologists know, that a little roughage in the mental food is just as good for man as a little roughage in the physical food: it aids digestion.

Keep in mind that his was an ultra-sophisticated adult audience! The others were not wanted, or at least not welcomed until they knew how to " take " the Hot Stuff.

❡ I have heard him say: " I never met an individual who seriously found offense in anything printed in *The Philistine.* Always it was all right for *him*—it was the Other Fellow he feared would be shocked."

More than once Hubbard set out deliberately to razzle-dazzle the uninitiated, to make them think, to react, to stimulate them—because most of us are so unearthly self-satisfied, smug, and sanctimonious—in public. So many subjects are so sacrosanct—in public.

Surely he secured his effects, yet he testifies, " I never use profanity except in print." And that was true, and it was equally true he never told smutty stories under cover, in private, behind doors—nor did he specialize in pornographic or psycho-sexual literatoor of " extraordinary sexappeal "—which is being done—I say which is being done! His worst as well as his best was always in full view for the carping critics to see and settle on: and one or two obnoxious and inconsequential individuals constituted themselves selfappointed censors to see that he held to the straight and narrow path (in print) which he did not do—not always.

⁋ After a lapse of years—and taking into consideration the progress the world has made since the World War in achieving personal freedom—his stories seem harmless enough ๑ ๑

By comparisons with some stuff which is current his offerings seem to be contributions from the Age of Innocence.

⁋ For my own divertisement and amusement I have gone through twenty years of *Philistines* and I can find but two stories that seem to be over the line, and that might better be left unprinted—but then I recognize that *What is Humor* is a matter of personal choice and opinion. For instance, *I* can't find the Jokes in the London *Punch*.

Or perhaps it is that I work at a disadvantage in knowing the play-boy spirit in which these absurdities and exuberances were written.

Further, I hold no license to pass judgment. Nor have I the inclination, for I well remember he never felt apologetic, and that he had a special contempt for the man who left the room when somebody said " Pooh," because he marked that man for the hypocrite he was.

Here then are fair samples of what he called *Humor* culled
and collected from a large number of *Philistines* and adult
America may judge for itself whether or not Elbert Hubbard
was the " shocking individual " that the professional Hell-
Dodgers made him out to be!
These excerpts are " run of the mill "—neither better
nor worse, funnier nor duller than the average. You shall
be the judge.

The subject was literature, but it got switched off on sur-
gery because Bloxom said that Clangingharp had appen-
dicitis and was to be tabled.
" It 's queer," said Bloxom, " It 's dam queer that there
has never been a single great surgeon among Homeopath-
ists! " and he knocked the ashes from his cigarette and
looked off wonderingly into space.
" How about Klue? " asked Bigelow.
" Oh, yes, I know, but you can't really call him a great
surgeon," answered Bloxom, still gazing into space ᴼ⊕ ᴼ⊕
" Or Chew! "
" Oh, Chew's reputation is merely local! "
" Or Glue! "
" Eh? " and Bloxom looked around, and it then came over
him that Bigelow was calling up from the yeasty deep of
his inner consciousness a list of eminent surgeons. He turned
red as a rooster's wattle and tried hard to laugh.
" One check," said Hendrick to the waiter, and the bill
was shoved at Bloxom to pay. He winced and protested,
but we told him if he did not pay Noxon would write the
whole story up in the *Journalis* giving full particulars,
with times and places. And he paid.

Some children in Rochester were selling lemonade for the
benefit of the Fresh Air Fund. There were two kinds—
five cents and three cents a glass. Asked why the difference,
they said they had reduced the price of one " because the
puppy fell into it."

Speaking of " Q " reminds me of a story of Ike Bromley.

One evening Ike was at a billiard saloon, accompanied by a friend. An accomplished amateur was displaying marvelous skill at the game. At Ike's request the friend introduced him to the player. " Mr. Squat," said Ike, " really you are one of the most remarkable players I have ever met." ᔓ "Scott," said the player and the friend, simultaneously. "No," said Ike gravely and firmly, "a man who can play billiards like that must spell his name with a q."

At a swell and crush affair in Buffalo a short time ago the cake was being passed by Afric's dusky sons. A certain sweet young lady, deeply engaged in conversation with a nice young man, glancing over the plate, said, " I like the chocolate best—oh, yes, here 's a piece! " But someway it failed to come. She wriggled it slightly—it surely was stuck—she wriggled it again. And then Eph said, " Beg yo' pahdon, Miss, but dat 's mah thumb! "

A certain doctor in East Aurora has achieved a tuppence worth of fame as an obstetrician. When a farmer calls him on one of these delicate events and fails to pay, the doctor refers in the matter as a case of R. F. D.

Here is a vaudeville crack not used on the Orpheum Circuit: It seems that a monologist was annoyed by a baby in the audience crying. It was a little bit of a baby, but it made a big row. Finally, the " act " stood it as long as he could and then addressed the mother thus:
" Madam, can't you keep that baby quiet? "
" No, I can't! "
" Well, why can't you? "
" Because my dress is buttoned behind."
And the trap-drummer crashed the cymbals just once ᔓ

In California I went out camping for a few days. There was a preacher with us in the party.
On Sunday the dominie declined to fish, and moreover, gently admonished the rest of us for so doing.
And what do you suppose he did while we were fishing?
¶ I 'll tell you, Terese: he went out and caught grasshoppers for bait, so he could fish on Monday.

A colored gentleman, on being asked why he did not get a job and go to work, replied:
" Ah go to work? No, indeedy, chile; if I done went to work and made money, my mudder-in-law would come foh shuh and eat up all I could earn! "
" Well, if you don't work, some one must feed you. Who do you live with? "
" Me? Why, I lives wid my mudder-in-law! "

Charles Dudley Warner was once talking informally to the students of the Art League in New York. His theme was " Refinement," and it goes without saying that he carried his auditors with him on and up.
" And how may one best attain to this ideal of refinement? " asked one young man.
Mr. Warner stroked his whiskers very earnestly for a space, but this was the utmost he could find of encouragement:
" A very good way is to inherit it."
Let us hope the young man did not go away sorrowful ❧

" You have a model husband," said the lady who was congratulating the bride.
The next day the bride bethought her to look up the word " model " in the dictionary, and this is what she found:
Model: A small imitation of the real thing.

Richard Mansfield is such a stickler for the poetic unities in art, that when he plays Othello he blacks his cosmos from Land's End to John O' Groats.

Ella Wheeler Wilcox says that the climate of New England is not favorable to love-making. Oh, I don't know about that! Why, once in Boston—but never mind, you would n't believe it, anyway.

" I say," said the little old lady with the high-pitched voice, as the Jerk-water slowed down at Grigsby Station. " I say, what is all this fuss about educatin' boys to be civil engineers; the thing this ere country really needs is a few civil conductors and less sassy brakemen."

" He also acts, I believe? " said a woman to Whistler of
an all-round genius—and Whistler replied: " Madam, he
does nothing else."

> One can bear grief alone,
> But it takes two to be glad.

That is the way I wrote it. I thought it was pretty fairish
and so I flashed it on Ali Baba. It was a rainy day and we
were in the barn, picking the sprouts off of potatoes.
The first time I passed it out, the ol' man said nothing,
and so I tried it again. I guess Ali was doing what he calls
thinking, for this time he said," Hell! there 's nothin' in
it—just sounds well. Literature is deceivin' folks into the
idea that you are smart. How 're these:

> One can be good alone,
> But it takes two to be bad.
> One can be bad alone,
> But it takes two to be good.
> One can get an education alone,
> But it takes two to be wise.
> One can be reckless alone,
> But two should be careful.

Beatrice Barebax will in this department answer all Questions concerning abnormal conditions of the Cardiac Region
and Questions of Proper Conduct, and will give Information
to the Obtuse in All Affairs Roycroftie.
Question: What is meant by the " Gabbyjack Perserve? "
                                                    —W.
Answer: It is a Perdigested Breakfast Food. However, it
is not my Perogative to answer Questions on Dietetics—
the Heart is My Perovince.
Question: What is the difference between Domestic Science and Keeping House?
Answer: It is the same Difference that exists between
reading " Hints to Housekeepers, or One Hundred and One

Ways to Cook Pigs' Feet," and holding the Baby on your Left Hip while stirring the Hash with a Large Iron Spoon wielded by the Right.

Question: Is it proper to eat Peas with a knife?

Answer: By All Means, if you are a Juggler.

Question: I am a Young Woman of Thirty-five and am keeping Company for the First Time. Do you think I should allow my Gem'n Fren to Kiss me Good Night when he leaves at Ten?

Answer: Yes—if he Will!

Question: I am engaged to a Press Feeder. He is a Dear, Good Boy, but he smokes Cigzrettes. I have given him John's Book on the subject, but—it 's Nothing doing ✒ It 's up to you now, Miss Barebax.

Answer: I should advise you to let the Poor Boy alone on the subject—You probably Chew Gum Yourself.

School-teacher: " Now children, I read to you yesterday from Greek mythology and you remember I told you about Achilles. Is there any one who will give me just one fact about Achilles? Hands up now, all who know one fact about Achilles! "

(Jimmy Jones holds up his hand with glowing assurance.)

Teacher: " All right, Jimmy, tell us one fact about Achilles."

Jimmy: " His mother dipped him in the River Stinks and after that he was impossible."

A Fable: Two sons of Milesia were once delegated to sit up with a corpse, and keep the candles burning.

Towards midnight the whisky which should have lasted all night, was consumed.

Both men were thirsty and very nervous.

Pat proposed that he should go to the saloon next door and work the growler.

" Not on your life! " said Mike, who amended the motion by proposing that Pat should remain with the corpse and himself go to the saloon for drinks.

" In God's name, I 'll never agree to that," says Pat ✒

Neither one being willing to stay alone with the dead man, and both having promised the priest that they would not leave the corpse, a great thought came to Pat.

The plan was this: they would take the corpse with them.

❡ No sober man would ever have thought of such a thing, but these men were just enough under the "inflooence" to be inventive.

Now, the dead man was not very big, and he was dressed in his "best" just as the watchers were.

So they stood the corpse up, clapped a stove-pipe hat on his head and pulled the tile down over his face.

Then, one on each side, they half-dragged and half-carried the dead man into the street and into the saloon.

They stood the dead man up against the bar, and he tipped at an angle, not unlike that often taken by convivial parties at the midnight hour.

"Two whiskies!" ordered Pat in a voice of authority so "Make it three!" shouted Mike, who had n't quite lost his ability to reason.

Pat and Mike gulped the whisky in nervous haste. And just as they were setting down their glasses, a commotion was heard outside, and some one yelled, "Dog-fight!"

❡ And by habit, urged on by their nervous condition, both Mike and Pat shot through the screen door, leaving the corpse leaning up against the bar, the high hat pulled over his face. In his fine Sunday suit the corpse looked like a man who had been to a party.

"Vell!" said the Dutch bartender.

No response.

"Did n't you hear me already—I said, 'Vell?'"

Still no response.

"So you don't like der visky, eh? You ordered it, and now you von't drink it. And your two dirty Irish chums has run avay and left you to pay already. Vell? All right, you need n't drink, but you vill pay, or my name is not Vilhelm Schneider. You hear me?"

And still no response.

The Dutchman reached for his bung-starter. He took the mallet in one hand and then the other. "Pay up, or I 'll

schmash your high hat vorse around your ears than it is.
Pay up, I said. Ein—svei—drei—! "—And the mallet de-
scended with a thundering whack on the Saint Patrick's
Day hat.
The corpse toppled, slid, fell. And just as it hit the floor,
Pat and Mike came back.
They rushed forward, and stooping in tearful solicitude,
cried, " Are you hurt, are you hurt? " And then in wild
wrath they shouted to the Dutchman, " Oh, Oh, Oh!
You have killed him! you have killed him! you have killed
him! "
" Vell," shouted back the Dutchman, " the sunovagun
pulled a knife on me! "
Moral: Any man who hits another with a bung-starter
always says it was in self-defense.

Mr. Ragged Haggard, familiarly called by his friends,
" Cave-of-the-Winds," stopped off to lunch with me the
other day. Among other things he informed me that when
poor people call upon assistance, the Secretary has the
Inspector investigate the case and if found worthy the
applicant is given an order on the American News Company
for a copy of *What to Eat.*

In many hotels you will see a brass plate on the door of
each room, reading thus: " Stop! Have you left anything? "
❡ John Bunny tells me that in most of the big hotels it
should read as follows: " Stop! Have you anything left? "

A very bald-headed man went into a barber-shop at East
Aurora, and plumping himself down in the chair said:
" Hair-cut! "
Jed, the barber, looked at him a moment and replied:
" Why, man, you don't need no hair-cut—what you want
is a shine! "

Ali Baba stoutly contends that this earth is hell, and we
are now being punished for the sins done in a former life.
" We are living in hell now as much as we ever shall," says

the old man, " and the only way to get out is to accept all that comes. Kicking makes the matter worse. If you don't take your medicine in this life, a worse hell is in store for you the next time, the Devil tells me."
" What do you know about the Devil? " I asked.
" Me? Why, I am that man," was the stern reply.

Charles Warren Stoddard relates that he found in the South Sea Islands a tribe of savages so meager in intelligence that they could not lie. In other words, the thought of deception, untruth, affectation or pretense had never come to them. However, there were neighboring islands where missionaries of several denominations had settled, and there the savages were not sunk quite so low.

When in Chicago, Mr. Zangwill, being a Jew, was taken by the Smart Set in the Fine Arts Building to see the Cudahy Packing Establishment. He saw pigs jerked to Kingdom-Kum in a jiffy. As he looked upon the scene a debutante of mature years asked him a question thus: " Oh, Mr. Zangwill, how do you like Chicago Pork? " " I like it," said Mr. Zangwill, " much better than Chicago Tongue."

I was out in the orchard, back of the barn, recording truth as it seemed to me, with a lead pencil on a pad. No one knew where I was but the Red One, and he, being wise, knew better than to call me, unless the matter was very urgent ✺ ✺
And the matter being very urgent the Red One came to me, there in the orchard, bearing in his hand a small, neat visiting card, on which was simply the legend, " Mr. Richard Stoddard."
" He will see you! " said the Red One apologetically.
" He will see you. I told him you were very busy, that you were in Europe, that you were sick abed, and that I could fix him out, but he would not explain his business —simply must see you! "
Now, lots of people want to see me—I am so eccentric,

you know. Then, besides, perhaps I knew this gentleman,
although I could not at the moment recall the name.

So I laid down the pad and pencil and went over to the
Shop to see the distinguished and reticent gentleman
who owned the neat copper-engraved card.

He greeted me effusively, and talked me into smirking
imbecility, because I could not for the life of me remember
when I had seen him before.

"You are such a great book-lover," said the Strange
Gentleman for the fourth time, "and I came out from
Buffalo on purpose to see you—you are such a great book-
lover!"

I gasped and managed to say, "Yes, I 'm a great book-
lover (damnation!) and you are a great book-lover—I 'm
delighted, I assure you "—

Just then Minnie Gardner went by. Now Minnie is one
of my brightest and best Roycrofters, and among her
other duties shows visitors over the Shop.

"Oh, Minnie—Miss Gardner—here please! This is Mr.
—Oh yes, Mr. Stoddard! Mr. Stoddard, let me introduce
you to Miss Gardner. Now, Minnie, show Mr. Stoddard
around, please. He came out here on purpose to see us.
He is a great book-lover—show him Mr. Kinder's bindings,
and those last illuminations, please. And, say, yes, don't
forget to present him to Sammy—I know he 'll like Sammy,
for Sammy is a great book-lover, too, as well as an artist"
—and I slapped the gentleman on the back in a friendly
way, determined not to be outdone in affectionate effusive-
ness. He tried to say something, but thinking my cordiality
had embarrassed him a little, I slapped him on the back
again and assured him he must make himself at home.
And my tall, fine girl, Minnie, led him away.

Then I escaped hastily by a secret stairway, and went
back to my work in the orchard.

That night Ali Baba said to me nonchalantly, "I bounced
him!"

"What?" said I.

"I gave him the G. B."

"What do you mean?" I demanded.

"I trun 'im down," explained Baba.

"Who?" I asked.

"Why, that fellow who wanted to see you so bad this afternoon."

"Goodness me! you have no right to insult visitors!" I exclaimed ◦◦ ◦◦

"Well," said Baba doggedly, "I give him the run. I was washin' windows, and just after you left I heard him ask Minnie, 'Who is that long-haired man in the flannel shirt, anyway?' And then he asked what it was we made here. Next thing he flashed a perspective of the 'War in Cuba' to come in four hundred parts, at thirty-five cents a part. He was just a plain, dam book-agent—never heard o' you, never heard tell o' the Shop—been in town two days canvassing every house. An' when I saw him git Minnie in a corner and ask her to subscribe, I just took him by the collar, led him to the door, and pushed him down the steps —see? Minnie's a nice girl, and I'm not goin' to stand around and see her imposed on by any razzle-dazzle peddler of bad literatoor—am I—see?"

"Baba," said I, "you are getting worse and worse—not only do you use your own vocabulary of slang, but you are acquiring that of the tramp printer we hired last week. Here is a dollar Major Pond left for you when he was here yesterday; you are to have this on consideration that you will shut off your argot and not use a single swear word for a month."

On his way to Boston, Bath-house John stopped over a couple of days at Buffalo. Being told by Jakey Stern and Norman Mack that Hamlin's Stock Farm was located at East Aurora, and being further assured that I was one of the greatest book-makers in the country, the Great Man came out to see me.

He wired me of his coming, and so I met him at the station. When he alighted from the train the gorgeousness of his apparel quite knocked the village loafers speechless. John tipped his high white hat to the crowd, and then looked me over deliberately. At length a smile played upon his

classic County Down features, and he held forth his hand:
" You are me own—me ownest own," he said. " The
cloze is wot caught me—the make-up. A book-maker got
up like a buck-wheat—see? Dinky Dink would fall over
hisself givin' you his roll to take care of—see? You look
that honest. Say, lead off for yer joint."
The faultlessly clothed one lafft softly.

When we reached the Shop there was pain and perplexity
on the face of John. He showed small interest in anything.
After he saw the boys running a printing press, he turned
to me and said, " I 'm it, but I don't blame you—you
was n't in the game. But they told me in Buffalo that you
was a book-maker and dressed regardless—the real ting
see? and here you are nawthink but a feller who makes
books. It 's one on me, and it'll cost me fifty when I gets
back to Buffalo. Say, can I go to Albany widout goin' tru
Buffalo? "

When I explained that the only way to reach Albany was
via Buffalo, and the first train back did not go for five
hours, John was more dejected than ever. I offered to
take him to the Stock Farm, but he declined with thanks,
remarking, " I 've had enuff of the razzle for one day."
He went over to the Tavern and interviewed the Landlord. A crowd assembled and John entered drinks for
everybody, assuring the Landlord, " It 's on me."
At dinner the waiter-girl asked John whether he would
have roast beef or lamb.
" Say now, gimme fish—see? " was the answer.
But although it was Friday the East Aurora Tavern did
not have fish.
" Well, if ye have n't got no fish, then bring me some
beef—and say, have it rare and fat, wid plenty of gravy—
see? "
The beef was brought and John ate one dish and ordered
more. As he polished the dish for the second time he crossed
himself devoutly and turning to me said, " Gawd knows
I ast for fish! "

An East Aurora farmer went into Buffalo, and while there

celebrated a bit as farmers sometimes do when they go to town ◠ ◠
This farmer-man wandered into the Silver Dollar Saloon, and as he entered, he saw an electric fan on one end of the bar—one of those small brass things that whirls.
Our friend gazed at the whirling fan and it seemed to fascinate him.
He stood stock-still and looked at it as if hypnotized ◠
"What shall it be?" asked the bartender.
"Jus' a moment, my frien', don't get in a rush—I 'll tell you all right in a minute."
Still, he stood and stared, swaying slightly to right and left. Five minutes went by, and the farmer took out a big silver watch and looked at it with lack-lustre eye, holding it in his hand.
"Well, if you don't want anything, you better take a walk," said the bartender.
"Don't get excited, neighbor," said the farmer; "I 'm tryin' to find out how long that dam squirrel can keep 'er a-goin' without gettin' tired."

Ali Baba's son got married.
The Roycroft Band escorted them to the railroad station. We wired ahead to the Biltmore for a nice room for them. 'T was the first time that Ali Baba's son or his bride had ever left East Aurora. We wanted them to have a good time.
❡ When they reached the Biltmore, the room was waiting, the boy showed them up.
They looked at the gorgeous curtains and draperies, the luxurious arm chairs and the shaded lights—they were delighted—until Baba Jr. saw the Twin Beds!
Then said he, disappointed and disillusioned, "Shucks! I thought we were going to be alone!"

"I say, Miss Johnsing, befoh I can obfuscate myself to perpose to you, I would like to know how much Amonia de Courthouse granted you when you was divo'ced de las' time?"

Fra Elbertus
of East Aurora

☙ "We shall slide out of this Life into another, and the day of our Death like the day of our Birth shall be shrouded in forgetfulness ⚜ and if we do remember any of our Trials and Troubles it will only be to Smile that they have cost us a Pang"

Good Bye East Aurora

IX months before the World War was declared a notorious disturber made the statement, " I hate the American Flag and despise the things it stands for." That provoked Hubbard to see Red, and White and Blue ❧ ❧

In the very next issue of *The Philistine* (the size of which issue he announced to be two hundred twenty-five thousand copies) he printed the American Flag in full colors on a special insert with this verse:

SALUTE TO THE FLAG

Flag of our great Republic
Symbol of human Liberty,
Inspirer in battle
Guardian of our homes—
Whose stars and stripes
Stand for courage, purity and union,
We salute thee!
We, the children of many lands,
Who find rest and safety
Under thy folds,
Give our hands, our heads
And our hearts to thee:
We pledge our lives
And sacred honor
To guard and revere thee
And our beloved Country
       Forever.

The phrase, " our heads, our hands and our hearts " and the fact that this poem is not signed suggest that perhaps Hubbard himself wrote it.

Certainly it was his sentiment!

This man was an American of Americans and it was not quite an Accident of Fate that he died the death on the *Lusitania* the victim of the enemies of His Country!

Lest we forget, the *Lusitania* was torpedoed off the Irish coast May the Seventh, Nineteen Hundred Fifteen.

* * * * *

Sunday evening, April the Twenty-fifth, Nineteen Hundred Fifteen, Elbert Hubbard gave his last talk to the Roycrofters assembled in the Music Room of the Inn.

Within a week's time he was to sail away on the *Lusitania*. He spoke: " Elbert Hubbard II will be your chief while I am away. You know Bert as a man who will give you a square deal. His hands are clean, his head is clear, his heart is in the right place. He is your friend. * * *

" Mrs. Hubbard and I congratulate ourselves that during our absence the work will not in any way be retarded. We know that you will all work together for the common weal and welfare of the Institution. And we also feel that should we not return to East Aurora, and the Roycroft, the little work we have done—the Ideals we have attempted to materialize—will be appreciated and carried forward."

℄ Three hundred of us sat there and listened. Probably not one realized that we were hearing his Last Farewell.

℄ Days before, through some agency, he had been warned to " keep off the *Lusitania*." But Hubbard was not the man to be bullied or bluffed or turned aside from his purpose, and that to see the War with his own eyes.

Even when he said *" God be with you till we meet again"* I could not feel finality—it simply seemed that he was to be gone for a few weeks and then to be back among us twice as interesting as ever.

There was no sadness in this man—and yet this was a time for sadness ✎ Apparently he felt it, too. Though he joked a little that night there was a tear behind the smile ✎ Like all super-sensitive men he was something of a mystic— and as he talked there must have been a premonition of death. There was a catch to his voice and a tear trembled in his eye.

Unlike most meetings of his, it ended in silence.

There seemed very little to say when the men and women went up to shake his hand, and to bid him God speed and a safe return.

* * * * *

The weirdest thing I have found in Elbert Hubbard's writings was his oft-repeated reference to death in the Irish Sea! ❧ Twenty years before those waters closed over him he writes of death and disaster there! No other body of water seemed to exert the same fascination! Permit me to quote from *The Philistine:*

November, 1896
Page 192

" The literary gang-plank is very slippery and the Irish Sea is not yet full. Keep your eye on our obituary column."

December, 1896
4th pg. insert

"All persons finding themselves floundering in the Irish Sea "—

February, 1897
Page 192

" After just four issues and no more it slipped off the gang-plank into the Irish Sea, weighted with thirty pounds of debt"

January, 1899
Page 37

" Why, I thought you were drowned by the Irish—See? "

Aye! " Keep an eye on our obituary column! "

Yet, did he fear death?

I don't think so.

Scattered through his manuscripts I find sentences like this:
" The fear of death is the monopoly of young people. The man who has kept right at his work, living one day at a time and not bothering other folks any more than he has to, doing each task the best he could, keeping an interest in all good things—that man is not afraid to die."

* * * * *

He left East Aurora to fill a lecture engagement or two some days ahead of his sailing date.

The night before his departure I asked him, " At what hour do you plan to leave tomorrow morning? I want to go into Buffalo with you."

" The automobile will be ready at six a. m., and that precludes you. The ' late Mr. Felix ' will get up as usual at seven-thirty; and by that time I shall be gone away."

" Tomorrow morning I will break my inflexible rule, and be on your door-step at five-fifty—I intend to sit up all night! "

We both laughed, and he retorted: " Well, we shall see."

I thank my stars I kept the appointment.

What did we talk about on the trip in?

Not a single serious thing.

When he found me waiting outside his door, it provoked several and sundry humorous remarks, and that gave the tone to the conversation on the twenty-mile ride.

He was very fond of Negro stories and that morning I told him several New Ones, and he laughed and laughed.

¶ To add to the fun, in dressing in haste he had put on one black sock and one royal blue one—and that invited some more mirth.

When I said Good-bye and Good Luck to him at the door
of the old railroad station in Buffalo—he was still chuckling.
❰ I like to remember him that way—with a smile lighting
up his face.

* * * * *

When the German torpedo struck the *Lusitania* Elbert
and Alice Hubbard came out of their cabin onto the boat
deck, arm in arm.

He called to a friend, " Well, Jack, they have got us. They
are a damned sight worse than I ever thought they were! "
" What are you going to do? " The Fra shook his head.
Alice replied: " There does not seem to be anything to do."
❰ Then they turned away, still arm in arm, and entered
their cabin. They were not seen again.

The telegram which reached East Aurora said in so many
words: " Both lost at Sea." I can't believe it yet!

Down to the depths went Elbert Hubbard, with smiling
eyes that knew no fear, and all the lovely mermaids rub-
bered, and Neptune shouted, " See who's here! " Well
might there be a great commotion throughout the sea,
from East to West, for seldom has old Father Ocean clasped
hands with such a splendid guest. The inkstand waits
upon his table, his pen is rusting in the sun; there is no
living hand that's able to do the work he left undone.
There is no brain so keen and witty, no voice with his
caressing tones; and Elbert, in the Deep Sea city, is swapping yarns with Davy Jones. And all the world that reads
evinces its sorrow that he's dwelling there; not all the
warring kings and princes are worth a ringlet of his hair.
Death keeps a record in his cupboard of victims of the
monarchs' hate; " a million men and Elbert Hubbard,"
so goes the tally, up to date. If it would bring you back,
Elbertus, to twang your harp with golden strings, it would
not worry us or hurt us to drown a wagon-load of kings.

Emporia, Kansas   —Walt Mason

Upon the huge boulder on the lawn at Roycroft
is a bronze tablet with this inscription:

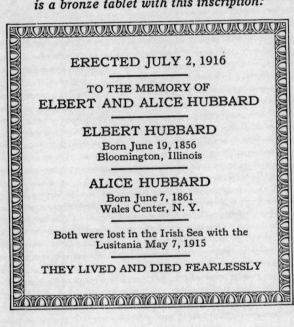

ERECTED JULY 2, 1916

TO THE MEMORY OF
ELBERT AND ALICE HUBBARD

ELBERT HUBBARD
Born June 19, 1856
Bloomington, Illinois

ALICE HUBBARD
Born June 7, 1861
Wales Center, N. Y.

Both were lost in the Irish Sea with the
Lusitania May 7, 1915

THEY LIVED AND DIED FEARLESSLY

SO HERE ENDETH "ELBERT HUBBARD OF EAST AURORA," AS WRITTEN BY FELIX SHAY. THE BORDERS, INITIALS AND BINDING BY ROYCROFT ARTISTS AND CRAFTSMEN, AND THE WHOLE PRODUCED BY THE ROYCROFTERS AT THEIR SHOPS WHICH ARE IN EAST AURORA, COUNTY OF ERIE AND STATE OF NEW YORK, MCMXXVI